W9-BWI-058

Thinking about Video Games

DIGITAL GAME STUDIES

Robert Alan Brookey and David J. Gunkel, editors

THINKING ABOUT VIDEO GAMES

INTERVIEWS WITH THE EXPERTS

DAVID S. HEINEMAN

INDIANA UNIVERSITY PRESS

BLOOMINGTON & INDIANAPOLIS

This book is a publication of

INDIANA UNIVERSITY PRESS
Office of Scholarly Publishing
Herman B Wells Library 350
1320 East 10th Street
Bloomington, Indiana 47405 USA

iupress.indiana.edu

© 2015 by David S. Heineman

*Manufactured in the
United States of America*

Library of Congress
Cataloging-in-Publication Data

Heineman, David S.
    Thinking about video games :
interviews with the experts /
David S. Heineman.
    pages cm
    Includes bibliographical
references and index.
    ISBN 978-0-253-01715-4 (pbk. : alk.
paper) – ISBN 978-0-253-01710-9 (cloth :
alk. paper) – ISBN 978-0-253-01718-5
(ebook) 1. Video games. 2. Video games –
Design. 3. Video games industry. I. Title.
    GV1469.3.H45 2015
    794.8 – dc23

                            2014049741

1 2 3 4 5   20 19 18 17 16 15

Contents

Preface

THIS BOOK IS A COLLECTION OF INTERVIEWS AND CONTEXTU-
alizing essays that function to bring together and bridge various kinds
of expertise about video games. Participants in this project come from
a wide range of backgrounds: there are video game designers; current
and former chief executive officers (CEOs) and high-ranking executives of video game companies; well-known figures from video games'
history; widely respected contemporary artists, authors, and editors;
people closely associated with video game culture and related communities; and several professors who study and teach about video games.
The basic idea of this book is that people who care about and approach
video games from different perspectives would benefit considerably by
holding meaningful cross-field and cross-discipline discussion about
their shared interests. This book attempts to model and, ideally, further
facilitate this kind of dialogue.

I teach a first-year seminar course for undeclared students at a state
university entitled the Art, History, and Culture of Video Games and
am regularly surprised by the sheer variety of topics across the history
of video games that interest students in the class. Of course, video game
history, the origins of which date back to the period just after World
War II, now encompasses almost seventy years of technological innovations, people playing with those innovations, and people writing about
the impact of people playing with those innovations. The volume of
commercial games released worldwide in that period is in excess of one
hundred thousand titles across more than one hundred platforms.[1] In
2013 the Entertainment Software Association (ESA), which releases an

annual report that tracks changes in gamer demographics and habits, found that 58 percent of Americans play games and that slightly more than half the homes in the country have one (and in most cases two) game consoles. The video game industry has almost tripled its annual revenue in the past decade. What these numbers suggest is that there are a *lot* of people interested in video games and that, in addition to the games themselves, there has been a lot of game-related writing and research produced by a wide variety of expertise.

In my course students are charged with uncovering as much of this material as possible that is relevant to their topic of interest. The hope is that, when undeclared students research multiple approaches to studying video games, they will also discover a potential major. What also happens, though, is that they regularly uncover examples of disconnect between academia and industry, fan communities and developers, designers and players, and so on. As the amount of material written about games has grown, it seems that the disconnects among people with something interesting to say about the medium have multiplied.

There was a time, when video games were a newer medium, that there was a much more collaborative atmosphere among those interested in the medium from across areas of personal and professional expertise. By contrast, what too often happens today is a kind of "siloing" of interests, where scholars talk to scholars, developers talk to developers, and so on, and the benefits of shared knowledge and regular collaboration are not apparent. For the most part, mutual understanding and appreciation across fields have given way to echo chambers and decreased relevance within them.

It is my hope that this book is able to find an audience among those who play games, research games, make games, or otherwise have a strong interest in the medium. While connecting to such a broad audience posed some unique challenges in researching the book, preparing interview questions, and writing the various sections found herein, I have done my best to offer a balanced, accessible approach to the subject areas addressed. Though this is a university press book, I have tried to avoid needlessly heavy citation, esoteric academic jargon, and the kind of methodological nuance that might alienate nonacademic audiences. I believe it is possible for a reader to learn how seemingly disparate approaches to video games can intersect without needing to become fully conversant in any one of them.

*   *   *

The interviews in this book were conducted over a span of about fifteen months in 2012 and 2013, during which time a number of individuals were instrumental in making the project come together. First and foremost in this regard are the participants included herein, each of whom was gracious and accommodating to various scheduling needs, logistical considerations, and other concerns surrounding the interviews themselves. In addition, I received help and feedback from a number of colleagues, students, and video game community members while preparing the manuscript. Specifically, Jeff Gillingham, Bradford Allison, Nick Reichart, and Jonathan Stringer were helpful for assisting with research, considering and offering certain ideas, and otherwise encouraging me during the process. Research was funded, in part, with a grant earned through Bloomsburg University of Pennsylvania's Office of Research and Sponsored programs.

Participants

IAN BOGOST is the Ivan Allen College Distinguished Chair in Media Studies and Professor of Interactive Computing at the Georgia Institute of Technology, where he also holds an appointment in the Scheller College of Business. He is also a game designer and an author of multiple books about video games, including *Unit Operations: An Approach to Videogame Criticism, Racing the Beam: The Atari Video Computer System,* and *How to Do Things with Videogames.*

NOLAN BUSHNELL is presently on the advisory board for Anti Aging Games, LLC. He is perhaps best known for introducing and popularizing video games in the arcade (*Computer Space, Pong*) and for cofounding Atari and Chuck E. Cheese's restaurant.

EDWARD CASTRONOVA is a professor of media at Indiana University and has published widely on the economics of video games, including *Wildcat Currency: The Virtual Transformation of the Economy, Synthetic Worlds: The Business and Culture of Online Games,* and *Exodus to the Virtual World.* He often consults with the game industry in areas related to his research expertise.

JAMIE DILLION is the program developer and coordinator for the Child's Play Charity, an organization founded by the creators of the webcomic *Penny Arcade* to raise funds for hospitals to provide games and toys for their patients. She has worked with multiple game-related communities and with various media to help raise millions of dollars in donations through various fund-raising endeavors.

ED FRIES is an adviser to multiple entities in the video game industry, serving on boards for companies like Ouya and Razer and for organizations like the IGDA. He is also a former employee of Microsoft, where he headed the games division for many years and worked as the chief architect and evangelist around the launch of the original Xbox in 2001. Fries has also done work as a programmer, including publishing an original Atari VCS title, *Halo 2600,* in 2010.

CHRIS GRANT is a founder and the editor in chief of Polygon.com, one of the most popular video game–related sites on the Internet. Formerly, he held the same position at Joystiq.com, where he also served as the editorial director. He has published widely on many topics related to games for much of the past decade.

CASEY HUDSON is a video game developer who is probably best known for being the executive producer of Bioware's *Mass Effect* series. Previously, he did work on series such as *Baldur's Gate, Neverwinter Nights,* and *Star Wars: Knights of the Old Republic.*

EUGENE JARVIS is founder and leader of Raw Thrills, Inc., an arcade game developer based in Skokie, Illinois. Jarvis is also an accomplished and award-winning game designer, with groundbreaking arcade titles such as *Defender, Smash TV, Robotron 2084,* and the *Cruis'n* series to his credit.

HENRY LOWOOD is the curator for History of Science & Technology Collections and Film & Media Collections in the Stanford University Libraries. He has done groundbreaking work related to video game history and to the preservation of old games and virtual worlds, some of which is cataloged on his blog *How They Got Game: The History and Culture of Interactive Simulations and Videogames.*

CHRIS MELISSINOS is the winner of the 2013 Game Developers Conference Ambassador Award, which cited his curation of the Smithsonian Institution's *Art of Video Games* exhibit as a crowning accomplishment in a career marked by promoting the role of video games across diverse platforms and in multiple contexts.

KELLEE SANTIAGO is currently the head of developer relations at Ouya. She is also a former TED fellow and a cofounder and former president of thatgamecompany, where she worked on award-winning titles such as *Flower* and *Journey*.

Thinking about Video Games

Introduction

VIDEO GAMES HAVE SOME OF THEIR EARLIEST ROOTS IN THE university. Indeed, the first full decade of video game experimentation is bookended on one end by the efforts of pioneering students who hacked multimillion-dollar machinery at schools such as the Massachusetts Institute of Technology (MIT) and Stanford in the late 1950s and early 1960s to create games like *Mouse in the Maze* and *Spacewar* and, on the other end, with work by people such as Don Rawitsch, who created *Oregon Trail* in 1971 at Carleton College and Bill Pitts and Hugh Tuck, who created the first coin-op game (*Galaxy Game*) at Stanford that same year. The origin of a modern-day technology industry, such as the video game industry, in student projects and university research labs is a common narrative of the twentieth century. It is one that informs the recent advocacy for increased funding for science, technology, engineering, and math (STEM) education in the United States, advocacy that suggests there are economic imperatives for investing in the kinds of invention and innovation found in engineering, computer science, math, physics, and other technology-driven areas of the academy. In this story, video games are regularly presented as an example par excellence of how twentieth-century university research might lead to profitability in industry and increased economic power globally for the state.

And though the video game industry has always had a foothold in academia (and vice versa), it is only for the past decade or so that there has been considerable and rapid growth in the nebulous field of "game studies," an area of research that brings together researchers from a wide variety of fields in the sciences, humanities, and arts to address video

1

games through scholarly activity. The initial publication of several key journals signaled this emergence (notably the online journal *Game Studies* in 2001 and the Sage-backed *Games and Culture* in 2006), and today there are many degree programs dedicated to game development, analysis, design, history, and research at both specialized colleges like DigiPen and in more traditional universities such as New York University (NYU), the University of Southern California (USC), or the Georgia Institute of Technology. Grant money exists to do research on games in a way that it did not even a decade ago, and gradually the "serious" study of games has become a topic of interest in major online and offline press venues.[1] As the twenty-first century began, there was a palpable academic interest in understanding why people were increasingly enamored with video games and what the consequences of their growing ubiquity might be.

The growing academic interest in video games has, not surprisingly, coincided with the growth of the video game industry itself. Though figures sometimes fluctuate from year to year and from region to region, the general trend for global video game revenues is upward. In the early part of this decade, the video game industry in the United States reached virtual parity with the profits found in the film and music industries, realizing a kind of pop culture milestone that argues for its prominent position in the public imaginary. Both video games and video game players have migrated in interesting ways in the recent past, with gaming becoming increasingly mobile, experiences becoming increasingly persistent, and with more players finding virtual homes in massively multiplayer online (MMO) environments ranging from virtual modern warfare exercises to virtual simulations of life's other experiences. It is more likely today that new video games will find their way into a classroom than they will into an arcade, that games will require input from more than a player's fingers and provide feedback to more than their eyes and ears, and that the average "gamer" will be both a creator of games as well as a consumer of them.

None of this is news, of course, to those who have followed the evolution of the industry even a little bit. What might come as news, however, is that many of the luminaries who have led the charge for making games a larger part of our lives have usually done so without directly engaging the resources of the university, where the medium originated. Over time, the initially close connection that existed between the nascent game industry and the institutions that birthed the medium has been largely severed. Though some academic institutions appoint "designers in residence" or invite various developers to campus to speak to students, the institution's role has increasingly shifted to one of observer and analyst rather than of participant and progenitor. At the same time, the industry has taken on greater responsibility in training its workers in (what are often studio-specific) best conventions and practices for making modern games. In other words, while there have been dramatic increases in both the number of people making games and the number of people studying them, there has not been much of a corresponding conversation between these areas of expertise, the kind of conversation that might productively inform the work done on games as a whole. This introductory chapter provides a series of three vignettes ("questions," "communities," and "competition") that reflect on this possibility.

QUESTIONS

In 1983 object-oriented programming pioneer Alan Kay spoke to a gathering of researchers at an academic conference at Harvard University. What is notable about this speech was that Kay did not speak about what one might expect him to address in most contexts at Harvard (for example, his own recent work in computer science, his thoughts on the challenges of programming in the early 1980s, and so on), but he instead spoke about his vision of the future for the video game industry. In that speech Kay laid out a type of research agenda for advancing the medium; he discussed gaming and treating disability, gaming and enhancing education, gaming and the development of artificial intelligence (AI), and gaming and artistic expression.

Kay, himself a well-known computer scientist who would go on to win a Turing Award, came to the conference that day as a representative of Atari, Inc. He functioned as a type of representative figure for a potential marriage between academic research and the video game industry. Kay's work at Atari as the company's chief scientist was to bring his expertise about how new technologies could advance human understanding to bear on how video games might become a significant part of that advancement (and, of course, to evangelize that connection). That kind of direct engagement and interaction between the game industry and academic research is, today, not a common enough phenomenon.

That conference in May 1983, held by the Harvard University College of Education, was titled "Video Games and Human Development: Research Agenda for the '80s." The three-day event brought together researchers from around the country who were considering, at a very early time in the medium's ascent toward cultural significance, the modes through which video games might become important objects for academic research. The published proceedings of that conference address these areas: "Video Games & Social Behavior," "Video Games & Cognitive Skills," "Video Games in Medical Rehabilitation & Learning," "Video Games & Informal Settings," "Video Games & Formal Education," "Video Games & Atari, Inc.," and "Video Games & Human Development." At almost all of these panels, there were representatives of video game and technology companies there to help shape the agenda, offer thoughtful feedback, and provoke further dialogue about the application and utility of various research projects.

From a certain perspective, it is humbling to recognize that game studies has been grappling with many of the same questions addressed in this book for at least the past thirty years. It puts current "hot topic" questions about the role of games in education (for example, the institutional backlash to Valve's "Steam for Schools") or about whether major publishers value their bottom line more than artistic creativity (for example, much of the popular criticism of employment practices found at large publishers Activision or Electronic Arts) into a historical context. There is evidence in these proceedings that gaming has been dogged with the same questions for decades and that those who are invested in understanding the social and cultural impact of the medium have struggled to find satisfactory answers. That is, in and against multiple periods of growth and change, some perceptions of the industry have gone largely unchanged.

There are also many interesting little moments in these proceedings that suggest things *have* changed in significant ways. For example, in a statement that would seem alien to most major game publishers today, Atari's vice president and chief scientist, Alan Kay, foregrounded his remarks about the future of games by suggesting that "children are our main clientele" and then geared most of his speech toward the future of games as a medium for children to learn on. In another now-bizarre interaction, a representative from Apple suggested during a Q&A session about the costs of funding computers for schools, "The term 'computer literacy' does not make a great deal of sense to me. You don't have to go out and teach a kid how to use the TV. It is of interest, he or she should be able to use it and learn on his/her own." These kinds of statements today come across as anachronistic, relics of an era when digital technology was only beginning to find its way into middle-class homes.[2]

Despite its many vestiges of a bygone era of game research, the conference also offered extremely compelling questions that have been of increasing importance in contemporary game studies. Questions about gender representation both in the industry and among players were broached. Detailed discussions of design decisions, artificial intelligence, and some early thoughts on what might now be considered platform studies were addressed in ways that are still relevant and accessible. There was interesting research presented on games in noncommercial contexts beyond education, and despite the framing of his company's products as directed toward adolescent audiences, Alan Kay's remarks were thoughtful missives on the potential of the medium to function as art through which unique transcendent experiences might occur. He explained, for example, the possibilities of moving past "shoot-'em-up games" and toward games that simulate, from an animal's perspective, what it would be like to visit a coral reef. He suggested that "a computer is not only a gadget for manipulating numbers. It is a container for a new kind of kinetic art. . . . [I]f we think of the visual arts as the imitation of life, then the computer arts are the imitation of creation itself" (61). This idea, now institutionalized in something like the Smithsonian's *The Art of Video Games*, was, in 1983, a revolutionary way of thinking about games. But then, as is true now, there is a pervasive impulse to dissociate "shoot-'em-up" fare from games that are "actually" art.[3]

For another example of persisting issues raised by the conference, consider the introductory remarks by Harvard librarian Inabeth Miller, who warmed the crowd before the keynote by highlighting an award-winning essay by a ninth grader entitled "Video Games . . . Are They Hip? Or Is It Just Hype?" The essay, which touched on the impact of the arcade craze on the young author and her peers, included the lines:

> Children can no longer understand machines that don't gobble money. How sad it is to see Junior vainly trying to stick a quarter in the mixmaster. And what of their minds?
>
> "Junior clean up your room."
>
> "If I do it in under fifteen minutes do I get a bonus?"
>
> Grisly, ladies and gentlemen, but highly feasible if the youth of America stays this course. (3)

In 1983 we see a measured response to the perceived threat of gamification. Thirty years later, many herald gamification as a promise.

The Harvard conference is not the earliest point in the history of game studies, but it is a significant one because of what it suggests about what an interdisciplinary approach to the field might actually mean. Today, the conferences and publications dedicated to academic game studies are markedly distinct from those dedicated to the game industry's various creative and fiscal interests. What has not changed, though, is that there is both intellectual and economic gain to be made by bringing these camps together. Perhaps conferences are a natural place to rekindle those associations.

COMMUNITIES

One way to think about the contemporary relationship between the game industry, its most invested fan base, and the researchers who study both is to consider the occasions where these groups have an opportunity to congregate.

For example, the largest annual game industry event is the Electronic Entertainment Expo, usually held in Los Angeles. Every year at E3, most of the major game companies (for example, Sony, Microsoft, Nintendo, Electronic Arts) make important announcements about upcoming hardware and software, reveal pricing strategies and release dates, hold both large public press events and small private meetings with select press outlets, and conduct many private business meetings. A large amount of networking, recruiting, and strategizing goes on at E3, and though members of the general public can purchase exorbitantly priced tickets, for the most part attendees are composed of the press, various industry stakeholders, and exhibitors.

E3 is largely about putting merchandise on physical and virtual store shelves. Most major companies use the expo as a mode through which to raise the profile of their products, hoping to land more release-day orders from big-box chains like Wal-Mart and Target, to encourage preorders through game retailers such as Gamestop, and to bump their stock values by putting together an attractive presentation that demonstrates attention to shifting market trends. They do this by creating attractive and pricey floor displays, promising exclusive demonstrations and interviews to the most influential media outlets, handing out promotional items and hosting free "invite only" parties, and engaging in an all-out public relations blitz. Despite the fact that the event is monitored closely by so many "core" gaming communities (especially online), the audience for E3 is decidedly not the "gamer" but rather the "consumer," the individual whose game purchasing is likely more informed by retail displays, television commercials, and word of mouth than it is by gaming-press reviews or online message-board debates. It is very much an expo that is put on for people who are financially invested in the industry, who buy and sell studios and intellectual properties, who place product orders and sell advertising, who are looking for industry jobs, and who cover a few stories a year about gaming for major news organizations like CNN or the *Washington Post*.

In practical terms, this means that E3 often leaves a lot of "core" gamers and a lot of game researchers searching for relevance where it is not apparent or does not exist. The former audience is left puzzled and perplexed when, for example, Sony spends a half hour of their major E3 press conference promoting something called a *Wonderbook*, a PlayStation hardware-software bundle centered on interactive reading and aimed at the ages five-to-ten crowd, instead of using the time to preview gameplay footage of the newest *Killzone*, *God of War*, or *Uncharted* title. As for researchers, to the extent that they might even pay attention to E3 (and there is little to no evidence that they do), it seems likely that they would see nothing more than hype and marketing about products that are not yet ready to be analyzed. Even though there is a lot to process about the game industry's philosophies, their understandings of their audiences, and their internal and external communication practices, the event is not one that, on its face, lends itself to an engaging application of pet models of game studies research.

Pet models of game studies research *are* the focus of the biannual Digital Games Research Association conference. DiGRA conferences are meant to bring together what are often disparate and disconnected strands of research on games over a period of several days of panels, lectures, workshops, and other meetings. At any given DiGRA conference, much of the research presented will have been conducted by professors or students with appointments or interest in some form of a game studies program, some will have been presented by individuals in other disciplines who have an interest in game research (for example, English or computer science), a smaller amount will have been done by independent scholars, and a relatively low percentage will be presented by people actively working in the game industry. A quick glance at the 2013 DiGRA conference website, for example, lists a dozen featured speakers. Of these, nine of the speakers are advertised to be faculty or students (most from departments that are structured, at least in part, around the study of games), and the other three are advertised as nonacademically affiliated individuals who are noted for working in or speaking about game design ("DiGRA Conference 2013"). The conference is clearly focused on academic research and is advertised as a conference of interest to an academic audience.

Academic conferences serve some of the same important networking and strategizing functions for academia as an expo like E3 serves for the game industry. Their insular nature is, by many accounts, one that is productive to scholarly debate, to the incubation of and experimenting with new theories and methods, and to the application of research to pedagogy. In other words, the academic conference is a predefined context wherein people can freely talk about the study of games and game-related culture in a space that is specifically set up as one removed from those where games are made or played. They are sites of reflection, analysis, agon, and conceptualization, not sites for hands-on engagement, observation, and practice with the actual texts being discussed. As such, they tend not to attract many presenters who are actively involved in game design or production, nor do they attract many attendees who are primarily interested in playing video games in social settings (for example, as a way to experience community). These folks are present, but they are in a minority. In other words, there is very little, if any, cosplay at academic conferences, even when those conference are about video games. Those audiences are just not in attendance at these gatherings.

There *is* a considerable amount of cosplay at the Penny Arcade Expo, a gamer-centered convention that is held annually in several locations (PAX Prime in Seattle, PAX East in Boston, and more recently PAX Australia in Melbourne and PAX South in Houston). PAX, the invention of Penny Arcade webcomic-strip creators Jerry Holkins and Mike Krahulik, was created, in part, as an answer of sorts to E3. That is, if E3 is a game-centered conference whose primary audience is the industry itself (and its shareholders), PAX is a game-centered convention where the primary audience is those who self-identify as part of gamer culture: individuals for whom video game playing is a primary hobby or passion, who situate themselves in various video game–based communities, or who are conversant in video games of the past or present.

A consideration of what takes place at PAX further clarifies its audience(s). For example, a central attraction of the convention is the exhibit-hall floor space, where many of the major studios, publishers, and distributors showcase their most recent or upcoming games with large eye-catching displays featuring artwork or characters from the game, multiple large televisions, and lines of players waiting to try out the offering. Like similar displays used at E3 (many of which recycle the same components, in fact), these displays are meant to stoke enthusiasm for a game. Unlike at E3, the people playing these games are generally doing so from the perspective of someone who plays games for fun instead of playing them as part of their job description. This distinction becomes most apparent when observing the kinds of interactions that take place between the people showing the games and the people playing them. At E3 these interactions are often marked by explanation of basic mechanics, emphasis on marketing-friendly features, and details of release strategies; at PAX they are marked instead by discussion of the game's relationship to others in the genre (or in game history more broadly – for example, "What are the game's influences?"), by competitive banter with others playing the game, and with a more informed exchange of feedback about nuances of game design. In other words, at E3 the assumption is that the person playing the game at any given booth might not be familiar with games in general or might be visiting a booth only to produce a story or make a purchase order decision;[4] at PAX the assumption is that the booth visitor is well versed in a variety of gameplay styles and, as such, might offer useful comments about the game for consideration by those who created it.

Beyond this main attraction, PAX is also filled with other markers of "game culture." There are nightly concerts by musicians inspired by games (for example, the *Mega Man*–inspired rock band Protomen), who create music that is based on game music (for example, chiptune artists), or who include game-related references in lyrics, songs, or stage presence (for example, Jonathan Coulton). PAX has rooms where people can meet to play against or with each other in LAN configurations, on classic consoles such as the Sega Genesis and Vectrex, or on vintage arcade machines. Most interesting, perhaps, PAX hosts a variety of panels (proposed by anyone and programmed by the organizers) that cover wide-ranging topics, including the various challenges of game development, tips for better community management, discussion of specific aspects of game culture, live podcast recordings, and sessions that feature game studies researchers talking about concepts as varied as game preservation, the use of games in teaching, gamification, and issues of identity (gender, race, sexuality, class, and the like) as they relate to game culture. Insofar as some of these panels are composed of and attractive to people who play, make, and research games and thus offer an opportunity to look at a mutual topic of concern from various perspectives, they are probably the best analogue to the kind of discussion this book attempts to foster.

COMPETITION

One way to think about the overlapping communities presented in this book is to think about how each was, from its inception, defined and thus problematized in different ways by an ethos of competition. Competition is not in and of itself a negative force in game-centered communities (it functions contextually), but it has an effect of turning the attention of each community inward, toward concerns of hierarchy, strategy, position, and status.

Competitive behaviors – like PvP (player-versus-player) excursions in *World of Warcraft*, Major League Gaming events, the EVO fighting-game tournament, or other elements of contemporary cooperative, competitive, or communal gaming – have their roots in some of the earliest expressions of the medium, most of which were created specifically for fostering rivalry. The golden age of the arcade might conjure images of packed boardwalk parlors and sweaty dens at the strip mall, but these gatherings were facilitated by the introduction of the concept of the "high score" into video games in the mid-1970s (*Sea Wolf, Space Invaders,* and the like). The social interaction that attracted the crowd to physical space was largely one that occurred between disembodied citizens; the arcade was defined by discontinuous (and spasmodic) member interaction. It was a community founded through discreet expressions of competitive mastery by previous visitors to the virtual space of a game (and the physical space of an arcade cabinet). These earlier users set a mark, made a statement, attained momentary ascendency, and indicated their position in a community of other users, all of whom were also attempting to indicate their place in "Today's" list of high-scoring community members or perhaps in the list of those who were there for "All-Time." Walter Benjamin's *Arcades Project* suggested that the nineteenth-century Paris arcades were a place where art, architecture, and community blurred, took shape, and decayed according to a logic of space and movement. The twentieth-century video game arcade, by comparison, was a place where community became shaped by competition across an incongruous temporality.

From the outset of video games as a commercial enterprise, a number of high-profile lawsuits have signaled the power of competitive, capitalist forces to shape game development and sales. Perhaps the most famous early case entangled the interviewee featured in chapter 1 of this book, Nolan Bushnell. In the spring of 1974, Bushnell was Atari's president, and his PONG had spent the past couple of years becoming the first megahit in the arcade. That same year he also found himself part of a lawsuit issued by Magnavox and Sanders Associates, the companies that had been developing Ralph Baer's Odyssey home gaming console since the mid-1960s. The suit surrounded questions of possible patent infringement on the gameplay and design of PONG that were extremely similar to those found in Baer's work. As Marty Goldberg (2007) explained in his essay "Video Game Misconceptions: The Magnavox Odyssey Is Analog and Not Digital":

> In 1974 Magnavox and Sanders filed a lawsuit for patent infringement against Seeburg, Bally-Midway and Atari in what would be the very first lawsuit in the industry. During Atari's pretrial hearing with Federal District Court judge John F. Grady, Nolan tried to testify he had never seen the Odyssey and its Tennis game before the advent of PONG. Luckily Magnavox and Sanders were able to produce an attendance log for the *Magnavox Profit Caravan* stop at Burlingame, CA that Nolan signed on May 24th, 1972. The *Caravan* was the very series of traveling product demonstrations that introduced the Odyssey to dealers that Spring. Nolan had no choice but to change his position, and settle out of court by becoming Magnavox's first sub licensee.

Bushnell, commenting on the case in later years, would regularly argue that although he had seen the prototype, he found the gameplay to be crude, unintuitive, and erratic. He suggested that PONG was significantly different because of the refinements it offered in gameplay and control over Baer's "Brown Box" prototype. Baer, in a 2013 interview with the video game website Polygon, remarked that "[Bushnell] has been telling the same nonsensical stories for 40 years. . . . [H]e just cannot let go of them because they affect his legacy. As for how I feel about that? Life's too short to hold grudges" (Campbell). Though the industry has changed dramatically in the ensuing decades following PONG, much of this intercompany, interdeveloper, and interstudio rivalry persists, often surrounding copyright and patent issues and almost always concerning profits. In 2012, for example, the website gamepolitics.com tracked more than a dozen ongoing lawsuits contesting rights to and usage of game-related technology from every major video game hardware developer.

Competition also shapes research on video games, albeit in slightly different ways. The use of certain terms, for example, can attract or repel people to the content of a manuscript such as this book. Misunderstanding of a key term can drive someone to take on a project under false pretenses, pursue the wrong degree, or speak to an audience on issues in a mode that diverges from audience expectations. For those who work with and study games, this is a present conundrum. For example, this text is part of a new series that takes the title Digital Game Studies. However, it purports to address subjects that, at various points, might fall into a variety of closely related (yet sometimes distinct) field-defining terms, including *game studies, digital game studies, video game studies, critical game studies, ludology, critical ludology, digital ludology,* and so on. Associated with these "umbrella" terms are distinct and sometimes overlapping subareas of research in the humanities, including video game criticism, video game analysis, video game history, the rhetoric of video games, the philosophy of video games, the psychology of video games, games and pedagogy, and others. Furthermore, there are, of course, many career fields related to games that may or may not match up to these subjects or areas and all of which may be institutionalized (in classrooms, in textbooks, and elsewhere) in academe. These include video game journalism, video game design, video game programming, video game art, video game sound, game hardware development, and so on.

Though these terms offer a lot of overlap and potential for collaboration, they also risk becoming arbitrary dividing lines in what, in chapter 11, Ian Bogost calls the "gold rush" of game research, research on which people's careers, institutions' profile, and grant funding might rest and for which there exists competition. There are, as in the game industry, material concerns for researchers that are rooted in definitional exercises about their practices.

The relative recent growth of game-related areas of academic research and training is, on the one hand, a good problem to have. It suggests an interest and awareness of the cultural impact of the medium, and, like other disciplines tied to particular media before it (for example, film studies, television studies, and the like), it is evolving at a rate that is quicker than the slow pace of the academy is able to accommodate. The result is, in part, the creation of specialized universities entirely related to games (usually seen as "technical schools" for the industry) and the majority of the most well-developed game-related programs existing at newer, smaller private universities. (Game studies has a way to go before it reaches the ubiquity of film studies.) On the other hand, such rapid growth and expansion are a more serious problem for creating a sense of focus, for understanding the relationships between these often polysemous terms, and for communicating the connections between academic research, industry considerations, and player interests. There is a messiness here that, while perhaps necessary and inevitable, is also an obstacle to those looking to get involved in a meaningful way with these various fields, subfields, and so on. To the extent that competition functions as a constitutive component of academia, it exacerbates these obstacles.

MODELING CONVERSATIONS

As indicated in the preface, the interviews in this book attempt to model the kinds of cross-field discussions that might help better frame and more astutely answer questions about video games, thus encouraging communities interested in the medium to further collaborate. Formal interviews are, of course, a kind of "staged" conversation, one in which both interlocutors are aware that their dialogue will extend beyond those present and become artifacts for public scrutiny. So while the included interviews are generally more formal than conversations that might occur more organically, they are nonetheless useful models for a number of reasons that bear elaboration.

First and foremost, agreeing to participate in an interview demonstrates a kind of openness and eagerness to share one's ideas with a larger audience. This basic attitude is an important starting place for fostering meaningful cross-field dialogue. Those selected for inclusion in this particular collection are individuals who ostensibly share a strong collaborative interest and see benefit in bridging disciplinary divides and the "siloing" effect that occurs among those interested in games, and so the way that they answer (and ask) questions should be considered in this context.

The interview is also a useful mechanism for pushing toward elaboration or clarification, two more important processes in cross-field dialogue. In many of the chapters that follow, those interviewed are confronted with critiques, concerns, and questions that they might not encounter regularly within their own area of professional interest. Sometimes, like when Casey Hudson addresses academic and public criticism of some of his studio's design choices in chapter 10, this engagement prompts new ideas and compelling reflection; other times, like when Bushnell reacts to Neil Postman's views on education in chapter 1 or Chris Grant weighs in on the value of college in chapter 7, it leads to a more immediate clarification of boundaries.

In any case, a collection of interviews that brings together individuals who may be of interest to different audiences is an attempt to foster wider collaboration, to bring more people with similar interests to the table. It is very likely that some readers will pick this book up seeking fresh insights from well-known scholars, others will want to read reflections on gaming history from those who shaped it, and still others will be interested in a link between one of the sections or chapters and their own specific interest in video games. All of those audiences should find what they are looking for, but the accessibility of the interview format and the curation of collaborative-minded participants are intended as an invitation to also consider new perspectives on games.

The rest of this book is divided into three broad sections – history, economy, and culture – that are meant to encompass a fairly wide cross-section of academic, industry, and player interests in video games. These divisions are shaped both by the expertise of the various individuals who are interviewed in each section and by many of the themes they discuss. In truth, one will find some discussion of economic models in the section on culture, some discussion of the culture found in contemporary game communities in the section on history, and so on. The concluding chapter brings these sometimes displaced and disparate ideas back into perspective while suggesting what might be garnered from the emergent themes found in the preceding chapters.

Each section of the book is preceded by an introductory essay that explains the connections between and the context informing the relevant interviews therein. Each interview is then preceded by a very brief biographical overview of the interviewee and an orientation to the relationship between their expertise and the topics covered in detail in the interview. The interviews are, of course, the focus of the book and where the type of cross-disciplinary and cross-profession conversations alluded to above are posited, pondered, and, on the most interesting pages, modeled. They are presented as they took place (with appropriate editing for readability), so any apparent jumps in logic or breaks in flow across the topics covered in each interview are the fault not of the interviewees but rather of the interviewer. The questions in each chapter were driven by a confluence of research about the careers and work of the individuals interviewed; by academic scholarship that, directly or indirectly, referred to each participant's expertise; and, in some cases, by issues raised in a previous interview.

Finally, while this introduction has emphasized the overarching purpose for and structure of the book, each section and each interview stands alone as a considered study of the topics presented. The choice of participants was driven in large part by a deliberation over who might be able to speak with authority on topics that are of growing relevance across different communities interested in video games, and there is significant insight into contemporary video games, their study, and their culture offered in each chapter.

Games and History

FOR A MEDIUM WHOSE EVOLUTION HAS BEEN LARGELY DEFINED by continued breakthroughs in interactive technologies, it seems odd to think that video games have now been popular for close to fifty years or that many of the medium's best-loved eras and artifacts are now as ancient as eight-track cassettes and dot-matrix printers; the golden age of the arcade took place more than thirty-five years ago, and the Nintendo Entertainment System was first released thirty years ago. Atari was founded more than forty years ago, and the earliest video games date back to a global post–World War II boom in technological innovation in the mid-1940s.[1]

By comparison, fifty years after Thomas Edison's theater showed the first commercial film in the late nineteenth century, the film industry had already produced both *Citizen Kane* (1941) and *Casablanca* (1944), two films that to this day rank atop the American Film Institute's "Top 100 Films" list at as two of the three best films ever made. On the other hand, film studies as a recognized academic discipline had not yet emerged by the 1940s (either for formal university training in film creation or for critical film analysis), but game studies in some form or fashion has been associated with games for much of its history.

I have written elsewhere (Heineman, "Public Memory") about the contemporary function of nostalgia in video games; invoking the past is a potentially contentious act that has consequences for group and individual identities and, because of this, often drives consumer habits, marketing choices, and certain industry trends. In part because of the functions of advocating for a particular public memory, writers from various backgrounds have been historicizing, canonizing, and reflecting on various developers, specific games and game series, and other components of the video game industry for much of the time that video games themselves have existed.[2]

The interviews in this section of the book all address, in various ways, what it means to think about video game history. There are two interviews with individuals who are often associated with some of those earliest successes for the industry (Nolan Bushnell and Eugene Jarvis), one person charged with preserving that history through a perspective more closely associated with an art museum curator (Chris Melissinos), and one person who has spent a lot of time thinking about the unique historiographical questions and material constraints of doing video game history as an academic (Henry Lowood). Each of them is grappling with large questions: How and why should we preserve artifacts of gaming's past? What lessons from that past are worth learning for the present? What is the best way to evaluate a medium that is so closely tied to rapid technological change? Most important, there is a common concern here: Does video game history matter at all? If so, what parts of it are important and why?

THE HISTORY OF VIDEO GAME HISTORY

Approaches to writing about video game history have taken several forms that can be loosely organized into three categories: popular histories, generally written by and for the "average gamer" or "general public"; industry histories, produced and curated in the interest of image management or profitability (or both) by those who make and publish games; and academic and institutional histories, which consider game history from specific methodological and theoretical approaches for interested scholarly audiences and educational purposes. Understanding the differences and relationships between these categories of historical approaches to video games is useful for considering the interviews that follow in this portion of the book.

Popular Histories

Prior to the growth of retrogaming-related content on the World Wide Web in the early part of the twenty-first century, much of the writing about older games and industry history that occurred was found in magazines that had features or columns dedicated to such content. For example, *Electronic Gaming Monthly* published its inaugural "Best 100 Games of All Time" list to coincide with its one hundredth issue in 1997, and *PC Gamer* published its July 2000 issue with a bundled compact disc of full games dating back to the mid-1980s in a "Classic Games Collection." This emphasis has continued in the years since in publications such as the British magazine *Retro Gamer* (published initially in 2004) and in long-running features such as *Game Informer*'s "Classic GI" (which ended in 2009).

More substantive, long-form works about video game history have been published since at least the 1980s. One of the best-known early works is Scott Cohen's *Zap! The Rise and Fall of Atari,* which was published in 1984 and, as the title suggests, provides insight into the company's meteoric rise and the eventual market crash that would forever change Atari and those who were associated with the company. Around the same time that EGM and *PC Gamer* released their definitive lists of classics mentioned above, Steve L. Kent authored both *The Ultimate History of Video Games, from "Pong" to "Pokémon" and Beyond: The Story behind the Craze That Touched Our Lives and Changed the World* (2001) and *The First Quarter: A 25-Year History of Video Games* (2000), Rusel DeMaria and Johnny L. Wilson collaborated on *High Score! The Illustrated History of Electronic Games* (2002), and Van Burnham published *Supercade: A Visual History of the Videogame Age, 1971–1984* (2001). Coinciding with all of this was a growing online interest in retrogaming (for example, AtariAge.com launched in 1998), the creation of the Classic Gaming Expo in 1999, and the production of the G4TV show *Icons* in 2002.

It is difficult to characterize these turn-of-the-millennium histories as a homogeneous collective, as they vary considerably in depth, tone, and focus. More significant, it seems, is the temporal proximity of their publication to one another; they launched what has since become something of a popular genre of game history books, video series, and various physical and digital features that cover almost all corners of game history. Though work in video game history existed prior to the twenty-first century, it has existed *in earnest* for the past fifteen years.

Increasingly, the best examples of "popular game history" have focused on a specific game, series, studio, platform, or era. Books such as David Kushner's *Masters of Doom: How Two Guys Created an Empire and Transformed Pop Culture* (2003), which chronicles the history of the game's development at iD studios, and Jordan Mechner's recent books that chronicle his journals from the time he spent developing *Karateka* and *Prince of Persia* (2012) are examples of studies that provide significant depth on a specific topic. Though they are published by MIT Press, the books in the Platform Studies series offer histories of various gaming or game-related hardware that are very accessible to the nonacademic reader. Other examples of note would include Kurt Kalata's (2011) tome on classic graphical adventure games and Blake Harris's (2014) recent book on the 1990s console wars.

Industry Histories

Coinciding with the boom in retrospective popular histories at the turn of the century, the video game industry itself has presented its own past in some very specific ways. Most notably, it has chosen to canonize some of its titles in various rereleases. The advent of optical drive technology helped usher in a deluge of "classic" game compilations starting in the mid-1990s and continuing today (though digital distribution has begun to replace this approach). *Wikipedia,* for example, lists more than two hundred published compilations of games, many of them coming from arcade stalwarts such as Namco, Midway, Taito, Sega, and Capcom. These compilations often offer descriptive texts about the specific games or developers, feature audio and video interviews and features, showcase production and concept art, and otherwise present games from the 1970s–1990s as historical artifacts.[3]

Beyond rereleasing games, the industry has increasingly made efforts to publish their own histories in encyclopedias, art books, or other print materials. For example, there are recent licensed books such as *The*

Sky: The Art of "Final Fantasy" (Amano, 2013), *The History of "Sonic the Hedgehog"* (Pétronille and Audureau, 2013), and the *Official Complete Works* of the Mega Man/Mega Man X franchises (Capcom, 2009). In another recent example, in 2011 Nintendo collaborated with the comic book publisher Dark Horse Comics to publish the 276-page *Legend of Zelda* history *Hyrule Historia* (Goombs et al.), which chronicles the series' development and offers many details and images related to various *Zelda* games, Nintendo developers, and physical memorabilia associated with the franchise.

Hyrule Historia is an especially good example of the kinds of histories that the industry itself typically produces in that it highlights "positives" associated with a particular company or property (commercial or critical successes, long-running franchises, and more) and ignores or de-emphasizes comparative "negatives" (commercial or critical failures, litigation histories, and the like). *Hyrule Historia,* for example, purports to chronicle every game in the *Legend of Zelda* franchise but deliberately eschews mention of the three *Zelda* titles that Nintendo licensed to Philips to produce for their CD-i console in the early 1990s (*Link: The Face of Evil, Zelda: The Wand of Ghaleon,* and *Zelda's Adventure*). These games are considered non-canon by Nintendo and are largely derided by fans of the other games in the series, but they nonetheless are part of the series' history.

Academic and Institutional Histories

Much of the peer-reviewed work about video game history has been published in journals associated with the field of game studies. For example, in 2013 the Sage journal *Games and Culture* featured scholarship that addressed topics such as the original VCS game *Adventure* (Lessard, 2013), emulation (Murphy, 2013), and a "genealogy" of *Second Life* (Veerapen, 2013); in the past they have tackled game preservation (Barwick, Dearnley, and Muir, 2011), the presentation of history itself in computer games (Schut, 2007), and hardware histories (O'Donnell, 2010). In another example, the December 2013 special issue of *Game Studies* features essays affiliated with the "History of Games" conference held in Montreal the previous June; the issue features essays on subjects as wide ranging as the role of hobbyists in game preservation, the history of gender representations in video games, and the origins of Japanese video games in the 1970s.

In the editor's introduction to that issue of *Game Studies,* Aarseth (2013) suggests, "What has been lacking is not the writing of game history, but the *institutionalization* of the study of computer game history in the shape of enduring structures: archives, museums, journals, conferences and international networks." There are, however, some well-known, ongoing efforts to create many of these things. Stanford University, for example, has a rich and well-cataloged collection of video game–related hardware, software, video and print materials, and more (much of which has been highlighted on Henry Lowood's "How They Got Game" website). The Library of Congress also has a large collection of games and game-related resources included in their Moving Image Materials collection. Increasingly, other university and public libraries are archiving and lending both older and newer video games in a fashion similar to how they treat video and audio media.

As will be addressed in chapter 2, the Smithsonian's *Art of Video Games* exhibit offered a recent and prominent example of video game history being recognized by a major public institution, but there are also other examples of video games finding their way into museums. For several years the Videogame History Museum has been touring conventions and trade shows and raising funds for a permanent home; its founders have more than twenty thousand unique items they hope to move into exhibition. Outside of the United States, there are museums such as Tokyo's new Huis Ten Bosch Game Museum, which opened in 2014, and Rome's video game museum Vigamus, both of which feature curations of older and newer hardware and software as well as exclusive and rare pieces from both private collectors and game studios.

THE FUTURE OF VIDEO GAME HISTORY

There are some looming concerns for those who are interested in video game history moving forward. Most urgent, perhaps, is preserving both experiences and memories of the medium's earliest history (from the 1940s to the 1970s), as much of the original hardware and software deteriorates or becomes harder to find and as the people who created the industry age and die. Poor documentation of early game creation and those involved, poor archiving of original production materials, and increasingly obsolete storage formats compound the historian's task, but a recent uptick in interest for publishing and reading video game history and for archiving and experiencing its most obscure components offers hope that these obstacles can be largely overcome in the near future.

Another concern of note is the rise of digital-only content; increasingly, video games do not have physical releases, or, even when they do, they are augmented with downloadable patches and add-on content. Most of this media is accessible only behind some kind of digital rights management barrier (for example, access to a service such as Steam or Xbox Live), and much of it can become unavailable when licensing rights change (for example, *Outrun Online Arcade* was removed from the PlayStation Network and Xbox Live when Sega's contract with Ferrari expired in 2011). For someone interested in preserving contemporary games for future historical research, the impact of services that provide licensing of games and the growing ubiquity of DRM will increasingly become areas of challenge.

Beyond these issues, contemporary video game historians are potentially tasked with identifying and documenting significant events that might occur within the tremendous volume of ephemeral virtual worlds. There is also the need to address a rich history of video game subcultures that exist(ed) both before and since the rise of the Internet, very little of which has been substantively historicized. There is still a large need for industry histories that are not produced by the industry itself. For example, compared to what exists for other entertainment forms, there is a relative dearth of biographies or case studies focused on specific game designers, directors, artists, and studios. There is almost nothing on the history of underrepresented groups in gaming history, nor has there been much written about the history of game journalism, game advertising, or game merchandising. To facilitate this kind of work, there needs to be increased public support for and training in methods of historical media research, in library sciences, and in digital curating. There is evidence that such support and training exist and are on the rise globally, but the long-term success and viability of video game history and preservation will be at least partly dependent on the quality of the work being done in these areas in the near future.

SUMMARY

This section of the book addresses questions about video game history, an area of growing interest to professional historians, game-industry content developers, and some enthusiast gamers. Specifically, it engages several carefully selected individuals about their perspectives on video game history itself, the archiving and presentation of that history, and the future challenges of doing historical work related to video games. They are responding, in large part, to the idea that doing work to preserve video games and their history for future publics is a pressing task in the wake of the medium's growing popularity, its aging early hardware and software, and its transition to more ephemeral online contexts. These interviews meet that urgency with a compelling mix of expertise, perspective, and strategy.

ONE

Nolan Bushnell

LEARNING FROM THE PAST

NOLAN BUSHNELL IS THE PERSON MOST OFTEN ASSOCIATED
with the origins of video games as a commercial enterprise. His list of
"firsts" in the industry reads like an outline for the study of early gaming
history: he created both the first commercial arcade game (*Computer
Space*) and the first commercially successful one (*Pong*); he was a founding partner of the first wildly successful video game company, Atari;
and he was instrumental in developing and curating content for arcades
in both its "golden age" and in its "Chuck E. Cheese era," named for
the gaming-themed chain of family restaurants that he created. Though
video games' earliest beginnings would predate the launch of Atari by
almost thirty years, their migration out of university computer laboratories and student unions coincided with Bushnell's emergence as a shrewd
evangelist of their potential to capture both a wider audience's attention
and, importantly, their coins.

Bushnell's enthusiasm for games started early. He was one of the
fortunate few who had the opportunity to play *Spacewar!* on the PDP-1
with the game's creator, Steve Russell, an experience that Bushnell re-
calls as "mesmerizing." "I spent every minute I could in that computer
lab" (Bushnell in Melissinos and O'Rourke 24). He has been a longtime
advocate of games that are centered on repayable, challenging mechanics
over those that feature bloat, spectacle, and easy titillation.[1] His influential perspective on game design was succinctly explained in 1971: "All the
best games are easy to learn and difficult to master. They should reward
the first quarter and the hundredth." Recently, he has suggested that his
"great hope" for such game design principles "is that video game meth-

odology has an ability to communicate with young minds in an amazing way" (Bushnell in Melissinos and O'Rourke 25).

In the twenty-first century, Nolan Bushnell is in a unique position of being able to weigh in on how game history has been preserved, presented, and framed by those who write about it despite, in more and more cases, not having lived it directly. In addition, he is well suited to reflect on what elements of that history are especially important to carry forward into new game designs, game industry decisions, and, with his current focus, educational endeavors that involve games.

Given that Bushnell has spoken and written at length about his own time in the industry, this interview forgoes a recapitulation of that past and instead begins with his insights on the way that this history has been told and, specifically, his understanding of what has been underappreciated and underemphasized. The interview also includes Bushnell's thoughts on links between classic game design principles and human learning, links that he has emphasized in his own work to create games for lifelong education. He also shares his thoughts on game studies and on retrogaming fan culture.

—⁓—

HEINEMAN: You've commented previously about whether or not people have done a good job of thinking about and writing about video game history, and you've mentioned that journalists and historians often focus too much on individual programmers at the expense of teams or at the expense of projects. What are your thoughts on the status of recording game history as you're familiar with it?

BUSHNELL: Well, I think that the general flow of what's been recorded is pretty accurate. There's nuances that I disagree with, but nothing really big. I believe one of the areas that is often overlooked is how creativity is a driving force in game development and that, much like any entertainment media, it thrives on "different," and that the ability to provide "different" and to create games that are new and somewhat revolutionary has been part of the legacy of the game business. We've gotten some of the most creative people in the world as a result thereof.

The other issue is that with games, because of their tremendous use of graphics and real-time computations, we've actually forced an awful lot of growth in computation, graphics processing, and other things that have been very beneficial to other industries. We're really driven by the economics of the game business, so now, if you can see molecules and DNA and things like that, an awful lot of that computer power and algorithms were actually created by the game business. That emphasis has not been brought out [in gaming histories].

HEINEMAN: One way to think about the history of the game industry and how it's been successful economically is by tracing the ways in which it has responded to shifts in spatiality, both in terms of designed game space and in adapting to the spaces where we game (e.g., the arcade, the living room, mobile devices). From your perspective, is the understanding of space something that has driven success?

BUSHNELL: I think so. One of the things that I'm very fascinated with right now is augmented reality. There was artificial reality, which made everybody seasick, and fifteen years ago everybody thought that was going to be the big thing. But, unfortunately, if you make your customers sick, it tends to have limited commercial appeal. It turns out that there's some interesting things with that. Everyone thought that [the limited appeal] was because of lag time and lack of computing power. But the problems haven't gotten much better though some of those technical obstacles have been solved. There's some real interesting things going on in the brain that I don't think we totally understand in terms of that artificial reality push. Augmented reality, of course, really means that you can now start to have game dynamics in a physical space in which you essentially view the world through the porthole of your cell phone, but it's matrixed over a square, or a mall, or a physical location, and I think that's very interesting.

HEINEMAN: There have been attempts to characterize gaming history as an evolution in a medium (for example, as an "art form"). Given your previous answer about the history of games as one of technical innovation, do you think that these classifications (e.g.,

"art," "entertainment," "technology") are useful in informing
our cultural understanding of games? Is there a danger in trying
to look at them through the lens of another industry or another
discipline?

BUSHNELL: No, it's always important to focus on the interstices or the
links. I mean, clearly, game development is an art form. No matter
what people say, it is.

Some wonderful music has been created. I don't know if you've
ever been to a Video Game Live concert, but they're fantastic.
They have full symphony orchestras and choirs that were used
to create the soundtracks for video games. To bring it alive in a
cultural, orchestral setting is really cool. The Smithsonian exhibit
was wonderfully done. Clearly, there's some great art that's been
created there.

HEINEMAN: Has your interest in augmented reality manifested itself
in a particular project?

BUSHNELL: I'm not working personally on it, but my son is, and he's
got a couple of interesting projects that are in that area. I'm right
now primarily focusing on the gamification of learning. How do
we use some of the brain science that we have used in making
games viral and addictive in some ways to allow people to learn
faster and have more fun? In some ways, every minute of boredom
in a school robs a student of a certain amount of enthusiasm and
curiosity, and I believe that we can, through game dynamics, bring
academic subjects alive in a very interesting way.

HEINEMAN: What sparked your interest in that?

BUSHNELL: I have eight children, and it's very hard to have children
without bumping up against the education establishment and
seeing the fact that it's no longer doing a good job.

HEINEMAN: How do you approach design of a game differently when
the intent is to use it in an educational setting, as opposed to one
made strictly for fun or for commercial purposes?

BUSHNELL: There is some interesting research that was (pretty
much) pioneered by a guy named Mihaly Csikszentmihalyi on
the concept of flow, and I would recommend you see his TED talk
or read his book. The concept is quite simple. It's what we call the

"Goldilocks Point," and that is you want a game to be hard enough
to be difficult but easy enough that you can succeed, and that
by staying right in the middle of those two constructs – not too
hard, not too easy, but just right – you put yourself into a state of
flow, which is sort of an ultimate happiness. You can do that with
educational projects, and, when you do that, all of a sudden the
learning becomes stickier. A student can be working on a project
for a couple of hours and not blink, whereas most students tune
out after fifteen minutes of lecture. We have some games right now
that are accomplishing an awful lot of that.

HEINEMAN: Can you point to an example or two of a game that you
see as exemplary of what you'd like to see in educational contexts?

BUSHNELL: Go into any of the anti-aging games on our site. If you go
into Wordplay, which is our test alpha project for teaching Spanish
vocabulary, you'll see that these are very simple games, but they're
engaging, and they force the student to be an active learner as
opposed to a passive recipient, and that is a big difference.

HEINEMAN: Is the application of these design principles any different
for creating an educational game versus creating a game that
doesn't have an educational purpose?

BUSHNELL: No, they are the same.

HEINEMAN: Do you see games having utility in a classroom from
preschool all the way through to something like a doctoral degree,
or is there a particular point at which one finds diminishing
returns when using games in education?

BUSHNELL: Oh, I think that it's pre-K to post-gray. I used *Putt-Putt*
and some of the Humongous Entertainment games with my kids,
who sort of grew up with those things. I believe that in many ways
it was extremely neurogenic.

HEINEMAN: Are you familiar with Neil Postman's work at all? He
wrote a lot about television and its impact on the education
system. Have you read any of his work?

BUSHNELL: I have not.

HEINEMAN: He was a student of Marshall McLuhan, if you're
familiar with McLuhan, and his work.

BUSHNELL: Right.

HEINEMAN: He argued that television, when it was introduced in the classroom in the form of educational videos, was doing more to harm education by packaging education as entertainment, whereas, beforehand, education wasn't seen as something where kids were meant to necessarily enjoy it.[2] They were meant to learn, benefit from it, and gain things from it.

BUSHNELL: I violently disagree with that.

HEINEMAN: Do you think there is any risk in packaging education as play, if that's what games do? Is there a point at which students aren't able to make a distinction between the two?

BUSHNELL: I believe that the principle is incorrect. The ideal life is one in which you can't tell the difference between work and play, and that's what I've always tried to focus on. It turns out that if you're playing and you're enjoying something, the only people who think that's a bad idea are the latent Calvinists who believe that without pain, there's no gain. I think that's absolute bullshit, and that a proper education should be fantastic, engaging, and highly enjoyable. Can you build a trashy game and put a label on it that says this is education? Of course you can, but our stuff is teaching ten times faster in the classroom, and kids are enjoying it, so I think that's a win-win.

HEINEMAN: What's the distinction between a "trashy game" that clearly is play and might "parade" as education without providing students with useful learning and something like what you're doing, which is still a game, still play, but does have educational value? What is the difference there? How do you tell?

BUSHNELL: Outcomes. Are you learning something? Is it demonstrable? I'm an engineer, and if you can't measure outcomes, then don't do it. If you're measuring outcomes, it's very easy to tell whether your stuff is working well or whether it's trash. So, the determination of success or failure is outcomes.

HEINEMAN: Expanding on this idea of play a little bit, you've spoken in the past about an element of fun being necessary in order for the game to be worthwhile. You and other well-known designers have also lamented that in the last ten or fifteen years, there seems to be a decrease of "pure fun" in the most mainstream, critically acclaimed, and biggest-selling games.

BUSHNELL: What I believe happens is there's an awful lot of games that are highly repetitive, and I think that repetitiveness in a game context can be okay, but it's not neurogenic and what you really want. The core principle of neurogenesis is different, and I think that by introducing more diversity of your game style and game play, you're actually treating your brain better and giving it a better opportunity to grow. I'm not sure if that's quite answering your question properly, but what I don't like is some of what I call negative social messages that happen in some of the games. I dislike that.

HEINEMAN: Meaning messages about violence or those kinds of things?

BUSHNELL: Yeah, I think *Grand Theft Auto* is a trashy game, and I don't see a lot of social benefit to taking on the role of a mugger and a car thief and a woman beater.

HEINEMAN: Well, then, how do you quantify "fun"? Many people enjoy those games, and they find them to be fun. So even if you believe they are sending negative messages, is there a way to hook that same population of players on games that are teaching them or making them do more productive things?

BUSHNELL: Well, I think that there's *Fifty Shades of Grey* and there's Hemingway, and are we going to be able to excise prurient interest out of a population? I don't think so. But that doesn't mean that we shouldn't always try to illuminate positive aspects and create games that have substance and learning, and some people are going to enjoy them and some people aren't.

HEINEMAN: To what extent do you think the possibilities of games in education are due to the fact that gaming has now been a major industry for forty or fifty years? People who are teaching now grew up playing games that you were designing in the '70s or '80s. Do you think that it's a generational thing? Why do you think now is a good time to start seeing increased gaming in the classroom?

BUSHNELL: Mankind has always been in a contest for "How do we capture imagination?" and the answer is competition. If you have a world full of high-production-value video experiences, whether they be commercials or television or movies or games, and compare those to a teacher with a piece of chalk and blackboard, they're outgunned in a real way. People expect information to be coming at them at a very, very high rate of speed, and their brains have actually been modified to expect that kind of experience, and so the schools became increasingly antiquated.

When I was going to elementary school, school was the most interesting thing happening in town. The alternative was watching the river flow and the corn grow. That's not what our kids are involved in today. I mean, we didn't have a television set until I was in the fifth grade. So, really, we cannot view the golden age of schools in the '30s, '40s, and '50s as being anything that's useful today. It's just wrong. It's different, it's inappropriate, and all of these things have trained brains to actually be smarter and to be able to take data faster, and for us to not give data faster creates boredom and tune-outs.

HEINEMAN: Fans of games have created communities, conventions, and other activities around contemporary gaming but, increasingly, also around classic gaming. What is your thought on the ways in which that has grown over the past ten or fifteen years, especially the retrogaming scene?

BUSHNELL: Oh, I love it. I've keynoted several conventions of fifty thousand gamers, who've come in with a sleeping bag and their computers and hook up in a convention. I was at one in Bilbao in which, basically, people came and gamed almost 24/7 for a week. What a fantastically engaged environment that was, people coming to conventions in full regalia of their favorite video game hero/heroine. This is fun, it's just fun, and I applaud it all.

HEINEMAN: Is there anything about gaming that you think makes it especially ripe for this kind of activity?

BUSHNELL: Absolutely. Gaming presents a very compelling universe that operates under predictable values and predictable outcomes. So the experience can be very intense and very satisfying in a world that is increasingly chaotic otherwise. All this stuff works really well to create a fan base and people that basically want to emulate their heroes, even though their heroes are constructs. I was at a PAX conference in Seattle a month ago, and I'd say that a third to a half of the attendees were in some kind of costume.

HEINEMAN: How familiar are you with game studies as a discipline, and do you think that it has had positive, negative, or negligible influence on people in the industry? Do you think that there's a good conversation there?

BUSHNELL: I look at it as being really in its infancy, and so the impact has not been huge. But it's growing, and I expect it to continue to grow and become more and more important. It's always good to have academic understandings and underpinnings for two or three reasons. First of all, I think that any industry, any science, any group of technologies start out with an awful lot of anecdotal evidence, and I always think that it's important to have scientific, empirical outcomes to separate myth from reality, and that is the role that the academic community does wonderfully. I'm one of these guys that believes that there is a truth and that we should always be questing it, and, again, there's a lot of difference between belief structures and knowledge structures, and I think that we always want to bias society toward truth structures as opposed to opinion structures.

HEINEMAN: One analogy that I often make for people is to compare the field to film studies and to consider the ways in which film studies, at its inception, taught people either to make films or to study them. Over time, those two foci increasingly came together so that the best filmmakers were those who had also spent a lot of time doing critical film studies work. Do you see that happening in the future for game studies, where it becomes important for people who study game design and programming to also have a healthy dose of the humanities in which they can study gaming's social influence, the politics and economics of games, and so forth?

BUSHNELL: I think that it will come together. I'm always concerned about teaching too much formulaic analysis, i.e., if you have to scare the shit out of somebody every ten minutes in a movie and then you follow it up with a romantic interlude. It leads oftentimes to formulaic movies, which, while they may be successful, don't push the boundaries of creative thought. I would be hesitant to have the world converge so that all future games become a variant of *Bejeweled*.

TWO

Chris Melissinos

ART AND VIDEO GAMES

IN HIS YEARS AT SUN MICROSYSTEMS, CHRIS MELISSINOS'S official title was, in part, that of an "evangelist," a role associated with street preaching, door knocking, dogmatism, and conversion. Those who hired him for the position of "chief evangelist and chief gaming officer" were no doubt themselves initially taken aback by his infectious enthusiasm for technology and, specifically, for video games. Talking about his time at Sun some years later, in an interview addressing the opening of the exhibition *The Art of Video Games* that he curated for the Smithsonian Art Museum, Melissinos reflected on having the opportunity to express his hope for technology's future while at a Java Developers conference in 2009. "I made the point that technology is wonderful, and it gives us the opportunity to do many things, however none of it matters if we don't find the humanity in it" (Bednarz).

If *The Art of Video Games* attempted to argue one thing, it is that a productive route to finding the humanity in technology is to approach that technology as an art form. Melissinos's exhibit made a strong case that video games in particular might be understood as the work of artists who skillfully write beautiful code on the constrained canvas of a particular platform, who design experiences that provoke complex thoughts and actions from their audiences, or who merge existing art forms (music, illustration, acting, and more) into a novel expression of humanity.

The 2012 Smithsonian Art Museum exhibit came at an interesting time in the history of the medium. Two years before its grand opening, film critic Roger Ebert stoked a long-simmering debate about the status of video games as art by penning a widely read editorial piece proclaiming the medium's innate inability to ever produce experiences that could be considered art. Ebert's lofty status as a prominent art critic certainly contributed to the volume and voraciousness of the response by those seeking to refute his claims. The debate persisted in earnest for some time afterward in many online forums and game communities, but in many ways the Smithsonian's institutional power to confer the status of "art" on games functioned as a visible and powerful refutation to the spirit (if not to the specific arguments) of Ebert's controversial statement.

Whether and how to consider games as art has also been an increasingly recurrent theme in game studies scholarship, with articles in prominent journals (several of which are alluded to in the interview) taking up the issues of aesthetics (Deen, 2011; Kirkpatrick, 2009), of creative algorithms (Burden and Gouglas, 2012), and of artistic design (Gillespie and Crouse, 2012; Kirkland, 2010). In some ways, this scholarship reinforces the arguments presented in Melissinos's exhibit. In others, it challenges some of its core assumptions.

The interview featured in this chapter addresses the exhibit in light of some of that scholarship and offers a discussion of the relationship between state institutions and the funding of game development, exhibition, and preservation as well as games as public experiences. Melissinos also shares some thoughts about definitions of art and about the future of games exhibited in public contexts.

—⁂—

HEINEMAN: What were the goals of the Smithsonian exhibit, which recently came to a close? Did they change over time? Did you feel you accomplished them all to varying degrees?

MELISSINOS: The root of the goal of the exhibition was formed back in 2009. I was asked to come to the Smithsonian to participate in a program called Smithsonian 2.0. This program was basically the initiative of incoming secretary Wayne Clough, who wanted to understand how to better utilize technology to meet the patrons where they lived their lives. The museum was a space that was somewhat disconnected from that, so they wondered how they could engage audiences through technology to basically deliver

the message of the Smithsonian museum to patrons that either
come through the door daily or who have an affinity or connection
to the museum or to its materials from a distance. We spent three
days there, about twenty or twenty-five senior technologists from
all across the computer industry. It was myself, as the chief evangelist and chief gaming officer at Sun Microsystems, all the way to
the guys from MySpace and Facebook, and Microsoft and Google,
and so on. What most people were saying is, "Oh, yes, after spending three days with you curators, you should write more blogs, and
you should tweet more, and you should do podcasts."

I took this very contrary position of saying, "I've spent three
days with you curators, and what I have discovered is you don't
want to talk to the public. What you want to do is curate. You want
to apply yourself in the process of curation, to have this deep body
of understanding. So, rather than force you into something that
may consume more time than you would like and may not necessarily be the best way for you to address your audience, and rather
than look at just the standard modes of communication, through
tweeting and blogging and running a Facebook page, instead
think about how do you speak to people who walk through the
doors every day with iPods in their hands, with DSs in their hands,
with PSPs in their hands. You have dozens of schoolkids coming
in your doors every day that live their lives in this electronic communication medium, that live their lives in this interactive space,
but you're not meeting them there."

It was during that time that I got connected to the museum
through one particular person, Georgina Goodlander, who had
done an alternate-reality game at the museum called *Ghosts of
a Chance.* The head of the art museum said to Georgina, "Hey,
look, video games seem to be important in terms of how they've
been adopted and the reach that they've attained. From an artistic
standpoint, how do we feel about that? What is the compelling
argument to be made for video games as art?" and she said, "Well,
I don't know video games, but I know a guy that does, and he was
already out here, and let's invite him back in."

They brought me back in, and what was supposed to be a
thirty-minute meeting turned into a three-hour meeting of all the

different things that we could do, and, from that, I said, "What you need to understand is that for those of us that grew up programming games and playing games, I mean these are so much a part of our lives that it's impossible to extract ourselves from them." We always knew that the games that we were making, the things we were doing, the earliest forms were more than what we believed them to be. We just didn't have the maturity or vocabulary to describe what it is we were actually creating or why it was so important.

So the goal of the Smithsonian exhibition was to look at video games as an art form, not just the art within the video games. It could have been very easy to create an exhibition that says, "We'll look at all games that are really from an impressionist artistic point of view, or a watercolor point of view, or a pointillism point of view, or an abstract point of view." You could have skinned it any one of those ways, but the problem is that you are only focusing on particular pieces of art within the artwork itself, and that's what's so difficult sometimes when trying to wrap your head around video games as an art. People say, "Well, it's not like painting." Well, not only is it like painting, there are painters involved in creating art that goes into games, as well as sculptors and modelers and writers, and musicians and historians; all of these different practices go into the creation of a video game.

To that end, I think we achieved what we set out to achieve, which is not to look at any one particular game for a particular piece of art or art style or art component, but rather video games as a whole as an art medium. While it wasn't necessarily as deep as we could have gone, it was more of a cursory examination, more higher-level examination, because you're trying to acclimate the idea of this notion to members of an audience that may not have ever considered it to be art before. I think, to that end, we achieved our goal, which was to lay the foundation work for video games as an art form.

HEINEMAN: Since you opened the exhibit, you've found yourself often answering this question about, "Well, how does one define art, and why do video games count as an example?" In the book that accompanies the exhibit, you explained art thus; you said,

"When the viewer is able to understand the artist's intent in a work and find something in it that resonates on a personal level, art is achieved. If it elicits an emotion, from disdain to delight, it can be viewed as art" (Melissinos and O'Rourke, 9). The first thing that I'm struck by in that definition is that you define art as, above all, the work of an intending artist.

MELISSINOS: No video game is made without some intent. Just like any other form of art, it isn't something that manifests itself out of nothing. There is definitely intent, and sometimes within that intent can come compromise, can come an adjustment of position, and these sorts of things. Am I correct in assuming that you mean by an "intending artist" that you are asking, "Does the artist intend to call themselves an artist?" That what they are then producing is artwork? Is it that the artwork can emerge out of something that they never even intended to be viewed as an art?

HEINEMAN: Well, actually maybe it's neither of those things. I guess the question is if a game becomes definable as art at the moment of "understanding" a certain intent. The reason I'm asking is because some might suggest that art is *not* about understanding intent; it's about interpreting meaning.

MELISSINOS: I am allowing for both of those things. Let's take a game that has very clear intent, a game like in the *Metal Gear* series of games. The games are informed by Hideo Kojima's world, his personal world. In my interview with him, he went on to talk about how so much of it was informed by the life that his parents had led, and how he views war and diplomacy, and the failure of diplomacy, which causes war, and these sorts of things. So, when you look at a game like *Metal Gear*, it is really an antiwar message that is inventing this game, which is when diplomacy fails, this happens, but you need to try diplomacy first, and that's boiling down to its very basics.

So, anybody that's ever really played the game and played through the *Metal Gear* series can understand that's his position. It emerges within the story. However, on the road to understanding that intent, there are all of these small decisions that are made along the way that personalize the experience for the player

themselves. In a game like *Metal Gear,* you can get through most
of the game without physically harming the NPCs [nonplayer
characters]. You can choke them out and kind of move them to
the side, or sneak your way through many, many of the scenarios
without actually having to exercise this overt kind of attack. There
are some people who will just run through and mow everything
down to get out of the way. Other people will take a very different
approach to it.

But, at the end of the day, while that is a very personalized
experience, it all is framed within the intent that Hideo Kojima
had for that universe to exist, and people that play those games
can understand what Kojima was trying to say, but have a very
personalized experience that then speaks to their moral code,
how they view the world, and the things that they would want to
see occur. Video games are the only medium that allow for both
of those pieces to fit within the same body of work. Books don't
provide that. You can go back after reading a book and reflect upon
it and say how it differs from the way you do things or the way you
view the world, or the choices you would have made different, but
that has never presented itself in the experience of reading that
book. You're at odds and conflict with it, but it never allows you to
personalize the words off the page. It is the same thing in movies,
the same thing in music (well, music is a bit more abstract in that
regard).

HEINEMAN: What about other types of games, whether that be something like chess or poker or Monopoly, or even maybe something
a little bit closer to video games, like *Dungeons & Dragons,* with a
game master who does this creation of a world, which has this sort
of defining player choices, and so forth? Would those, because of
what you're suggesting, also count as art in the way that you mean
it?

MELISSINOS: Absolutely, and specifically *Dungeons & Dragons.* That is
a game about a personalized character story and interaction within
the combatants. The adventurers in the game sit within a gameplay
framework that is ultimately, on a very macro level, controlled by
the dungeon master. So, the dungeon master can control where

monsters are placed and trenches are found and traps are to occur and the history that comes out in the module. But that dungeon master cannot control the individual choices that the players make: "I'm going to choose to use this spell." Well, that may not be as effective. "Well, that's not your choice, dungeon master, to make." That is the choice of the person playing in that character. So, they can get these micro choices made that still fit within the entire framework that the dungeon master has set forth. In *D&D* both pieces are emerging at the same time. They are in parallel working together in concert. It isn't really hard to understand the intent there because you're basically told, "This is what's standing in front of you. This is what you chose to ignore. This is exactly your only way out." It's written right there for you.

HEINEMAN: One of the other things the exhibit has emphasized is the way that there's a certain amount of artistry in the programming of game software. Certainly, Ian Bogost's work in *Racing the Beam* with Nick Montfort addresses the notion of the intense creativity to be found by working within certain constraints. Does this understanding of the "artistry of programming" thus extend to other nongaming software?

MELISSINOS: If I assign to three separate programmers the same problem, they will all come at it from a different perspective. I expect the same output, I expect the same occurrence to happen, but there are three different approaches that more than likely will materialize out of this. You have programming methodologies, like Agile and Waterfall and Scrum, and these sorts of things, and it's supposed to push some of those things out of the way and get everybody into a similar system and kind of build upon those things, but, at the end of the day, it's about individual choice.

When you listen to somebody like R. J. Michael talk about coding, what he said (and I just love this) is that "when I write a piece of code, I write it like I'd write a good story. My comments are very clear, people can understand what I intend to do, and so I try to make those as clear and forward as possible, and when I write code in that manner and it executes well on the screen, it moves me in a very profound way." He said it's much like observing the beauty of a 3-D object in our world and then building that within his. It's an incredibly moving thing for him; what he's really doing is he's describing code as prose. I've long maintained that writing those video games is a form of poetry; it's just spoken in an abstract language we don't directly understand, but computers certainly do. Every bit of these games, when they're written, every line of code is written with the intent that it's written against the overall objective, the position that the designer or the author or the game needs to either communicate to the player or a message that it needs to deliver to the world, so there's no real arbitrary code that sits in there. It all goes toward that end, right? It's not as if they're writing a bunch of incidental pages that can get thrown out that have nothing to do with it, right? It's intent.

When you look at Ed Fries and the work that he did with *Halo 2600*, he said, and I'm paraphrasing him, that basically "writing for the 2600 is like writing haiku, because each character matters." Every small little bit, because of the constraints of that space, it is a requirement to be very thoughtful, to take a very considered approach to writing it because every single character will matter in terms of getting the game to fit into that space in the way that they want. If you talk to people who program for a living, they can speak as passionately about the type of work that they do in the same way that an artist can about the work that they do.

HEINEMAN: When any new medium starts to be understood as an art form, then we also begin to think differently about the ways to productively critique the medium. A "good" film critic might not be the professional film critic who writes for your local paper; it might be the person who teaches in a film studies program and has studied film academically. Do you think that there's a need to, as we reconsider games as art, reconsider how we write about and think about games publicly?

MELISSINOS: I think that will happen naturally over time, and you have a variety of different things that are occurring right now that will lead to change. For example, the democratization of technology is at an all-time low in terms of cost and acquisition for very powerful tools, which means that you now have a system that is receptive to any and all forms of games and intent and imagination to come screaming out into the Web, and that's what we're seeing today. There's no shortage of games to find. In fact, there's almost more games than we could ever possibly hope to take a look at.

What you get is the other side of the pendulum – that's where all this content comes flooding in. Now, it takes time to sort through that, to understand, "Wow, this piece is actually a very compelling thing, and actually it mirrors a message that is being delivered in society," or "This is mirroring a specific political position," or "This is somebody who is trying to invoke these thoughts in the players from their childhood," or so on and so forth. So, I think over time, as we sift through this, we will find the body of work we need to have that critical discourse. Today, you're right, most of it is "Well, the graphics weren't as good as they were before, the story line was pretty good here, the voice acting, I give it a 7 out of 10," right? That's most of where we are today; it's mostly kind of newspaper criticism. That doesn't in any way, shape, or form devalue that work; it's important because they're helping the world to kind of sift through these things.

One has to be really careful, I think, when we create art games versus being critical of the art within games. By that what I mean is there are several games, I won't mention them, but there are several games that people kind of hold up as, "Oh, this is an art game," and in many ways it ceases to become either. It becomes neither game nor art, because it overtly is saying before it's even pushed out, "I'm making an art game," so you're announcing art without any sort of critical discussion or adoption by the observer, and you are removing a lot of what makes a game a game by lumping it specifically within an art discipline, and I think we have to be very careful about that. What we need to understand is that video games are a form of art that is still extraordinarily young compared to other forms of expressive media, and, with that, we have to give ourselves time to understand the implications of games, how they affect a society, what are the messages that they're trying to teach, and how we can best understand the world. So, the short answer is yes, we will get there; it's just going to take some time.

HEINEMAN: Is part of the issue an appreciation of technique? With painting or film, I think the technique is easier to just "see." In a game, the coding is often proprietary – we can't actually "see" how it's been coded; we might be able to see interesting particle effects in an engine or something like that, but if you're suggesting that a lot of the underlying artistic components that provide full appreciation of a game as art is at this level that is fairly inaccessible to both players and critics, how do we move toward changing that?

MELISSINOS: When you look at the movie industry, for example, you can go and find these communities of camera buffs who talk about fit and finish and polish and architecture of cameras and camera bodies. There is a discipline to that which people recognize within that very specific field. They notice things that were done better in this model camera or that model camera, or this sort of rigging or that type of approach, and that's one level of creation that occurs. That tends to be more insular; it tends to be narrower in terms of a social discussion. It's kind of the same thing in the car industry. Within the automotive industry, you have designers and artists of note that sculpt these incredible cars. You and I probably couldn't name a single one of them or even recognize them walking down the street, but car buffs, people within that space, absolutely could and talk about, "Well, this is during his period, and he was focusing on futurism out of the '6os." So, you are going to have these subsections of the culture, of the technology, of the medium that will have kind of these critical discussions and critical eyes.

When you're talking about the broader segment of society that's never going to touch it, it's kind of like when Peter Jackson did *Lord of the Rings*. He set out and said, "Now, look, I need the technology to do this. You know what? I don't care if they're using nylon bushings in this camera or they're using German ball bearings in some components of this. What I care about is being able to tell my story." He wasn't going back and rebuilding new cameras every single time he was creating something. So, I think you get this kind of separation of the two critical components.

Are we ever going to see a public that, when they pop in a game, say, "Oh, the programming on this is astonishing. I mean, this guy knocked off one hundred milliseconds in this frame of animation by using Bender's decomposition technique!"? That's not going to happen there, but it will happen in academic circles, it will happen in the technical circles, it will happen on that side of it.

What I find really interesting is more and more people are starting to discuss the beauty and the economy of fonts, and you hear more and more people today, even in the general public, talking about font foundries, and the fact that kids are going, "Well, kerning," and you go, "Okay, well, yeah." When you read websites like *The Oatmeal,* and stuff like that, and you get kind of this introduction to these more esoteric things through something that is a widespread medium, like a comedy site, like *The Oatmeal,* then yeah, people are starting to pay attention. Will they ever become critics of it? No, but in that world of font creation, absolutely. They look at it as art, except it's a very, very narrow band of society that does that, right?

HEINEMAN: What is your sense of the importance or weight of the "video-games-as-art" discussion outside of a U.S. or even a Western context? Is it a question that's being explored there with the same interest in places like Japan?

MELISSINOS: Since we've launched the exhibition, I have been contacted by people all over the world who are trying to do very similar things to illuminate video games as an art form within their culture, promoting Japanese artists and Korean artists and European artists, and game designers and developers. In fact, I know of one game company in Korea whose CEO is using his personal money to actually build a full-on, dedicated museum to video games, a public institution.

This is something that, collectively, people around the world are looking at games and saying, "We need to understand what this means to us, to society." As our children are engaged in this more and more, as society is engaged in this more and more and more, as academic institutions are providing degrees in game development, and these sorts of things, what does it mean? How do we really observe it as art? It's just going to rocket from here, which is great: more conversation to try to at least answer important questions or build a basis for further discussion.

HEINEMAN: My next question is about the treatment of games as art in academia. The discussions you've been alluding to seem driven first and foremost by gamers and people in the industry, not by scholars. Why do you think that this question of gaming as art or, more broadly, about the cultural significance of games is taking longer to catch on at the level of scholarship in academia?

MELISSINOS: Because I think, by and large, people (not just in academia, to be very clear) were kind of dismissive of video games, specifically as art. I know in several programs at several universities, where they were trying to start game developer programs, and you would have faculty members go, "Why would we ever do that? Video games are what we want to teach our kids to do?" Well, it turns out that in order to program video games, you need to understand advanced mathematics, you need to understand physics, you need to understand English and history and creative writing, and all of these individual disciplines that are kind of this amalgam that creates video games, right? Games are an amalgam of many different forms of art, and it's all these different forms of practices that create this.

Remember, video games are only forty years old, as far as popular society and popular culture really understand them and have played with them, and so we've gone through this incredibly fast, hyperevolution of video games as a fixture within modern society. I think, when you have this mass adoption of it, typically, at least from my observation, it's always been, "Well, just because the masses have decided this is important doesn't mean it has academic merit."

HEINEMAN: Casting aspersions down from their ivory towers.

MELISSINOS: Exactly, and it's a good discussion to have because one of the things that I think we have to be very careful of is to not overanalyze this. If you want to talk about the technology and you want to talk about the technical expertise and merits of it, great. You can actually have a discussion that builds a course of practice that's based on prior work, it's based on history, it's based on fore-casting of technology and trends, but there's a huge psychological component to games, there's a huge emotive component of games. Typically, the humanities and technology within the university structure are at odds with each other. It's no different in creating these games, "Well, I don't want that artist telling me, the pro-grammer, what to do." Well, guess what? The only way to do games is if you have this understanding of both technical development and the humanities. I think you have this kind of bifurcation of video games within that space.

A lot of times when academia tries to throw their arms around games in such a broad way, they may get a good body of work or useful information out of their research but may miss the larger point. Even within academia, we have to be very careful to not overanalyze this stuff, but to try to meet it head-on, to meet it from a place of kind of ingesting and interacting with it versus totally from an observational standpoint.

HEINEMAN: I want to shift to some questions about the relationship between games and the federal government. Because of its loca-tion on the National Mall and prestige of the Smithsonian, did the exhibit ever become politicized in any way (e.g., as an example of government waste)?

MELISSINOS: Not only did that not occur, but the embracing of this exhibition, from just about every group that I met with coming through, whether it was political, educational, or otherwise, was extraordinary. People, even if they didn't play games anymore or didn't fully understand them, understood that they were more than they could articulate. Even if they had stopped playing, they understood that at one point in their lives, games were important to them. To see multiple generations, and in many cases three generations within the same family in the exhibit, all observing it at once but from a different point of view and then finding connections was fantastic. We didn't receive any of that sort of pushback. It was incredibly well received and adopted because, I think, people recognize that these things are not going away; this is not a fad. Most society, even most people within their own homes, they observe either their kids or themselves playing these things, and here's an opportunity now, rather than to just come out and go, "Video games," to just go, "Hmm, video games. I never really looked at it this way before." In fact, that was one of the most interesting things.

I had to do docent training in the museum. The first group of docents were, by an overwhelming majority, women, probably over the age of fifty. I had to walk them through and explain why *Panzer Dragoon* was so important on the Saturn, what *Halo* meant and these sorts of things. Of the people that came up to me at the end of the training, which were quite a few, the comments that were made were all within this camp: "I've never considered video games in this way before, and I will never look at them the same way again. I never understood that there was so much meaning and intent behind these things. I didn't realize the artistry that goes into these. I had no idea that there were this many types of video games. I thought they were all a violent game." They said it has helped them to better understand culture and the things they observed, even within their own families. I think, overall, the exhibition just gave us an opportunity to say, "Okay, yeah, video games. I can get behind this. I can understand why. I can see more merit in it than I'd been told that they embody."

HEINEMAN: There was an essay last year in the journal *Game Studies* by Philip Deen. In that essay, he suggested about *The Art of Video Games* exhibit at the Smithsonian that it was evidence of "games as art" under what can be classified as an institutional theory of art. He says, "Put very crudely, the institutional theory asserts that an object becomes a work of art when accepted by the relevant community of artists and critics," and he suggests that the primary function of *The Art of Video Games* is to bestow "art," not to make necessarily an argument about the intrinsic aesthetic value of a medium or of an object. Do you think that that is in any way a valid critique? Is it a legitimate concern that you ever considered, knowing that you were producing a state-backed exhibit, which, by its very existence, would function to authenticate and legitimize what it is you wanted to exhibit?

MELISSINOS: The words that greet visitors into the exhibition are my words, and, on the wall, the very last line says, "They may even be art." The goal is not to stamp definitively, "BOOM! Video games are art," because art is an incredibly subjective term. I can tell you, having been kind of thrust into this fine arts world for the past three years, of which I have no background in fine arts, what I think I have the ability to do is to describe on a very personal and emotional level the impact of video games on culture, on society, on kids that grew up in that era and never stopped, and now have the luxury and the benefit of reflection and looking back and to understand why it was so important. I sat in front of many a piece of artwork and just went, "I don't get it," like, "I can appreciate it – I can appreciate the technique, I can understand what they were trying to say, and it doesn't move me in the least."

HEINEMAN: To interject, it seems that he's suggesting that, for example, if you look at a painting hanging on the wall that you have no real appreciation or interest in and it doesn't move you, the suggestion is that its very existence in a museum lets you know that it has value and forces you to see it that way anyway, even if there's nothing in the piece to actually make that argument for itself. Is there a concern that an exhibit on video games might create the idea that "games are art" simply because it's exhibited as such, and not because they understand it at a deeper level that they might get through understanding all these deeper components we've discussed?

MELISSINOS: If people draw that conclusion without going any deeper, then they're making the same mistake that people made when they said video games could never be art. They took a very cursory look, and they said, "Oh, well, if they say it, it must be true, so there you go." That's not what this is about. It is about presenting video games as an expressive form, even as worthy of examination as art. It's worthy of having the conversation, it's worthy of understanding there's more to these things than there seems to be at first blush, and so it presented at least the opportunity to start having the discussion. Whether or not some people say, "Well, if the Smithsonian American Art Museum says it's art, it must be art," well, again, that is just as quick an adoption as it is a dismissal, of just deciding, "Oh, they're just video games," right?

I think in some cases you're going to have that effect, where the people say, "Okay." My hope is that at best, people look at it and say, "You know, this is really something that is so new and means so much to so many people, not the people that just make them, but the people who play them, that we should be studying this. We should understand its greater meaning in society, in artistic intent, in better exploring the human condition," all of those things. That's my hope, that at least people will walk away with the ability to have this, or at least, as we were talking, the permission to say, "Okay, yeah, let's have the discussion."

So to answer Philip Deen's question very directly, sure, there are some people that are going to say, "Well, it's in the Smithsonian," right? But, again, I'm sure there are many pieces people walk by that are in any of these institutions and say, "I know it's in here, but I don't get it," and that's okay. Not everybody has to agree with it. That's what's so wonderful about this. I've stood in front of Jackson Pollock's work before and said, "Great, I get it . . . I understand his technique for painting and everything else, great." But I've shed a tear playing *Flower*. If I had to talk about understanding the intent of a piece of work, a creative endeavor, and have it presented within the same framework and answer which one has moved me? *Flower* has; Pollock hasn't.

HEINEMAN: In 2009 the National Games Registry was created. In 2012 video games became something that could be funded through NEA [National Endowment for the Arts] funding. After all this institutional recognition, might there be a future for a gaming "equivalent" of PBS or NPR or other state-funded "public interest" game development?

MELISSINOS: I think right now there are many different groups in the government that are trying to figure out exactly how to do that, the question of "How can we use this to teach?" everything from civics to ecology. The first lady did this campaign that also involved video games to teach health and better health practices for kids. I think as they realize the potential of video games as not

just an artistic medium but as a communication tool, a communication framework, one that is engaging, one that people are willing
to give themselves up to, one that people are willing to suspend
other things to do, one in which they're learning and the retention
of what they engage in is that much greater than through other
forms of communication, sure, we're going to see that happen.
We are already starting to see it. You're seeing from the side of the
government, and we're seeing it purely from the side of the public
in crowdfunding endeavors like Kickstarter.

HEINEMAN: PBS produces and broadcasts compelling drama; NPR
has plenty of hours devoted to the appreciation of a wide variety of
different kinds of music. Can you see a near future, or is it maybe
down the road, where we could have something like a AAA, big-
budget title that's purely meant to be enjoyed and consumed (and
not to teach) funded through the federal government?

MELISSINOS: There's an opportunity to do that. I think, again, we
have to give ourselves a little bit of time. We also have to give ourselves a lot of credit in dealing with a medium that was created and
exploded into the popular culture and has become an inextricable
part of cultural fabric on a global basis. That's happened within
at least my lifetime. I'm forty-two, and I've witnessed it from
the beginning; within my lifetime this has happened. That has
never happened before. So, we have to give ourselves some time
to continue to understand how best to apply our intent to these
things. All this has happened in such an incredibly and vastly short
window of time, it's astonishing, and with that, within the age of
video games, we've also seen the growth of personal technology
adoption for personal communication.

Consider the fact that a single individual can create a message
and broadcast it over the Web to the planet. This ability has never
been part of human social experience. Anybody can go into a
public library in the inner city that's equipped with a Web cam
and broadcast a message to the planet for free. Never before has
individual reach been as explosively global as it has in our lifetime,
and now we're not even talking forty years; we're talking about an
approximate fifteen-year window. Video games exist within this
framework, and its medium is one that had to be adopted very

rapidly by a culture and society that's still trying to understand what it all means. Thus far, society has done a pretty good job of figuring all this stuff out. I think as time goes on, as we understand its bigger place in the world, it's only going to get better.

It was wonderful to hear my six-year-old son have to write in his first grade class, "What do you want to be when you grow up?" "I want to be a video game designer." Now, okay, his dad collects video games, we play video games all the time, but to see this stuff that they create and to listen to the way they talk about it and to hear the stories unfold, and to observe their interpersonal play, how they play with each other and how they communicate with their friends: it's magic. It's just this outpouring of creativity and empowerment. That's something that we didn't talk about it but something that I typically talk about when I'm speaking at universities.

Take, for example, my Commodore Vic-20. What's so awesome about this is that inside of this cartridge slot is a metal sphere that is a massive capacitor. I could literally stick my finger in there and get a 120-volt shock right out of it. So, the fact that we've released these things with components like copper grounding strips on the outside of it is astonishing. This could never be released today, because it could seriously hurt your children. However, in that 5-kilobyte system (3,193 bites available after booting), as a twelve-year-old kid, I created my first fully formed game. It was empowerment. It was gifted to me at a time in my life where I had no control over anything. I didn't control what I ate, what I got to wear to school, when I had to do my homework, what time I had to go to bed, where I had to go on Sunday after church – I had none of that. But, in this machine, I could effect this universe behind glass, and it was all for me. If I applied myself to this, I could understand its secrets; I could understand how to tell the stories I wanted to tell. We're observing that today. Look at a game like *Minecraft*, watching active, adaptive storytelling that's emerging in real time. What an extraordinary gift, right? It's astonishing to me.

So, where we go from here is a bit unknown. But, again, we have to leave ourselves open to be receptive to the fact that video games are more than what we believe them to be. They are a platform for creativity, for expression, for social reflection, for personal reflection, looking inside of ourselves and understanding whether we align with the story. It tests our moral compass. It puts us in uncomfortable situations, like games like *Shadow of the Colossus.* I often describe it as a game that I felt worse the more I played it because the protagonist's goals are at odds with my moral code. I know that these are creatures that have done nothing to me, and they're beautiful, and they're in this incredible environment, and I'm attacking them for a very selfish reason, and the more they fall, the worse you feel. I mean, what other medium do we have that allows you to engage that way but kind of self-check yourself as you're going through it? We don't have anything else.

That's what this opportunity at the Smithsonian was about. Again, will the government ever fund this stuff? I think eventually we'll get there. It may not be the same model that a PBS or an NPR had, it may find its way in other ways, but we're already seeing indications of that.

THREE

Eugene Jarvis

GAMES AND DESIGN

AS LONG AS VIDEO GAMES HAVE BEEN A COMMERCIAL MEDIUM, they have appeared in arcades. Their success there has waxed and waned over the decades, and for much of the past fifteen years the arcade business has seen most game studios ceasing production of coin-op games, have witnessed more arcades shuttering their doors than opening them, and have seen their historical role as a primary driver of industry trends shifted toward a contemporary role as a niche part of the video game landscape.

Eugene Jarvis, for all intents and purposes, is the "last man standing" in the arcade business in the United States. Jarvis cut his teeth programming classic Williams arcade games like *Defender* and *Robotron 2084* before working on popular titles like *Smash TV* and the *Cruis'n* series for Midway in the 1990s. The company he founded in 2001, Raw Thrills, Inc., is the only U.S. game developer regularly producing new arcade titles. In recent years they have produced arcade cabinets related to the *Fast and Furious* film franchise, the *Terminator* franchise, and the *Batman* films and have developed several original properties such as the *Big Buck Hunter* series. They have found success in placing their machines in Wal-Marts and truck stops and in bars and restaurants, as well as in many other locations outside of the traditional arcade space.

Though contemporary arcade games are no longer the driving force of game industry changes as they once were (in areas such as economics, game design, advertising, and so on), they remain a fascinating study in their own right. Arcade games have always had to address a different kind of audience than those games that appear on consoles or computers. Issues of player interest, of challenge, of novelty, and of other components of design are significantly different from what one finds in games that one might affordably own. Jarvis's work as both a designer-programmer and an executive has been regularly punctuated by an ability to take appropriate risks at appropriate moments, offering innovation for the right audience at the right price, creating intuitive gameplay experiences that quickly yield rich underlying complexities, and providing a reason to seek out games in public spaces.

By occupying various positions in the game industry over a long period of time, Jarvis has learned something about the patterns of inertia that have defined its history. This chapter's interview begins with him explaining this past, specifically highlighting how changes in game design, advances in game technology, and the needs of commercial enterprises have aligned across it. Furthermore, the interview covers several compelling questions of game design that have been considered at times by researchers in game studies (for example, tension, parody, and the like), offering a perspective on how these principles apply specifically to the context of arcade game development.

—⚬—

HEINEMAN: You are one of the few people who have been associated with the American video game arcade from its inception to its present. From your perspective, what have been the most significant moments in that history, and what were the catalysts for them?

JARVIS: Those early years of video games, that formative phase of the video game, was really what I would call the "laboratory phase," where you had William Higinbotham doing *Tennis for Two* at Brookhaven National Laboratory, and then a few years later you had Steve Russell with *Spacewar* at MIT. So it was the era of the big iron, the mainframe; computing was really confined to laboratories and academic institutions. Guys who had access to computers were like, "Hey, what can I do with this?" The creativity of humans with no economic motivation whatsoever is amazing. Those games, to me, were such important milestones in that they were so sophisticated and so fully formed at such an early era. It wasn't until almost twenty years later that commercial arcade games had that same level of sophistication.

HEINEMAN: So you view the origins of games as a moment where human creativity and ingenuity pushed the medium into existence?

JARVIS: Yes. The idea of creating an interaction with the video screen was preceded by work with manipulating oscilloscopes and by playing around with signals and stuff in these early interactive devices that then kind of evolved into video games. The next phase was the early commercialization phase, where, for example, Ralph Bear took the idea of interaction and asked, "How can I get this out into the world?" and "How can everyone have fun with it?" and recognized that there was a need to get games out of the lab, as not everyone could afford the million-dollar mainframe. He created the Odyssey. Or consider the game out of Stanford called the "Galaxy Game," which was an implementation of *Spacewar* on Deck computers that was actually coin operated. It was placed in the student union in the late '60s and early '70s prior to *Pong*. So that was really the first coin-operated video game; it was a one-off in the student union at Stanford.

A lot of famous stuff came out of the Artificial Intelligence Lab at Stanford in that era. It was interesting how that nexus of commercialization and the computer lab was there at the start, and obviously the next big thing was *Pong*. The Odyssey was in some ways just too early, and analog technology was just not the way to go; it was limited to a kind of cul-de-sac. By converting the principles of the Odyssey into the digital format, Bushnell created *Pong* and the first commercially successful arcade game. (Though I guess before then he had done his versions of *Spacewar*, which was kind of a commercial flop.)

That was the beginning phase, and then you had the golden era of the arcade in the late '70s and early '80s. I really think *Space Invaders* became the paradigm for the video games of that era where you had three lives, you theoretically could play forever, and it was almost like a pinball paradigm. In pinball you have so many balls and you can play forever, but technically you have three balls or five. Curiously, the video game just adopted that game structure. To the player it was incredibly appealing because you had this illusion of playing forever, that the reward of getting better and better was playing longer and longer. The player didn't feel limited to some time clock, as was the case in most of the early games, or by strict score, as was the case in *Pong*. So there was this illusion of playing forever, and that paradigm was then utilized in *Pac-Man* and *Defender,* and the vast majority of games of that era, when you felt you could play forever.

From that era the games evolved more, and you had a couple other big shifts. The rise of the driving game in the '80s became very significant in the arcade. There was a period where you had a rise in games that were designed as "buy-in" games, where when you died you just put in more money and kept playing. Where the old paradigm taught that your skill determined exactly how long you would play, the new one taught "Well, just let the guy pay." *Smash TV* was of course of that paradigm, as were a number of games in the middle to late '80s and into the '90s and even today. That proved to be a powerful economic model, but from a pure gameplay perspective it kind of mucks up the purity of a game. (This works in much the same way that, today, virtual goods muck with the purity of the concept.)

Another important event in the evolution of the arcade was the rise of the fighting game, which was kind of a return to the death-match model of the early *Pong* or *Spacewar* games, which were head-to-head. In the early days the CPUs really weren't that capable of doing much with AI, especially before microprocessors. It was almost impossible to have anything, any real component of sophistication. So using the human component was convenient, and a lot of the early video games had human components and there was no AI. It was fifteen or twenty years later in the late '80s and early '90s that the fighting game reminded players that "Hey! Human components are really cool! Let's kill other people and fight player versus player!" At the same time you had *Doom,* which kind of evolved into the death match and that whole FPS thing, and together with fighting games these games created this huge school of gaming, which is still very big today, that is based on player versus player, and the AI, while present, is not the focus of these games.

HEINEMAN: So the decline of the arcade in America in the late '90s was, in part, due to their own reinvigoration of multiplayer gaming, which caught on to such an extent that the arcade couldn't contain it?

JARVIS: The arcade, unfortunately, is limited by an economic model of needing money (previously a quarter, now a dollar) every two minutes; there are so many experiences that don't work. If you had to pay a buck every two minutes, how long would you talk to your mom? In response, the arcade became made up of limited experiences that were very intense and very high emotion, much like roller coasters. Things that are lower key just don't really work, and it just becomes very expensive. If you wanted to game for five hours a night, that would cost you three hundred bucks to play at an arcade. The economics really defeated the arcade.

It is amazing how, when I think of something like *World of Warcraft*, you can sit there for forty hours per month or more and pay sixteen bucks. It's like less than a penny a minute. It's so ridiculously cheap that you just can't compete with that kind of entertainment on that economic basis. So the arcade is really limited by its economic model, and that's just the way it works.

The biggest catalyst of these [changes in the history of the arcade] was technology. With *Pong* obviously the catalyst was the ability of digital hardware and the use of 7400 TTL [transistor-transistor logic] chips that were not economical to put in a box; I think a lot of the creativity has always been there, but it's the technology that makes it happen. If you look at the Apple Newton versus the iPad, it's the same fucking thing. But the iPad is in better packaging, it uses a better CPU, has a bigger screen, etc. It is the same concept, but the technology has all of a sudden made it a cool experience rather than some clunky pile. There is something like a "sweet spot" of technology that you have to hit; there has to be timing to your game.

HEINEMAN: So to adapt from one era to the next, especially in the arcade industry, means being on the technology at the right point?

JARVIS: When it becomes cheap, when it becomes possible. I did this
game *N.A.R.C.* in high definition around 1986, when we were all
first excited for HDTV. We had this high-definition screen, and
we had a ROM board that was the size of Cook County, and the
thing was very expensive. It was an awesome-looking game, and
to this day it looks awesome because the resolution was just crazy.
It was millions of colors and the pixel density of not quite as much
as the iPad. It was pretty insane and it was a great game, but the
economics priced it high so it wasn't as successful as it would have
been. It was weird how the game was ahead of itself on the technology curve, and that can hurt you from an economic standpoint
because the game becomes too expensive to produce.

As a commercial art form, there's always the concern of price.
That has always been a difference between video games and movies. It's one thing that has always hurt the video game business
since we are still, to this day, embodied in a piece of hardware.
You can take any movie and play it in any theater. I can make a
really piece-of-shit movie and play it in the same theater as James
Cameron playing a billion-dollar movie. With video games, a new
game has to play on the Xbox, it has to play on the PC, or it has to
also run on the Gameboy. I think we are slowly getting beyond
that, but it still is an amazing difference that's held us back in that
there is no universal format.

HEINEMAN: Do you think that the same creative environments that
made for innovative design in the early days of the industry, which
maybe were in part due to the technological limitations, are possible to reproduce today?

JARVIS: As hardware has evolved, it has removed a lot of these constraints. Now the constraints are more about the budget; before it
was just you "couldn't frickin' do it." Constraints were certainly a
huge factor in some of the early games, like *Space Invaders,* where
you were just stuck on a screen. That discipline yielded some very
interesting stuff and also made the game easier to understand.
Tetris obviously was again that one-screen idea. *Defender* was one
of the first games that got beyond that, that saw screens as boring
and let you scroll through the world.

HEINEMAN: So with *Defender* was there a particular technological innovation that came along that allowed you to do that, or did you figure out how to add something to an existing technique?

JARVIS: It was the technology. As far as scrolling, you could have done that with the existing technology. At the release of *Defender,* in fact, I think there were some already scrolling terminals at that time, so it was not a completely foreign concept. But the technology that actually debuted in *Defender* was that we used a bitmap screen, which was using pixels. Most of the games before then utilized hardware sprites. So we utilized the bitmap screen that made possible all of these effects, which are what's now known as particle effects (we called them explosions). When you blew up your spaceship, it was 128 bits flying across the screen; we had all these really cool showers, their bits and pieces going everywhere, and that really excited the players.

That effect added "spark." Trip Hawkins always talked about "simple, hot, and deep": a game has to be simple in the sense that you can grasp what the hell you are supposed to do, it has to be hot in the sense that it has to be eye candy (e.g., "Wow, this is a cool world I haven't seen yet. Look at those fucking reflections and the burning zombies!"), deep in the sense of replayability. *Angry Birds* totally has this because it's this super-simple concept of catapulting the birds into the pig, the graphics are very pretty, it's really beautiful and smooth, and it uses the touch screen, which has been coming into its own in the last five years. The touch-screen interface has allowed completely new paradigms in play that the joystick and classic controller does not allow; this has been a huge catalyst of this wave of creative game designs that come out of the mobile field.

HEINEMAN: What do you see as the biggest challenges and opportunities for designers looking forward?

JARVIS: Obviously, the holy grail is the holodeck. Virtual reality is a big thing, and there's the creativity of new game paradigms, and I guess we have seen this huge explosion with touch screens. But really, we have these huge high-resolution screens now, and it's amazing how 98 percent of all innovation goes to create more eye candy. The game really doesn't change; it's like *Madden*. *Madden* is kind of a paradigm for the whole industry: "It's still fucking football. It's still eleven guys. They just look better." In some ways we're doing that. We're all, like any entertainment medium, telling stories, trying to make that same old story cool. The creative side of things hasn't really caught up. We're all still just making the same old fucking game.

HEINEMAN: You gave a speech in 2008 about the "Evolution of Video Game Design" entitled "Intelligent Design or Artificial Stupidity?" Can you elaborate on how you understand the answer to that question?

JARVIS: It's been a slow progression. Computing itself has only been established for seventy years or so. I remember that back at the AI in Stanford in the 1950s and 1960s that we were sure that, in ten years, we would be past the Turning Test and into all this other great stuff. It happened that it was just a lot harder than people figured. The human brain and its software (or whatever the hell is running up there) are incredibly sophisticated and incredibly complex. By contrast, everything done in the AI community aimed at defeating a problem not with what we actually consider intelligence, but with brute computing force. Take, for example, AI designed to solve chess. Now computer chess programs can beat just about anybody, but they struggled with forty or fifty years of brute-force approaches to AI in order to get there. It got to a point where they didn't even take an "intelligent" approach to chess any-more; they just used the brute force of searching algorithm trees, doing some clever pruning of five trillion possible positions, and solving: that's not really AI. It's the same thing with speech com-prehension, which is now pretty well advanced after thirty to forty years but is not "intelligent" in the sense that we think of human intelligence. By contrast, in the gaming world there has been real progress in genuine AI. Progress is certainly frustratingly slow, but there've been some real victories.

Even in games, though, a lot of people can't tell the difference between a good random-number generator and a good AI enemy. You can program a good number generator in about ten minutes, and the problem with that is that like a lot of the time players don't want some AI enemy to use those generators to kill them. They don't want something that is smarter than them. No one enjoys playing chess with people who kick their ass all the time, because it's not fun. So in some ways gamers hate AI, they want something stupider than that, they want to feel superior, and so pretty much what we see in games is not AI – it's "artificial stupidity."

An example would be the work of Chris Crawford, who for years had a project that was trying to create nonplayer characters (NPCs) that, when you talked to them, it would be like actually talking to a real person. There has been this huge dream of trying to create that, and it just has been a very difficult problem. It has become a great frustration of those people who want gaming to be this interactive Shakespeare play where the guy is a real guy and you can talk to him. It's this dream of a more sophisticated game world that functions on something other than hit points. (It seems that we always get down to how many hit points, and I have a potion and you have an antidote, rolling dice, etc.) So there has been this one huge unsolved dream, which, when coupled with virtual reality, would allow this sense of being fully immersed in a beautiful and completely alien universe. You could travel to Pandora and talk to the blue guys and feel their pain.

HEINEMAN: Do you think that university-level education in game design is the future of the industry, or do you think that there are some weaknesses to learning in the classroom versus going straight into industry?

JARVIS: It's funny. Academia has become more and more important in the line of things. But would a musician need a bachelor's degree? Fuck that, man, just get a guitar and you're Bob Dylan! [*Laughter*]

That said, a lot of these programs are learned by doing. There are a lot of problems addressed in the classroom, there are a huge amount of projects that students work on, and I think it's been very successful to the point where, as an employer in the industry, you're leery of hiring someone who doesn't have one experience in game design or a degree. I really find it amazing how academia has grown and become very important in the field and has created some very talented people by giving them that boost. As the field became more and more sophisticated, there are a plethora of disciplines (sound-design composition of sound, music, art, graphical art, drawing, character design, 3-D modeling, environmental modeling, rigging of characters, animation of characters, lighting, etc.). My mind is blown by just how many specialties there are and how much you really need to learn to get on top of all these programming disciplines, the physics of game engines, collision detection, special effects, particle effects, game design, level design, and so on.

So I think that higher education teaches the tools and skills that enable the art of construction; the more skills you have, then theoretically you can express yourself in a greater variety of ways. On the other hand, you can have all this artistic training but end up spending months of coding on the reflection of a helmet or the texture of a shoe in the newest *Madden.* You have these armies of guys who are just immersed in the finest details of things, and in some ways it's just mind crushing to go from school where "Everything is possible – you're going to design the next *Tetris*" to "Here's your job: you're making the reflection on all the helmets look really, really cool."

In response to this soul-crushing machine, there is now this huge incubator of indie games. That's directly related to the university-level education of game developers. It used to be that you really had to spend years in the industry to learn how to do everything, but now people are coming out of school that are probably ten times smarter than I am; it's a flood of talent. The only thing that I worry about is how all of these developers are going to make a living selling games for ninety-nine cents. I've heard stories of guys who put their game up and publicize it, and in the first week only make sixteen dollars because only sixteen people bought it. So we've created a generation of starving artists, even though we are going to get some great stuff from them.

HEINEMAN: There's an analysis of your game *Robotron 2084* in a past issue of *Games and Culture* where the authors describe that game as interesting because of the tension between the notions of "level" and "wave." They are referring to the idea that a player can't just go into the game with the mentality of "This is a new wave and the enemies will be a little bit faster, but my same basic techniques will suffice," because in *Robotron 2084* the enemies change significantly from stage to stage.

JARVIS: I think that is probably underappreciated. It was a deliberate thing, because the problem with most wave-based games, typically, is that the first wave is real easy, wave 2 starts to get good, and then in wave 3 you just kill the player. It becomes a shallow thing because you're turning the dial on a player just like you would turn the speed up on a treadmill, and, eventually, they are just going to fall on their face. It's not that interesting because it just goes faster, faster, and faster until you're dead. So, in *Robotron 2084*, it was a deliberate decision to use a randomly generated play field that would give the appearance of new levels. It was an attempt to try to create a world that would overload the player with new stimuli and create a sense of tension. We were trying to create a richness. We didn't want a trivial game where the enemy sped up to a point where it was too fast and the player had to put in another quarter. Instead, we wanted to mess with the player and give them enemies that couldn't be killed, enemies that worked like a blocking thing, enemies that worked like a moving wall, enemies that shoot projectiles, etc. The game was trying to get beyond the trivial and really facilitate these interesting interactions that were much more complex and variable. I always think of it like a soup, like a recipe. You're making beef stew: you need some carrots, celery, and some beef; then the next wave is tapioca pudding. You're fighting the boredom of the player.

HEINEMAN: So how do you do that well? How do you tweak it to create that tension?

JARVIS: It helps, I found, if as a designer you are more of an average player (or just a "good" player). If you are a great player, you are at a huge disadvantage for successfully tweaking a game. Unless you are specifically making a game for the great players, you have to mirror your audience and you have to represent your audience. If you are a great player making a casual game for beginners, you might have a hard time because you just can't relate to how stupid and slow they are.

When I sit down to a game, I want to play it intuitively. This is like the Steve Jobs school of gaming where the point should be obvious; the creators should never have to tell you anything. In the era of *Robotron,* that game was a vicious hard game; it was almost like the players enjoyed being tortured – it was almost masochistic. It was like this challenge to your ego. It seems to me that players today have changed quite a bit: it's more the self-esteem generation, it's like "YOU'RE DOING GREAT!"

HEINEMAN: "Here's an achievement."

JARVIS: "You died in wave 1. You killed one robot. You're a hero!" "My God, we're putting you on the all-time list of this!," and "Oh, my God, you're fantastic! Play again!"

HEINEMAN: "And we'll literally give you trophies."

JARVIS: Right, exactly. It's funny how the social environment of the era is also expressed in the game design. If you're in the age of self-esteem, then everyone gets a trophy and everything is wonderful. I think, in the era of *Robotron 2084,* maybe the generation as a whole was more abused. I remember that my parents kicked the shit out of me when I was a kid. What we would call child abuse was just play. I think that was just what that generation was about: sink or swim. During that time it was a more brutal era, and games were brutal and you wanted that challenge. There was something about challenging the machine and fighting it. It might have been a carryover from pinball a little bit too. Where pinball was this physical struggle between you and the machine, you would shake it and kick it and try to do anything good to beat it, like pick the game up and slide it around a little bit.

HEINEMAN: In the last decade there has been this increased cultural focus on the early days of gaming and gaming history, retrogaming is a big craze, and a lot of contemporary designers cite influences from early arcade games and express a lot of reverence for that period. Do you think that the attention paid to this past is a noble thing, is it something that we should spend our time doing, or does it in any way stifle innovation? For example, a lot of the early arcade games established genres that are pretty much still the same genres that we play today. I wonder to what extent the process of constantly looking backward for inspiration and holding those projects up is stifling in any way to moving forward?

JARVIS: It certainly could be that we're creating a culture and that we're prisoners of our culture. From a commercialism perspective, there is always this need to clone things, which to me is even more stifling than history. I would say about 5 percent of the game business even cares about history; there's some small amount, but really what is most common is that you clone whatever last thing was that made money. Our cloning and our influences do blind us, and we get blinded by the current culture of gaming (whatever that is). It's hard to break out of that and get beyond it. I think that the history has been long enough now that you can actually, by studying history, revitalize a genre that has fallen away. It's fascinating just from an evolutionary perspective to see how the games developed and notice that there is some huge branch of the tree that is completely missing.

It's interesting how movies and games have always had a checkered cultural exchange. Video games made into movies are typically horrible, and movies made into video games often are terrible too. One thing that is surprising is that it seems like political games are very rare. Whereas politics and opinion are a very big part of our society, games that have any kind of message that's either religious or political or have any other sort of controversial message are very rare. Maybe it's just a commercial art form, and so you don't want to turn anyone off, but it is surprising because there are a lot of movies out there with certain political slants, and gaming has been less affected by politics.

HEINEMAN: Gaming doesn't have its Michael Moore, that's for sure. There is no one out there that's profitable that is doing political commentary with games.

JARVIS: Maybe it's just a young art form. That's the thing. We're only thirty years or forty years away from *Pong,* and if you look at movies starting with the early Edison movies in the 1890s, then maybe gaming is in the late 1920s. It's still a fairly early point in our development. I don't even know if we are there.

HEINEMAN: You've created games that have spoken to political or controversial subjects in some interesting and usually funny ways. *N.A.R.C.* addresses the war on drugs. The *Cruis'n* series offers all these little send-ups of the American and European landscape and culture. *Target Terror* lampoons the War on Terror. *Smash TV* is a parody of the violent entertainment that we have in the culture. Do you think that games are an important medium for providing social commentary? Do you think that gamers recognize those elements in your games and respond to them in any way, or are they just shooting stuff as it flies by?

JARVIS: I think it's hard to tell. Where arcade gaming is at, you don't really get a lot of feedback. I see some fans every now and then, and there is some small minority of people who totally get all of the little subtleties and the messages and the funny little parodies on a conscious level. On an unconscious level, who knows what happens? I feel that a game should always be playable on an unconscious level; in my view the ideal game should be very intuitive and almost unconscious. I always hated games like *Pac-Man* where you had to memorize patterns. Obviously, some people's minds are able to memorize more easily, but to me that was always work. I always wanted things to be different every time, challenging every time. To me, the ultimate game was one where you just go into a situation and you just intuit and do.

At the same time, though, you want people to care about a game. That's where the theme part comes in. With *Robotron*, the robots are taking over the world. The player wants a little bit of a backstory, something to care about. If the player can't relate to whatever conflict you are throwing out there, it's like, "Who cares? I'm just in Afghanistan killing people, and I don't know why. And this is not fun." So the medium can be a good one in which to make social commentary, but it is underdeveloped and it is a challenge because of the need for replayability and the fact that it is largely a commercial medium.

FOUR

Henry Lowood

ARCHIVING AND GAMES

HENRY LOWOOD IS CURATOR FOR THE HISTORY OF SCIENCE &
Technology Collections and Film & Media Collections in the Stanford
University Libraries and a leading member of the Preserving Digital
Worlds initiative funded by the Library of Congress. He has long been
an instigator and an innovator in the emerging area of archiving games
for historical analysis and has both produced prominent scholarship and
taken part in groundbreaking archiving projects that continue to shape
how we understand the historical importance of video games.

In 2011 Barwick, Dearnley, and Muir published an essay in *Games
and Culture* that offered an overview and analysis of the most recent efforts in digital game preservation, wherein they concluded, "The preservation of computer games at present is based on imperfect solutions – the
collection, storage, and display of computer games and paraphernalia,
with arguably the more important issue of preserving *gameplay* being
beset by legal ramifications" (387). These problems persist, they suggest, despite efforts by academic institutions, private and public museums, and state apparatuses to overcome them. Lowood's work is largely
directed toward proposing solutions for these obstacles, something he
has accomplished by modeling preservationist and historical research
that productively interrogates and successfully navigates a variety of
academic, legal, and material concerns.

Video game historians traditionally face two major challenges in
attempting to access useful sources for preservation and analysis. Those
challenges are found in accessing materials both before and after a game's
release.

69

As was the case in the early years of film, in the first decades of video game production most design studios, marketing departments, or other areas of creation and iteration did not think about the significance of their work for long-term scrutiny and analysis. Game production was (and still is) largely about shipping a stable and profitable title in a timely fashion, and any thought of archiving alpha or beta builds, concept art, meeting minutes, developer logs, or other artifacts that were generated in service of that final product was rare. During a panel called "Preserving the Digital Game Canon" at PAX East in 2011, it was revealed that many companies that were especially prominent during the golden age of the arcade or in the first few decades of home game console adoption discarded the materials that led to the creation of defining titles. Furthermore, for what does persist, there is often the problem of successfully accessing physically decaying media, re-creating the technological conditions under which the games were originally experienced, or struggling with imperfect emulation.

The other problem facing game historians is that of accessing and archiving player experiences. For pre-Internet-era games, there were not many avenues for players to express their thoughts on games publicly, to log or preserve their play sessions, or to otherwise create a record of what they were experiencing. The problem historians face is a dearth of accessible materials. For preserving and analyzing more recent games that feature online connectivity, the problem is the opposite. There are difficulties in accessing and parsing a wealth of data about player interactions and transactions that are collected by servers, safeguarded by companies for future game development, and sometimes protected by privacy laws. Many of Lowood's efforts have been directed toward understanding the causes of these problems and, in the process, offering models of solutions for how to overcome them.

In the interview found in this chapter, Lowood provides considered responses to questions about the difficulties outlined above; discusses the study of game history more generally; offers perspective on some of the ideas presented by Bushnell, Jarvis, and Melissinos in previous chapters; and discusses the relationship of his own work to various academic disciplines, sectors of the video game industry, and participants in video game fan culture.

—⚂—

HEINEMAN: As someone who works at the disciplinary intersection of game studies and history, how would you characterize the contemporary relationship between those fields?

LOWOOD: Very underdeveloped, unfortunately. Thus far, what passes for the history of digital games in game studies has been a very immature idea. It's been dominated by journalistic accounts, which is not in itself a bad thing, but the weight has been very much on either the chronicling of events or on storytelling. I think the discipline of history should bring to that an interpretive edge, including of course a critical perspective. If you look at somebody like Hayden White, who's written on historiography, it is perfectly legitimate and expected for historians to write in almost a "fictional" sense, to construct their stories to express a particular point. I think there's been almost none of that in game studies so far. In the next year or two I'm going to be trying to do a few things to kind of push this a little bit, and I think a few of the people I would put in that category are also trying in their own ways to sort of push it along a little bit (Ian Bogost would be one example with the Platform Studies series).

HEINEMAN: Your own historical research is focused primarily on the experience of individual players and on clans and communities, rather than on the broader work of developers, the mechanics of gameplay and how they've changed, or audience studies. When gathering research materials about these smaller communities and these individuals, how do you determine what are you going to preserve and what are you not going to preserve? Are some of the user experiences more representative or more significant than others, and, if so, how do you determine that?

LOWOOD: One thing about games as a medium is that we have this fantastic opportunity to do much richer work about the experiences of using a technology, of consuming a medium, of being entertained, and of studying all of those things that players do than we perhaps were given by older media. By contrast, reception studies (in literature) relies on a lot of indirect kinds of evidence, on "constructing a reading experience." With games, we have an opportunity to work on a much richer account of what it means to use a medium because there are so many more traces of that use by virtue of the fact that players co-construct what happens in gameplay; you don't have a game without players.

I don't think it is widely recognized (kind of surprisingly) that there have been events that have taken place in game worlds and in virtual worlds that were meaningful to communities of people, that have persisted in the shared culture of those communities, and that have survived as lore.

A very obvious place to start is with some of those events. What kind of documentation is available about them? What remains to tell the stories that can inform us about what actually happened around those events? I've been gathering documentation about the "Corrupted Blood Incident" in *World of Warcraft,* where we've basically identified an event that a lot of people know a little bit about. They've maybe heard of it or have a vague idea that something happened in a virtual world once that dealt with infectious diseases. Well, what really happened? What documentation do we have about what really happened? Who was actually involved? How did it start? To me, those are obvious places to start. That answers the question for how to look for certain kinds of documentation and for doing sort of "microhistorical" studies: focus on one event and tell that story.

HEINEMAN: Where do you often find that documentation or those records? Is it on discussion boards? Do you find saved replays, or videos, or all of those things?

LOWOOD: It's a lengthy process that involves pretty much all of the above. It's a kind of an archaeology of the Web. What's very interesting about the history of game worlds and the history of virtual worlds is that much of (if not all) the documentation does not exist in the worlds in which those events took place. You don't go to *World of Warcraft* to find that document, like you might if a historical event happened in Germany and you traveled to Germany to look for an archive. In a virtual world, at most you might gather some information around what the location looked like. Instead you go to the Web, you go outside that virtual world, and you find things in blogs or in guild websites where people might've posted things. You end up signing up for a lot of things, joining guilds yourself so that you can go to a private forum and ask them for their documentation and permission to use it, and generally follow a lot of traces.

Videos are important, but there is a major problem there with authenticity. The percentage of stuff on YouTube that was actually created by the person who posted it is surprisingly small, so many things are derivative instances of somebody posting somebody else's stuff. For example, some of the events we tried to document in the Australian "Moving Images" project led us to video that was clearly not authentic where people were claiming to be the first person to have been involved in an event that happened in *EverQuest* when, in fact, the video was not authentic. Sometimes you could tell it was inauthentic from the video itself, and sometimes you'd find out from the comments on the video or from discussions somewhere else on the Web. There's a lot of that kind of "historical detective" work that you have to do to even verify the authenticity of some of the sources.

It's pretty interesting, and a lot of fun actually, to do that work. Sometimes you end up, surprisingly, in a conversation with somebody who was involved in something that happened eight years ago in some virtual world, and they'll tell you additional information or provide you with additional documentation. That, of course, is very rewarding, but it's not an exact science at all. It involves following a lot of trails and being willing to work in a world where most identities are not "real" in the sense of "real-world identities." You don't have real names most of the time; you have a lot of game handles that may or may not persist across different games and may or may not be used by the same actual person in different games. There's a lot of that kind of sorting work that has to be done in order to find stuff and then document it. But it is possible to get a good outcome and to be able to put together a decent historical collection around some event that happened.

HEINEMAN: How do you select historical materials for more single-player focused games that don't revolve around a shared community event?

LOWOOD: The division you're making is between social events, experienced by or shared with large numbers of people in a community, and the single-player game. The single-player game is a little more difficult. There is a kind of "event" aspect to those experiences in the sense that that person who played that game might have been involved in something significant or may have broadcast an event that would have impact on people. An example of that might be a recent ten-year *Civilization* game where somebody played it for a long time on their own, nobody knew a thing about it, but the release of the replay of those ten years made it interesting on a couple of different levels.

It was interesting because it had an impact on a large number of people who read about it. It was also interesting in terms of the game situation that was documented, where you would see that *Civilization* could be played in this particular way, way beyond what the designers ever intended. It went hundreds of years beyond the game's normal end point. It had a very interesting outcome that you or I could then go in and read, or, maybe, we could even play the game ourselves to try to see if we could resolve that situation. A number of people did in fact do this.

HEINEMAN: You've also spent considerable time studying machinima, a form of movie making grounded in game performances. Does the field of performance studies offer something to the study of game history that maybe can't be found from more traditional historiographical methods?

LOWOOD: *Performance* is sort of the word of the late twentieth century or early twenty-first century. It has so many contexts. We talk about our stock performance. We talk about the performance of our computer, of our video card, and of course people performing expressively. Performance studies has theorized about expansion of the notion of performance, which is almost meme-like in its persistence through a lot of different parts of culture. By doing so, they've really expanded the notion of performance: it's not necessarily limited to formal theatrical or mediated performances but to many, many kinds of activity. The research in performance studies that I found interesting when looking at machinima was that addressing definitions of different phases in the performance process (e.g., preperformance, postperformance).

Some performance theorists suggest that performance really is nonarchival, it can't be preserved; you're there in the moment, or you're not. A videotape of a performance is not a performance; it's a media object. But other performance theorists have looked at performance as more of a continual process. That has helped me think about how, for example, gameplay might be thought of as a kind of rehearsal for something like machinima. How important is it that those sorts of "rehearsals" are private? Can they be? If you expose your preperformance, does it ruin the performance? I think most performance theorists would probably tend to say yes, but if you look at gameplay and particularly its role in machinima, it's a little bit different. It's very important for us to recognize what gameplay went into a machinima piece because much of our appreciation of that (at least for a lot of people) is seeing what special skills were brought to bear in making the machinima. That's a case where the performance studies discussion of an issue is interesting for somebody working in game studies.

Another thing that's increasingly important is a mediated performance, and there's a lot of writing about that right now. Gameplay, game environments, and virtual worlds are among the technologies that are being used for performance nowadays. That's an application of digital games that is interesting to think about, and people in performance studies are doing that. Those are the kinds of issues that I wouldn't expect historians to develop quite as richly as the performance studies people would.

HEINEMAN: Do you look at previous historical work, maybe outside the field of game studies, that incorporates ideas of performance and/or performance studies in particular and useful ways?

LOWOOD: The area of history that I use that way is more history of technology. User studies, for example, would be a field that I have found enormously useful, and those have been primarily historical studies. For example, I find the study of the unintended uses of the automobile informative for thinking about how machinima was, in a sense, an unintended use of game technology. There has been a lot of other work in user studies and in historical studies of technology that looks at all that's involved in the social construction of technology, the term of the artifact's stabilizing, that whole process of negotiation through which we eventually decide that "this is what an automobile is."

HEINEMAN: I think of some of that as existing in dead media studies as well, right? So that one of the ways to continue to have some relevance for a dead medium is to find some way to reinvent it and use it in an unintended context. The next question: some of your recent work focuses on the idea of archiving hidden code (which is documents and other bits of information left in the files associated with the game). What is the scholarly value of this data relative to the more complete and polished code?

LOWOOD: Game texts are not fixed texts in the way that we're familiar with written text. And by that I don't mean the interactivities, but the fact that they really aren't stable. There's obviously a period of development, but even when something is released, there's a lot of revision that still occurs. This is even more the case if you look at a game world or a virtual world like *World of Warcraft*; it's incorrect to think of it as a finished artifact.

It turns out, if you explore those things, there are a lot of glitches; there are a lot of these hidden spaces, a lot of stuff under construction. It is a necessity to understand games as a medium, as artifacts that are always under construction, which means that there's lots of documentation, pieces of code, ways to explore things, techniques (including video, machinima, screen shots, and a lot of things like that), and communication within communities about what's going on to describe things. I don't think that just buying the game, version 1.0 that's released, putting it on the library shelf, and then having that be the record is useful. For example, take a copy of *Warcraft 3* sitting there on the library shelf. Fifty years later, somebody comes along and says, "There's my book – there's *Warcraft 3*." It's not like that at all. There's a whole development of that game and a lot of history around that organic development and how it changes gameplay or affects tournaments because of changes that occur and the timing of them. Who's making the changes? Are they being made by developers? Are they mods that have been played within the game community? There's a lot of stuff like that, and it's all about this throbbing, evolving organism that a game is in a way. This is all in addition to the interactivity part; this is just about how difficult it is to pin down the artifact as being finished at a certain point, or having a definitive version. That's a decision you have to make. Which is the important version? Maybe there were multiple important versions of this game, and you want to have access to all of that information and be able to reconstruct different versions or to be able to run demo files that maybe require a specific version in order to be seen. That involves collecting a lot of different kinds of stuff. It doesn't stop with just the packaged game or a version of source code that led to that packaged game.

HEINEMAN: So then the value of that as a researcher is to get a picture of the game's development over time, to get a sense of maybe why certain decisions are made. I was reading a story earlier today that Blizzard is patching their *Diablo 3* code so that they can fix the end-game problems and so forth. As a historian, if you want to study *Diablo 3* twenty years from now, and if you go back and look at the user experiences, video files, or playthroughs from shortly after the game is released, can you, as a researcher, be able to look at these materials and somehow weigh the value or the effects of that code change? What does a specific glitch or a specific fix tell you in the grander scheme of understanding something about community experiences or player experiences with the game, especially since they are now changing more and more over time?

LOWOOD: I would look at it is as almost like a hierarchy of questions that you're asking. At the bottom layer it's "How did Blizzard patch *Diablo 3* at a certain time?" "How was this version of *Diablo 3* created?" That's the bottom-level question. And for that you have to gather some kind of documentation. You want to make sure you see the right things and so on.

The question one layer above that starts to get more interesting. It's "How does Blizzard, a content-creation company, respond to the consumers of its products, the players, in developing patches for its game?" Now it's more a question of how this particular medium works as a dialogue between the content creators and the players. That one example – you have a particular patch – is going to be a piece of that puzzle. It may or may not be enough to answer it. There's even one layer above that Blizzard question, which is more a history-of-technology question, which is "How do users of media technology interact with the creators of that technology?"

So now it's not even restricted to games. It's a much more general and broad question, and you can start going from there and consider questions like "Is this a characteristic of a media environment of the late twentieth, early twenty-first centuries?" because of the particular kinds of technologies that were in play, the expectations of users, the kinds of businesses that existed, etc. Answering that question at that highest level certainly requires you to have some well-documented cases at that lowest level, or else I don't know how you talk about it other than to talk about your own personal experience.

HEINEMAN: It seems like that's an increased trend. Ten or fifteen years ago, if there were problems with a game, patches were usually developed through play testing or maybe some player feedback. By contrast, Bioware recently changed the ending to one of their games based on player feedback. It seems like the end user is now having more direct influence on what the final code of a game ends up looking like.

LOWOOD: There are even games under development where the eventual players participate in game-development decisions. You're given one hundred tokens that you can vote with. If you preorder the game, you get more tokens, you get more votes essentially, and that kind of thing. I think we're dealing with a media economy that is changing in some important ways.

Games are, arguably, a very important part of those changes. In order to talk about these things at this upper, more analytical, more general level, we really need to have better documentation of the cases. Right now we don't have great detailed documentation of those cases or very many of them. Part of what we're trying to do by gathering more documentation is just make it possible for people to write critically about what's going on, so they can move on to those upper-level questions. Not that the Blizzard question isn't interesting. It is. But there is more that can be built onto that at higher levels.

HEINEMAN: Some well-known historical figures in gaming have expressed reservations about popular gaming history as it currently exists, which we started talking about a little bit at the top. So, for example, when I spoke to Eugene Jarvis, he suggested that popular gaming media tends to focus too much on individual designers as opposed to teams of designers and the evolution of a company and how they produced games. In other interviews Nolan Bushnell has suggested that popular history of gaming is, in general, poorly documented and largely misinformed. What do you see as the most substantive faults with popular histories of gaming?

LOWOOD: Well, one, right off the bat – and this is very meta, considering we're doing an interview right now – is that too much is based on interviews. [*Laughter*]

HEINEMAN: Fair enough.

LOWOOD: I don't think I want to name particular names, but I think there are definitely histories that are almost entirely constructed out of snippets of interviews kind of strung together. That's not historical methodology. If there's a discipline that works that way, its ethnographers, and they work differently with interviews than most of the books on the history of games that I've seen. I see very little in the histories I'm talking about that is based on what I would consider a critical use of documentation. They'll occasionally cite a particular document to fix a date because it's interesting, but there isn't the attention to the range of documentation that might be available out there, how the documentation interacts, comparing conflicting accounts, verifying sources, and those kinds of things. I think that's been a big problem with a lot of the game history. In addition to that (and I think this is in sync with what Eugene and Nolan said), a lot of it is too narrowly focused, I think partly because of the interview orientation where it's just sort of storytelling from a particular perspective.

Maybe it's better to say what I think are examples that kind of go against that a little bit. There have been a couple of really good examples in the Platform Studies series that I think have used documentation effectively, not just interviews, but also a documentation and an understanding of the technology based on that. What Eugene Jarvis is saying? I think that's true. I think there's still a kind of a "great person" phase in game studies where there's a lot of attention to these certain great designers or great designs, and not much social history. What we have in that vein is coming from ethnography and mostly people working in virtual worlds (T. L. Taylor, Castronova, and people like that), not so much the disciplinary historians. It goes back to what I said at the very beginning: that game history is very underdeveloped at this point as a piece of game studies.

HEINEMAN: How might you get at the social history of gaming for the pre-Internet era other than through interviews with people who made games or who ran arcades? What sorts of documentation, other than perhaps journalistic reports, are you looking for?

LOWOOD: We just got a collection a couple of weeks ago that was a collection of photographs by a photographer named Ira Nowinsky, who is not at all connected to game culture. He's a very well-known photographer that's worked on very different topics: Jewish culture in the Bay Area, the Holocaust legacy, Native Americans, and so forth. But, it turned out, he had made a number of photographs in the 1981 to 1982 period of video arcades in the Bay Area. That's a really interesting period: '81–'82. The Loftus & Loftus study on the psychology of video games came out in 1983, and they have that chapter on the arcade subculture. His photographs are essentially exactly from that period. He heard from somebody about the Atari *Asteroids* competition that was held at the Exploratorium and went there, was fascinated by it, and took dozens of photographs of what it was like there.

Obviously, there are different kinds of documentation, and you use photographs differently than you would a patent application or a letter, but these photographs do give you some really interesting insight into the atmosphere of this "arcade subculture," as Loftus & Loftus put it. You see people in arcades. One observation that I basically got from Ira, the photographer, that is also commented on, interestingly enough, in Loftus's chapter, is that the arcades are places where people are allowed to stare at what somebody else is doing without exchanging any conversation, and it's perfectly acceptable. There are photographs in Ira's collection that document exactly that. They show what it was like, the expressions on people's faces, somebody watching somebody playing an arcade game and just staring at them and what they're doing. Photography functions as a form of documentation for that.

There's also some stuff that, if you're interested in game competitions, for example, there's some television documentation and there are some memoirs. A few of the people that have been involved in that environment have written about it (for example, Walter Day at Twin Galaxies has written). So you look at that stuff.

One project we did in the past was to study the *Nintendo v. Magnavox* lawsuit. I identified the district court and just invested a little in figuring out what it would take to get whatever documentation was available at the court and did it. We learned a little bit about what is and what isn't [available] when there's a settlement and people agree not to disclose certain things. We got some of the documentation, but there were some very interesting things that we were able to get from that: lists of who testified, lists of what documents were submitted (even in cases where you weren't able to see actual documents), some of the documents that were included (depositions and things like that). There was some really interesting stuff, like early contacts between Nintendo and Magnavox that I had not seen documented anywhere else.

Ralph Baer: I have to single him out because he's done a great job of just basically laying bare all the documentation he's got and making it available. Patents are a great source of documentation. It's different. You may not find it all in the Web. You may not be able to do it all from your office, but if you do the legwork, you can find quite a bit of documentation.

HEINEMAN: You mentioned the Platform Studies series as one place where you see some really interesting historical work going on. In most of that (as I've read them), the focus isn't on the social component of the gaming. It's more on how the platform works and why it was used, it's difficulties, etc. Outside of that series, is there other good historical work? If most of it is bad, is there some other stuff you can hold up as an example of where you'd like to see more people going?

LOWOOD: It's more that it's absent than it's bad. Very few people who are trained in history have looked at games (but I think there are a few people who have done really good history work). James Newman is one person I would mention and his study of game players. Mia Consalvo also is in that vein – her book on cheating, for example.

But there are people like T. L. Taylor who have written what I would call ethnographies or sociologies, the difference being that the disciplinary guidelines of those fields require the authors to maybe not divulge as much about real-world identities and such that a historian would find essential. They are essentially critical historical accounts of how specific – for example, in T. L.'s work – game worlds were constructed, how they worked, and how the players worked with the developers.

I agree with what I think it is that Jarvis was pointing to: you have to want to say something more than just yarns and stories from the perspective of a particular character in the cast. You have to want to have a kind of a plot, as maybe Hayden White would say, or maybe as Steve Martin probably would've said in *Planes, Trains, and Automobiles:* it's a good idea to have a point to what you're writing. I think that's very important, and I think that's something that a journalist can certainly do.

HEINEMAN: Do you think that the discipline of history, as it's taught, is meeting the needs of students to do this kind of research? Do students have the interest in doing this? And does the discipline know how to train them to do the kinds of things that you are suggesting?

LOWOOD: It's a huge problem. One of the big impediments to this is the way that history is taught before students get to college. That approach actually ends up turning so many people away from history as it's actually done by historians.

HEINEMAN: Dates, names, places.

LOWOOD: Yeah exactly – just deadening kinds of factual information. And unfortunately, that, I think, seriously turns a lot of people away from touching history in college and learning about the ways that historians think about history, the least of which is probably dates. Historians are likely the least-reliable people as far as asking them a specific date. A question like "When was George Washington born?" or something similar? That's probably the last thing they're concerned about.

What ends up happening is it then separates. What's written later separates the people who are in the academic category and are kind of writing for each other, not really paying enough attention to bringing in a wider readership, on the one hand, and, on the other hand, people who are fans and write because they love something and they want to embrace that thing that they're attracted to and deliver a lot of details about it but don't get to that more analytical, critical side of history.

HEINEMAN: What do you understand to be the role of projects like the "Digital Game Canon" or the Smithsonian exhibit on the art of games, both of which function to hold up certain games, maybe at the expense of others, as artifacts that are of particular scholarly, artistic, economic, or general cultural importance?

LOWOOD: The primary role for both of the things you mentioned was symbolic more than practical. In the case of the "Digital Game Canon," it was a way to make the point that I wanted to make, and that is that you could treat games in a way that you treat other media that have been discussed in those terms. We should be able to have an equivalent of the American Film Institute list of films for important games.

There was a practical component to that, which was that a really difficult problem for game-preservation efforts was trying to figure out where to start. Because it's such an intense thing, at the moment, with what we have available, the projects we're doing required a lot of selectivity in terms of cases.

So we thought maybe by saying, "Here are some really fundamental games," maybe that could function as a case for preservation. Which, by the way, the American Film Institute list also guides preservation. The Smithsonian thing also was primarily symbolic. It was very similar to the canon thing, saying, "Art is shown in the Smithsonian. Games are shown in the Smithsonian. Games can be appreciated as art." It's almost like a syllogism.

The fact of the exhibit being in the Smithsonian is a very important part of that. I don't want to discount the intellectual work that was done or the interviews that were done at all. But to some degree, it almost didn't matter. Just the fact that that exhibit was shown in the Smithsonian is symbolically important.

HEINEMAN: So if they have a symbolic role that allows them to raise the profile of gaming in the general populist mind, and therefore funnel people into preservation efforts and rethinking the medium as something more than just leisure activity, do you think that there's a downside to them at all? The symbolic function seems perhaps the more obvious function. In that they can only select certain games or kinds of games, is that delimiting or detrimental to our cultural understanding of games in any way?

LOWOOD: For me, when I was doing the "Digital Game Canon" project, I had to overcome a resistance to canons very much. It's very inconsistent with the work that I do to have done a project like that. I'm very much willing to appreciate different kinds of auteurs, some of whom are game designers, some of whom are players – that kind of thing. So there was a kind of resistance there, but I thought the symbolic importance maybe made it important to do that. Is it negative? I think it might be negative in the sense that it pushes attention to sort of a "great deeds" approach, a "great person" approach that makes it seem like we can get sufficient appreciation of the history of digital games by identifying a small number of examples and just being able to say a little bit about them that indicates why they should be appreciated.

We maybe run the risk of that with game studies, which is very counter to anything that I'm interested in doing. But there is some external resistance to it as a field, and there is certainly some resistance to games as anything more than an entertainment form or maybe, at most, a popular culture form. When there are opportunities to show that games are an expressive medium and, if possible, even show how they might be expressive beyond just the finished games but also through the things that players do with them and so on, that just helps to show the possibilities for the field.

HEINEMAN: You've argued that the growth of game studies is akin to the development of the discipline of the history of science by talking about a similar tension in both between critical study and practice. I was wondering if you could elaborate a little bit on that. How is that tension different from what one might find in the history of other burgeoning fields as you look at their early history, especially in those that might initially seem to have closer parallels like film studies or television studies?

LOWOOD: The way that digital humanities has grown and some of the debates in digital humanities about, say, for example, whether you can be a serious digital humanities scholar if you don't know how to program have continued to move that discussion forward about the tension between productive practice and critical practice.

I think one of the big differences is that programming and many of the skills involved in game design are actually very accessible. If, by contrast, you were doing a history of television engineering, there are many more requirements to understanding what's going on. With film you have different kinds of practice involved. It's a very complex field. It's different if you're saying the practice that's required to be an actor versus the practice that's required to be a cinematographer, a camera operator, or that kind of thing.

Game studies reminded me a lot more of the discussions in the history of science where you had a lot of people who, in the early days of the history of science, crossed over from technical fields to do critical studies. So PhD physicists became historians of physics and were very important in the field; there was an intellectual debate organized around that for a while. It was actually a very similar formative stage in that discipline, as was the ludology versus narratology debate with game studies. That debate was between what was called internal and external history of science and was about whether you could better understand the dynamics of the history of science by a close reading of the development of the internal scientific knowledge versus an external study of the social, political, economic, etc., organization of science. It tended to be that the people who had PhDs in their field, for the most part (there were some significant exceptions), tended to be looking at internal history. And the people who did not have that kind of a background tended to have more of an externalist approach. What happened, as happens with so many of these kinds of intellectual debates, is after a while, there was sort of a meeting in the middle, and the most interesting work that was done involved aspects of both and being able to show the connections between a close read-ing and contextual kind of work.

　　With game studies right now, a lot of the interesting theoreti-cal and critical work is done by people who, as was the case in the history of science, have crossed over. The history of science example seemed very close in that the impact that practitioners had on the academic field was to create a kind of "sorting out" that had to happen. I would've expected that same tension to sort of work itself out by now in game studies, but I don't think it really has. In fact, that discussion has become broader as digital humani-ties–type fields have expanded. There's been even more discussion about this issue as a kind of hurdle that scholars involved in these fields have to get over: how much technical knowledge of those fields is needed in order to talk about them critically?

HEINEMAN: How has it grown?

LOWOOD: It has expanded to even more fields that are kind of like game studies. There are some digital studies – for example, the text mining that's done in literature – where there's a shared belief among a fair number of people who work in that area that you can't really be part of the discussion if you don't understand the technologies that are brought to bear on the work of scripting and the quantitative analysis that's involved in that. So it's expanded to other fields. Some of these other digital humanities fields are having the same discussion as game studies. I'm seeing among a lot of the graduate students who are working in game studies (and this I see as a positive thing) that they're insisting on being both involved in game development in some way doing critical work and having their critical studies have an impact on their game development. Their game development is probably not going to be the AAA-type games – they're probably more involved with indie-type games – but there is a conversation between, a meeting at the middle of, these two fields.

That's not to say that you have to program. Games are such a broad, creative platform that your technical knowledge might be knowing a lot about machinima, being a very good player, being a pro player, etc. There might be other backgrounds besides programming that would come into play that way.

HEINEMAN: In the "Preserving Digital Worlds" final report, you suggested that one major barrier to librarians who are interested in digital games is existing contract law. What specific significant challenges exist that are unique to the medium when negotiating with the legal infrastructure about archiving and preserving digital games?

LOWOOD: We knew that law was a problem and that there were things we would have difficulty doing because of legal issues. We thought that it was intellectual property law that was going to be the whole story: DMCA and copyright, maybe patents and that kind of thing, maybe other ways in which companies protect their intellectual property, that would keep us from doing the necessary data migration, copying when we need to do it, working with emulators – those would all cause problems.

What we found out was, yeah, there are problems there. But there are also a lot of problems that aren't necessarily purely intellectual property laws: for example, whether or not you have certain rights in a copyright law agreeing to something when you play a game. If you're in a certain virtual world or game world, there might be a restriction on what you can make screenshots or capture video about and then distribute. That might be important to a machinima maker, but that might also be important to an archive. Or it might be important, as in my case, to somebody who's curating a collecting of machinima.

It also comes into play with a world like *Second Life,* where there's a contractual but also implicit agreement between the player community and the developer about things like privacy, certain community standards about what you do or what you don't do if you're part of that *Second Life* community. And if you walk into *Second Life* and say, "Hey I want to copy your stuff because I want to put it in an archive," you may find out that they're quite hostile to that.

Or you may take the position that we need to get permission from somebody before we take something that they've created in *Second Life* and migrate it to some kind of repository. How do you do that? You need to get their real-life identity in order to get their permission. And you find out that Linden Lab in a sense has this contract with the players, the residents of *Second Life,* that they're not going to divulge that to you. I may have their avatar's name, but I can't go to Linden Lab and say, "Could you tell me the real-world identity of this person, please, so I can contact them about getting their stuff?" That's going to be seen right away as a breach of that implicit agreement between them. So you have to go through all these crazy hoops to try to do that, which we documented in the "Preserving Virtual World" report, and you end up getting a really, really low response rate. It's just too clunky a thing. You can do maybe what somebody like Jason Scott would do at http://www.textfiles.org of just going ahead and sucking up all the data.

Jason is somebody who's pretty courageous about that kind of thing, and he's willing to take the hits that he might take along the way. But in an institutional context, most repositories – which most repositories are in – maybe at a university, maybe part of a big museum, they can't do that. They can't just ignore the law and ignore the way that people will react to what they try to take. I thought we had a pretty good technology for moving stuff out of *Second Life* into another environment or at least getting started on that work, but we were just stonewalled by these soft issues around legal matters and by these kinds of agreements people think they have with the producers of virtual worlds and the like. It pretty much brought that to its knees.

HEINEMAN: Do you think that it's more likely that we'll lose more useful information from large companies like Activision or Electronic Arts than we would from a smaller, maybe independent group of developers and that our history is going to be skewed in some interesting ways? Because of all this legal baggage, will we know less about things that were more influential, had more people involved, and had more of an impact because they're owned by big companies that protect their information?

LOWOOD: There may be some skewing about it. I don't think it exactly follows those lines. The stuff you're talking about (large companies, small companies, who's going to get rid of stuff), I think, is pretty random in terms of what you could lay your hands on. I know of large companies that deleted stuff. I know of small companies that have completely disappeared. I know of small companies that have contacted us, and I know large companies that have contacted us. That's pretty random, and likewise with players, and likewise with websites.

I think the question is "How do you manage that randomness?" The thing is, the only way to do that is kind of an Old World word. It's not used that much anymore in the archival world. You have to develop "documentation strategies," which means you have to sit there and think about who you would contact to get documentation and then go through the process of contacting those various parties, some of whom will have stuff, some of whom won't.

The skewing is that the documentation strategy will naturally be skewed. It's an archivist's or historian's view of that event, what event is important, how to document it, and so on. That will mean that some things will be missed, some things will be overweighed, some things that even the person who thought of the documentation strategy would've wanted to get won't be present because of some random loss of information.

But I don't know a better way to do it. I think it's still the best methodology. You can think of it as the archivist creating documentation rather than just sitting back and waiting to see what collections are delivered to the archivist's doorstep.

I think the legal barriers hit hardest on the software-preservation side and with the virtual-world complication I mentioned. Our answer to that was, "Well, if we can't just grab data from the virtual world, from people, the alternative is documentation." We opted to do traditional documentation work about these events that occurred in virtual worlds if we couldn't just actually grab things from creators and the like. Likewise, emulation is a thing that's very much affected by copyright law. But that's primarily a software-preservation and access thing, less than a historical documentation thing. I think you're right. I think basically most of what archivists and historians have learned about documenting real-world events probably is applicable to virtual-world events.

Games and Economy

AS VIDEO GAMES HAVE GROWN IN POPULARITY, THEY HAVE also grown in profitability. Today's most expensive games often have production and advertising budgets that meet or exceed those of major Hollywood blockbusters, bring in global revenues that dwarf those found in most other entertainment industries, and offer a growing variety of opportunities for employment related to video games. This section of the book collects interviews with people who have a wide range of experiences across multiple areas of the video game industry. Ed Fries and Kellee Santiago offer firsthand accounts of both large- and small-scale ventures in hardware and software creation and curation, Chris Grant discusses video game journalism to provide the perspective of someone in an affiliated industry, and Edward Castronova offers a multilayered approach to game-related economies that bears much significance for those who wish to do research in this area.

From an economic perspective, much about the video game industry has changed in the past decade. This introduction offers a brief overview of the contemporary video game industry landscape as a way to hopefully frame the interviews in this section. In some respects, this is likely the portion of the book that will age most quickly, as the interviews were conducted during the emergence of a new console generation, an event that has historically offered some sea changes in strategies for game development and for other aspects of video games as a business. On the other hand, all of the interviews offer important historical contextualization for the present state of the video game industry that will continue to shape future decisions for those plotting a path toward profitability, popularity, or both.

The word *economy* is being utilized throughout this section in a very broad manner. In part, it refers to any and all linkages between video games and financial considerations. This includes game development and production costs, retail sales, share prices and stockholder interests, the used-games marketplace, online auction houses for virtual items, and other financials directly related to the buying and selling of video games and related content. There are also a number of economic interests that are tied to the popularity of gaming itself that one would want to consider in any discussion of the fiscal impact of video games; these include for-profit media surrounding video games (journalism, video/streaming services, books, music, films related to games, and the like), professional gaming leagues, retail stores that specialize in video games, and any number of interests that are not usually considered part of the "gaming industry" per se.

Beyond these associations, the term *video game economy* also might refer to designed in-game systems of transaction. This would include more obvious examples such as free-to-play games that reach profitability via microtransactions as well as less obvious examples such as the accumulation of experience points that can be used as currency (bought, sold, or traded) to acquire virtual items. In-game or virtual economies are not entirely insulated from the larger global economy, but they tend to operate on specific principles that make them a fascinating study in their own right, one that grounds much of Castronova's work.

Nick Dyer-Witheford and Greig de Peuter's 2009 book, *Games of Empire: Global Capitalism and Video Games,* functions as a near-exhaustive overview of the economics of video games and the parallels between industry business practices, game content, and an imperial model of finance:

> Since the production and consumption of digital games are themselves part of a world market whose profitability depends on dividing and controlling – when necessary by force – various unequal strata, from e-waste miners to gold farmers to "EA spouses" to game-publisher shareholders, it is hardly surprising that so many of the industry's virtualities reproduce and reassert the actualities of Empire.... [M]ost, though not all, of the other worlds that games explore are ... intensifications of global capital. (228)

The interviews in this section of the book attempt to interrogate some of these ideas and, along the way, to consider how the economics of video games might vary in different contexts.

In broad strokes, the contours of the video game industry look something like this:[1]

- *Large publishers and holding companies:* These are generally publicly traded companies that own multiple studios, licensees, and intellectual properties and often are vested in other types of industries. Prominent examples would include Electronic Arts, Activision Blizzard, Microsoft, Nintendo, and Sony.
- *Large development studios:*[2] These are places where games are made, qualified here as "large" due to the number of projects or employees or the amount of monetary investment by a publisher. These studios often make big-budget titles ("AAA games"). Prominent examples would include Rockstar Games, Bioware, Respawn Entertainment, Bungie, Infinity Ward, Insomniac, or Sega.
- *Medium-size publishers:* These are sometimes publicly traded companies that tend to be devoted solely to software creation and distribution, qualified here as "medium" due to a smaller "footprint" in the industry as a whole compared to companies like Electronic Arts or Sony. Examples would include companies such as ZeniMax Media (Bethesda, iD Software) or Capcom.
- *Medium-size development studios:* These are places where games are made, qualified here as "medium" due to comparative size, number of concurrent projects, and budget. Examples would include Crytek, Epic Games, and Platinum Games. In recent years, these studios tend to be most at risk of acquisition, bankruptcy, merger, liquidation of assets, and so on.
- *Small publishers:* These are publishers that often specialize in a particular kind of game, qualified here as "small" due to comparative number of employees, fiscal outlook, and the like. Examples might include Aksys Games, which specializes in localizing Japanese games, or Telltale Games, which releases episodic graphic adventure titles.

- *Small development studios:* These are usually newer or niche studios composed of relatively small teams of programmers, artists, and others. Examples would include developers such as Klei Entertainment, WayForward, or Hello Games as well as traditionally small studios like Cave, Stardock, or Psygnoiss.
- *Indie development studios:* At the most basic level, an independent studio with a resulting "indie game" is simply any game or studio not owned by a publisher, though the term has often been used to stand in for "small development studio" or "small studio owned by but with full artistic freedom from a publisher" or even "new developer that makes games with small budgets." The term is confusing, to say the least, as everything from thatgamecompany, which was in a contract with Sony when developing games such as *Journey* and *Flower,* to self-funded projects by a very small team (or even an individual) such as *Two Brothers* or *Crimzon Clover* are all classified at times as "indie games." Some of this slippage or confusion is addressed in the interview with Kellee Santiago in chapter 6.

As evidenced by both financial headlines and the amount of job postings found in various avenues, the video game industry sees a lot of change and thus a lot of personnel turnover. Furthermore, the industry has undergone significant periods of success and failure at revenue generation across its history and thus has witnessed several substantive restructurings of previously successful business models. In many ways, game development has become more costly and thus riskier; on the other hand, industry profits have increased steadily for the past decade.

ADDRESSING ECONOMIC PRACTICES

The economics of video games has already received considered attention by both popular and scholarly writers; it is also a topic regularly addressed by game-based journalism that covers the success and failure of various publishers and developers (and their individual products) across the industry. Websites like *Gamasutra,* for example, offer regular commentary penned by those who work in an array of contexts in the video game industry on topics such as questionable employment practices, corporate culture, tensions between artistic license and profit motives, and the relationship between content creators, distributors, and consumers.

From an academic perspective, the work of economist Edward Castronova, which is addressed in detail in chapter 8, is some of the most careful and influential thinking about the past, present, and future of a range of issues related to video game economics. Beyond Castronova's work are book-length treatments of some specific kinds of game-related economies, such as Dal Yong Jin's *Korea's Online Gaming Empire* (2010), which looks at that nation's multitiered game industry and considers its political economy, and T. L. Taylor's investigation into the world of professional competitive gaming in *Raising the Stakes: E-Sports and the Professionalization of Computer Gaming* (2012).[3] Other representative research in the area of game economics would include Malone's (2009) study on the relationship between community commitment and in-game economics in *World of Warcraft*, Smith's (2006) discussion of "economic game theory" as a principle of game design, and Steinkuehler's (2006) essay on the runaway economy of the MMO *Lineage*.

In recent years, a number of insightful essays and presentations have helped bring game economics to the forefront. For example, Ben Cousins's 2012 presentation at the Game Developers Conference (GDC), "When the Consoles Die, What Comes Next?," received a lot of coverage (and divisive responses) across major video game news sites (for example, Polygon and Kotaku) for its provocative suggestions about the implications for recent shifts in retail sales. That same year, one of *Gamasutra*'s most widely read stories addressed the pitfalls of developing "indie games" (Jan's "Congratulations, Your First Indie Game Is a Flop"). Stories related to games and economics have also received attention in more mainstream press outlets. *Fortune* has been covering games regularly for several years now, running stories such as "The 10 Most Powerful Women in Gaming" (Gaudiosi, 2013) and "Why Tablets Are the Future of Gaming" (Chou, 2012) that share the tone of their other articles that address the world of finance. A few years before, in 2010, Daniel Lyons published an essay in *Newsweek* titled "Why Behavioral

Economists Love Online Games" that focused on some of the ways that MMOs might function as a case study for "real world" economic practices.

Collectively, these individuals contribute some compelling examples of critical thinking about the economic structures and practices related to video games. Their work provides a kind of foundation for much of what is discussed in the interviews in this section of the book.

SUMMARY

As the video game industry has grown and the medium has gained wider global popularity, there has been considerable attention paid to its treatment of economics both at the level of business and as a concept used in game design. This section of the book offers an engagement on a range of issues that have emerged in recent popular and academic outlets on the subject of the game industry.

FIVE

Ed Fries

THE ECONOMICS AND POLITICS OF A LAUNCH

THE YEARS BRIDGING THE VERY END OF THE TWENTIETH century and the very beginning of the twenty-first were an interesting time in the history of video games. A few years prior to the millennium, the video game industry experienced a gold rush the likes of which had not been seen since before the infamous crash of 1983. In the six years between the initial sale of the Atari Video Computer System and the year when millions of unsold Atari cartridges were buried in a desert landfill, no fewer than ten game consoles were put on the market, many backed by major tech-industry companies like General Electric and Magnavox or toy companies like Mattel and Milton Bradley. By comparison, between October 1992 and September 1996 at least twenty video game consoles or video game console add-ons were placed on the market. These included the Sega CD, Atari Jaguar, Sega 32X, 3DO, Sony PlayStation, Sega Saturn, Nintendo Virtual Boy, NEC PC-FX, Amiga CD32, FM Towns Marty, Apple Bandai Pippin, Atari Jaguar CD, Casio Loopy, Tiger R-Zone, Pioneer Laser Active, Playdia, Neo Geo CD and CDZ, Supervision, Mega Duck and Cougar Boy, and Nintendo Stellaview (among others). This was a staggering amount of new technology flooding the game market in a very short time, and as was the case when a similar phenomenon occurred in the early 1980s, the vast majority of these systems failed to find an audience. In fact, the millennial transition period is probably more notable for the number of companies that found themselves forced out of the game console industry (including household names like Sega and Atari) than those that got their start in the period.

Given this backdrop, 2001 probably seemed like an especially risky time to enter the video game–console business. Microsoft, which had been involved in shaping the Windows-based operating system (os) for the rapidly failing Sega Dreamcast, had a front-row seat for that system's decline. Nonetheless, under the leadership of Microsoft pc Game Publishing vice president Ed Fries, Microsoft launched their Xbox console and brand that fall. The Xbox would prove to be a console that carved out a new niche in the game industry, one that was especially Western in its design, marketing, and overall economic structure. Many of these principles persisted at Microsoft through to the launch of its subsequent (and even more successful) console, the Xbox 360, a system that Fries also had early input in designing and planning.

Fries did a number of things at the system's launch that would help make the Xbox brand a household name. For one, he signed established development studios such as Rare (*Donkey Kong Country, Killer Instinct, Conker*) and Bungie (*Marathon, Halo*) to become first-party developers exclusively for the Xbox. He also accurately anticipated both the interest in and the possibilities for bringing long-standard pc features such as broadband-based multiplayer, a hard drive, and downloadable content to the console market. When companies like Panasonic, Apple, and even Sega had failed to create appealing game systems, Fries provided a viable model that demonstrated the value of carefully considering both audience and environment.

Given this success, when Fries left Microsoft near the launch of the 360, he found ample consulting opportunities in the game industry. Recently, he worked with the team responsible for launching the Ouya, a low-cost, Android os–based, open-source, and crowdfunded console that attempted to, once again, challenge the expectations for new consoles in a climate that has seen mobile phone gaming and pc-based gaming increasingly cannibalizing console-gaming profits.

In this chapter's interview, Fries outlines the story of the Xbox launch, the work that was done to overcome both internal and external complications before and during its launch period, and the relationship of the console to those that came before and after. Furthermore, he discusses the (then pending) launch of the Android-based system called the Ouya and why he thinks that certain strategies (and not others) make economic sense in the contemporary gaming landscape. Finally, Fries offers some thoughts on the past, present, and future roles of both government initiatives and university research that address the game industry.

—⚒—

HEINEMAN: Can you elaborate on some of the discussions that ended up resulting in Microsoft getting into the console business? What were you seeing as some of the obstacles, some of the opportunities, concerns, and compromises behind the creation of the Xbox?

FRIES: I was running the PC game publishing business for Microsoft at the time. The "console thing" had came up several times before. For example, if you remember the Windows CE guys had a deal around Dreamcast, and they had approached me and my group to do some things on Dreamcast, and it just didn't seem like that interesting a project to me, so I didn't support it at that time. Later, some guys from the DirectX team came into my office, and they had this idea for this direct Xbox. The way they originally described it was there would be a Windows PC running the DirectX APIs from a customer point of view so that it would look like and act like a game console.

So, you'd put a game in, and it would silently install on the hard disk (so you wouldn't have that kind of annoying PC gaming installation experience), and you'd have more of that "console experience" of just "drop in the disc and it works." For me, that was pretty appealing because I had grown our PC game business a fair amount by then, and I was starting to look at the console business as a way to continue to grow our game publishing business. The idea that I could get into a console business with our games without having to deal with different hardware than we were used to but with hardware that was PC-oriented hardware was very appealing. Because it would be easier for our group, I agreed to support them politically and help move the project forward, and that was kind of the start of it.

There were two competing console projects at the time. The group who had done the Windows CE project for Dreamcast also had a game console project. What ended up happening was, basically, two camps formed, and both of them had their senior executives and vice presidents behind them, and that went all the way up to a meeting with Bill and Steve, which was before the "Valentine's Day Massacre" meeting. This meeting was just to determine which group had the right to move forward with producing a plan to make a console. Both sides presented their plan. The Xbox side was very much what I just explained to you at that time, and then the Windows CE plan was very much like a traditional console, very much like what PlayStation 2 ended up looking like, very non-PC-like. Our group won that encounter and got the right to move forward with the project, and the other group basically got disbanded. We probably won because we presented a very "Microsoft-like" strategy. What we were presenting was basically a PC-oriented console at heart that ran Windows.

HEINEMAN: What were some of the other obstacles that came up in that meeting about the DirectX plan for the Xbox?

FRIES: We were very naive about the console business in general. Our group really knew a lot less about it than the Windows CE group, which had experience from working on Dreamcast. They also had a lot of ex-3DO guys who had joined the company through an acquisition, and so they really knew more about the console business than we did. I think we just presented a plan that was maybe palatable. For example, we said we were going to launch a year earlier than we actually did, and so we were naive about how long it would take to put a machine together. We said we'd run Windows, which we later backed away from. A lot of things were wrong about our plan, frankly. What ended up shipping, the final product, looked more like something between what they had presented and what we had presented. That, by the way, is what a lot of the tension at the Valentine's Day Massacre was about, almost a year later. The Valentine's Day Massacre was a meeting where the final real approval of the project to go forward was made, and it was also the first time we told Bill Gates that it wasn't going to run Windows, which he was not happy about and is part of why it was considered a "massacre." But once we got the right to do it, we learned more about the console business and thought more about what we wanted to build. The more we looked at it, the more we thought that running Windows was going to bring a lot of baggage with it, and we didn't really want that baggage. We wanted to make a clean break and just build an operating system that would be appropriate for this machine.

I wasn't involved in the operating system side. Jay Allard built the operating system, and I don't even think Jay was involved until after that first meeting (but I could be wrong). I think there are elements of Windows kernel in there and, certainly, the DirectX APIs are there. But it's really not Windows per se. The more we learned about it, the more we learned that we were headed toward a position somewhere in between that of the two groups. We learned about how long it was really going to take to build this system and to bring it to market, to build software for it, and how much it would cost for all of those different things, and that led us to design the Xbox that ended up coming to market. That took almost a year, and that was the plan that we pitched at that Valentine's Day Massacre meeting. At that point, it didn't really change much.

HEINEMAN: How much of the system's success (or sometimes lack thereof) do you think was a result of some of this internal conflict and of being new to the business? Most written histories of the launch of the Xbox really play up things like the Valentine's Day Massacre, but do you think those origins had as much of an impact on the launch of the console as other important external factors (a changing economy, the proximity of launch to September 11, 2001, etc.)?

FRIES: First of all, the Valentine's Day Massacre is a great story to tell. I love to tell it over a few drinks with people who haven't heard it because it's just a fun inside-Microsoft story. But if you extract out the few hours of suffering that we had in that meeting, the net effect was that we came in with a plan that we wanted to build this thing that was going to cost a lot of money, and we walked out of the meeting with approval to build what we wanted to build and with the money to do it. It's less interesting if you tell it that way, but that's what happened at the Valentine's Day Massacre meeting:

we got approval to build the Xbox the way we wanted to build it, which was to really be separate from Microsoft. We were ex-*Office* guys, and we knew how much interference the rest of the company could cause, and so one of the things we really wanted and asked for in that meeting was to have the freedom to be separate and to do this thing the way we wanted to do it. That was granted to us in that meeting, so that was great. Then we went off and we built the thing, and that went more or less pretty well.

9/11 happened two months before launch, so it didn't have a big influence on the content we were building or the way the box looked or anything like that since everything was pretty much being wrapped up. That doesn't mean it didn't have a big impact on us. Robbie [Bach] was in New York when it happened, as was Seamus [Blackley]. I was in San Francisco that morning and was meeting with game magazines to promote the Xbox, and it took us all a while to get back to Redmond. I ended up getting a flight out three or four days later. Robbie ended up renting a car and driving all the way across America back to Seattle and wrote a really fantastic e-mail that he sent out to the whole team about his experience and how that drive strengthened his confidence in America. It was a really inspiring piece of work.

But you have to remember that I'm also running the PC game publishing business where we make *Flight Simulator,* and *Flight Simulator* was used by the terrorists as part of their training program, so that had an impact. We were building a game called *Project Gotham Racing.* Well, *Gotham* is Gotham City, New York, and it had the Twin Towers, and we had internal debates about whether we had to stop selling or do something about *Flight Sim,* whether we had to remove the Twin Towers from *Project Gotham Racing* (which we ultimately did), and things like that. Another 9/11 impact was around *Halo.* We had already submitted *Halo* to the ESRB [Entertainment Software Ratings Board] to get a prerating on it, and we had been told that if we just made a few changes, it would be "Teen" rated. They asked us to take that blood out, and there were a few other minor changes like that, and so we did the three or four things that they asked us to do and we resubmitted it to be rerated, and then 9/11 happened and they came back with a new response that it was now "M" rated because of the intensity of the combat. We thought, "Well, screw that! We're not going to change the intensity of the combat: that's what the game's all about." So we put all the other stuff back in, and we just accepted that it was going to be "M" rated. It was really late in the process to have them change their decision, and we think it was 9/11 related, but we don't know for sure. We had boxes printed, we had advertising materials out in the stores that already had the *T* on them, and other things like that. It created some issues for our marketing people, but as far as the product team goes, it wasn't a big deal.

Those are the three things that I can remember as far as the impact of 9/11: *Flight Sim, Gotham Racing,* and *Halo.* The Xbox project itself was delayed a week as well, so we launched November 15, and our original plan was to launch November 8. That was blamed on 9/11 and the time we spent dealing with issues and being delayed, but that wasn't a huge impact.

HEINEMAN: What made you think it seemed like the right time for Microsoft to enter into the console business? Couldn't they have jumped in during the 16-bit or PlayStation and Saturn eras?

FRIES: There was an old Japanese system called the MSX that Microsoft was involved with and that had some game capabilities back in the old, old days. That was before my time with games at Microsoft. Like a lot of things at Microsoft, it probably wasn't the first time that they had looked at it or done it. I think part of the reason that this was the right time, which might sound funny outside of Microsoft, was that Microsoft really saw Sony as a competitive threat at that time. Sony was a strong and well-respected company and was starting to put PC-like components into the living room (a processor here and storage there, etc.). There was some internal feeling that Sony represented a threat to the Microsoft ecosystem, and I think that that was part of the reason that Xbox was approved at that time. The PlayStation business was a huge generator of profit for Sony's business overall, and so Xbox was a counterpoint to what Sony was doing.

HEINEMAN: That makes sense, on one hand. But, on the other hand, Microsoft also had involvement (at least with the OS) with the Sega Dreamcast, which, by 2000 or 2001, was already starting to show signs of having difficulty in the market. Didn't that give pause?

FRIES: I think you can accomplish a lot with being both a little naive and arrogant and having some money. I think we didn't know what we didn't know, and we felt like we could do this. You have to remember I joined the company as the seventh programmer working on the first version of *Excel* for Windows. When I joined, Lotus was bigger than all of Microsoft, and we spent several years doing better and better versions of *Excel* until we battled and beat *Lotus 1,2,3*. When I went over to run *Word*, we were battling *WordPerfect*. We battled and beat *WordPerfect*, and my boss, Robbie Bach, was from that same heritage. He was more of a sales and marketing guy, but he was involved with *Office* during those same battles.

So we went from being the underdogs doing spreadsheets and battling and winning to being the underdogs on word processing to battling and winning to then being a big underdog as far as establishing Microsoft as a credible presence in gaming at all. People were like, "What does Microsoft know about games?" So I was very used to being an underdog and people being skeptical about whether Microsoft should be in a particular business. So, to me, that was the normal thing. The console business was no different in that respect, and it played out in a very similar way from my point of view. We went out and we talked to the press, and they were very skeptical, and a lot of people told us all the reasons we would fail, and we ignored them and just tried to build the best product we could and bring it to market the best we could.

HEINEMAN: A lot of game studies scholarship has focused on how, especially during the present generation of consoles, gaming has signaled an important moment in the broader history of technology by realizing a type of convergence. Last generation, the Xbox (and to a lesser extent the PlayStation 2) showed some of the potential for that. I am curious about how decisions were made at Microsoft concerning what technological components would be put into the system and which would be left out. The Dreamcast, for example, had had some online functionality, but it wasn't extremely successful. Sony had only limited usage of their PS2 hard drive. Other previous consoles like the 3 DO and C D-i had tried to incorporate the convergence of different kinds of media within a console to only limited success. To this day, something that distinguishes the Xbox from the competition of that generation is the way in which it was able to bring together a variety of different devices and different technologies into one console.

FRIES: Early on, the most controversial thing was whether we should have a modem or not. At that time, very few people had broadband Internet at their houses. That was a decision that Robbie Bach made, and he just basically said, "No, we're going to bet on the future. We're not going to have a modem. We're not going to support dial-up gameplay. We're only going to support broadband Internet multiplayer play." People don't remember today, but back then every laptop had a modem; people used dial-up all the time. It was a very forward-looking and correct decision that he made. It's really nice when decisions like that get made because they're very clarifying for the team.

We almost backed into the hard disk. The original plan had the hard disk because it was a PC and every PC had a hard disk, but as we became more and more console-like, we started to ask if we really needed it, and we found ourselves in the position of trying to justify why we had it. We thought things like, "Maybe we can cache some of the game installation onto the hard disk so we can make our games run faster than Sony." We didn't even launch Xbox Live for a year after the launch of the console, and the early version of Xbox Live didn't support things like digital distribution, so the hard drive couldn't really be justified in those early days as storage for digital distribution. So the hard disk always was, and I think always will be, kind of a controversial decision.

I was always a big supporter of the hard disk, probably more than I should have been. I felt it was the one key differentiator we had on the Xbox when it came to hardware, and I thought we needed to have some reason Xbox was different from Nintendo or Sony's offering. But that was kind of a hard sell. I'm a programmer by training, so to me technical stuff like an included hard disk is neat. To a customer, though, they might not even know what a hard disk is or why it is important, and I don't think we did a fantastic job throughout the whole Xbox cycle of really coming up with the killer reason a hard disk was an important thing to have, even though we tried to include that in the marketing.

HEINEMAN: And what about things like DVD playing functionality? Sony had that in the PS2, but Nintendo made a choice with the GameCube to go with proprietary media (as did Sega with the Dreamcast). At what point did you decide, "Okay, let's do this and let's not do that"? Are there things you wanted to be able to put into it to create a richer converge?

FRIES: I always thought that the most important reason that we were making the machine was to play games. There are definitely other people, including my boss, Robbie, who saw other opportunities for the Xbox. If you go back and watch the E3 speeches that we did at the time, they were always talking about the Xbox being a broader entertainment device (they still do to this today). To some degree, that's become true, but the fact is most people buy it to play games first. It was my job to make sure they bought it to play games, that there were great games to play. I never worried too much about the whole convergence issue, that this machine can do other things beyond games, but it certainly showed up in my boss's speeches a fair amount.

One thing about DVD play is that the Xbox didn't include that feature straight out of the box. You had to buy an add-on to make it play DVDs. It was an add-on kit that had a remote and a little IR sensor that plugged into one of the USB ports on the Xbox. The reason for that add-on is that Microsoft didn't want to bundle into the machine the DVD playback royalties. There are royalties around the playback that you had to pay, and so having royalties on a machine that's had tightly controlled costs was to be avoided. That's why it ended up being a little bit awkward, I think, from a customer's point of view.

HEINEMAN: What kind of consumer analysis work was Microsoft doing when they were trying to figure how to best market the console? How did that analysis shape the eventual launch itself across various regions?

FRIES: It was my job to build the portfolio for both the launch and
beyond. I had been doing that for years on the PC, so it was more
a question about what could we get in the limited amount of time
we had. From the time we got final approval to launch, we had just
a couple of years, which isn't enough time to build something from
scratch. We had to look at what was available and be opportunistic.
So we convinced Lorne Lanning to switch from Sony with his
Oddworld franchise, which had been a recently big hit in the previous generation, to do his next game on our system. We thought
that was going to be a game called *Munch's Oddysee,* which was
one of our launch titles that we thought would be important. We
worked with the guys at Bizarre Creations who had done a game
called *MSR Racing* for the Sega Dreamcast, and so it wasn't a huge
step for them to basically take that game and port it to our console
and just take advantage of the better power to make the graphics
look better and have a new setting, new cars, and that kind of
thing. That was where *Project Gotham Racing* came from, which
was another launch title.

In the case of *Halo,* and in the case of almost every one of
these launch games, there is an illustration that the way the game
business works is less about strategy and more about relationships.
If you go to E3 and GDC for many years and you spend a lot of
time hanging out with developers and getting to know them, then
when opportunities come up, they come up. In the case of *Halo,*
a guy named Peter Tamte was somebody I knew from the game
business. He called me one day, and he said that Bungie was in
financial trouble, that they were looking to sell the company, and
that they already were talking with one party, and they figured if
they were talking to them, they should talk to some other people
too, and was I interested? That was the time when I was looking for
content, so I was definitely interested and said yes. They had this
new *Halo* concept that they had shown that got a good response at
a MacWorld, and that was the start of the conversation to acquire
Bungie.

HEINEMAN: When you look at that launch lineup of the Xbox and
compare it to those of the PlayStation 2 or the GameCube, it seems

to have a very different gamer demographic in mind. There are not, for example, a lot of fuzzy mascots. There is a much smaller percentage of Japanese-developed games. Was that a conscious marketing decision, or did it just kind of happen that way?

FRIES: Since I did it, I know why it happened. In a way, I guess a little bit of that is my style, but also you keep using the word *marketing*, and to me marketing had nothing to do with it.

Marketing would get involved later, trying to figure out how to sell the titles. But marketing didn't even report to me most of the time. It was Microsoft Games Studio's job to come up with the portfolio, and that's what we did. I think (and this is maybe a game studies thing) that what's really interesting to understand and probably what's most important about Xbox from a historical point of view is that we all came from a PC gaming world. We had a certain point of view on where gaming was headed and what was important. At that time, a big part of the PC gaming world was on-line multiplayer; you had games like *Doom* and *Quake* and others, and so the idea that we would do something like Xbox Live and that there would be multiplayer, first-person shooter games on a console only looks radical when you look at it from a console point of view. It only looks radical when you look at it from a "Mario point of view." It doesn't look radical at all from a PC point of view. In fact, a lot of people told us, at that time, that we were making a big mistake.

The early times when we showed *Halo,* we were told, "Wow, this really looks like a PC game, not a console game." Somebody from my group famously came into my office and did a color-palette analysis on *Halo* and said it was using PC colors, not console colors. Bill Gates and other people would often ask me, "What's our mascot?" You know, obviously, Sega had Sonic and Nintendo had Mario, so "What's your mascot?" We would basically say, "We don't have a mascot. We just have all these games we think are good." I think what Xbox really did was it Americanized console gaming, and it brought a lot of ideas from PC gaming into console gaming. Console gaming, up to that point, had been very Japanese focused from a cultural point of view. It was behind the times from a multiplayer-play point of view and even from a style-of-game point of view. There had only been really one good first-person shooter on a console before *Halo* came out, and that was Rare's *GoldenEye*. That is really the big accomplishment of Xbox, the thing that made it have a big impact. In a way, it matured console gaming and took it to a place that PC gaming had already gone.

But it would be a mistake to think that we differentiated ourselves to a different market on purpose. We did it because that was the set of games that we could get our hands on. We had more relationships among PC game developers than we did among console game developers. The idea at that time, that we could work with somebody like Rare, was just out of the question. It was just much more comfortable and natural for us to work with more PC-oriented partners and develop titles that were more PC oriented, even though we didn't know if that was going to work. It wasn't like we set out on this mission to take certain ideas from the PC and change the console world. It was more a situation where we could build a certain system in a set time and thought that there were certain kinds of games that we thought were fun and that we hoped that console gamers thought would be fun, too.

The fact that we embraced Lorne Lanning and *Munch's Oddysee* and similar titles is evidence that we were trying to hedge our bets as much as we could. We were trying to have console-oriented titles, too. The only reason we didn't have more Japanese titles is, from a first-party point of view, we had no Japanese production capability at that time. I started a studio in Japan, but it took years to ramp up, and ultimately we made games like *Blinx* and a few other things out of there. We just didn't have that capability. From a third-party point of view, we did get some Japanese games in over time, but the Japanese publishers were terrified to work with us. They really wanted to work with Xbox because they wanted a counterpoint to Sony, since Sony was incredibly powerful at that time. They wanted there to be this counterbalance to Sony, but they really couldn't afford to piss off Sony because if they pissed off Sony, Sony could very easily hurt them in their home market, the Japanese market, and that was critical to their business. So, they had to be very careful about how they approached Xbox and how they supported it.

HEINEMAN: Gaming journalism often talks about the original Xbox being important because of what it did for the Xbox 360 by establishing a particular kind of identity for what a Microsoft console is. Do you think that the identity of the Microsoft 360 is very similar to what you were trying to create with the original Xbox, or do you think that there are some significant differences?

FRIES: I was at Microsoft for a good part of the planning for the 360 as well, and the 360 was an extension of what we wanted Xbox to be and what we had learned from Xbox. It may not be obvious to consumers and journalists, but a lot of our learning with the Xbox over time was with the inside of the machine. For example, the original Xbox had an Intel processor and it had an NVidia chip and a graphics chip and a bunch of other PC-like components, and the problem with that was that it was almost impossible to cost reduce it over time. So a big part of the effort on 360 was all about building a machine with intellectual property that we could license and combine so that we could cost reduce the machine over time. There was no way with the original Xbox that we could have gotten Intel and NVidia to work together to merge the CPU and the GPU onto a single chip, for example, which is something that Microsoft could do on the 360. It doesn't really show through to the customer, but that was a big part of what 360 was about.

The fact that 360s shipped with a SKU that had no hard disk is sort of a reaction to the original Xbox as well and efforts to cost reduce it (because it was hard to cost reduce the hard disk). I still think that was a huge mistake, and it was something I was fighting for when I was there. I think it's terrible that there's an Xbox 360 SKU that doesn't have a hard disk because developers have to deal with the fact that this weird SKU is out there. I just think it's funny, because both of our competitors included either a hard disk or a hard disk–like function in all of their consoles. You wouldn't think that Microsoft, the guys who invented putting a disk in the console, are the only ones who have a console that doesn't have it included.

However, not including a hard disk did give Microsoft some ability to play marketing games around pricing that were hard for the competitors to match (though a lot of that is marketing strategy). The 360 also really had a goal of launching first. That was a critical thing in the planning for it, that it was going to hit the market first and get an advantage because of that. It would be established in the market before PlayStation.

Overall, to your bigger question about where Xbox has gone, I think that Xbox has been more successful in the West because it's just more of a Western brand. It feels more Western. It has a more aggressive, more mature sort of "Western feel" to it, and some of the Japanese stuff can come across as either foreign or kiddie in this market. I think that that's always been true from the first Xbox and also for the 360, and I think that that's important. Microsoft has also tried to broaden the appeal of the console and tried to reach out by representing it more as a multimedia device or an entertainment hub. I don't know; I'm kind of the worst guy to talk to about that because the people in the game business (game makers, game writers, etc.), if you sit at E3 and watch Microsoft talk about multimedia in their press conference, the game people always cringe. I consider myself part of that community, so I cringe a bit, too (but I use my 360 for Netflix and other things, so . . .).

HEINEMAN: Ouya's noted for being funded in part by using crowd-source financing built through Kickstarter. Can you discuss how the decision was made to pursue that avenue for revenue?

FRIES: From the time that I was approached to be involved with the project, that was always the plan. I think Ouya takes a certain point of view, which is that there's this opportunity that isn't being met. There's an opportunity to build a relatively cheap console, a relatively open console, and to get the kinds of games that are available that are currently difficult to get working on a TV onto the TV. If you're a developer right now and you make a game that you think would be fun to play on the TV, you have very poor choices for how to get that to happen. Basically, you could go to Microsoft and try to convince them to take you on as a first-party Xbox Live Arcade title, but they do very few of those a year. You could go to one of the other major publishers who have publishing slots on Xbox Live, and if they turn you down, you're pretty much out of luck, even if you're willing to fund it yourself and do everything yourself. Even if somehow you manage to convince people to publish your thing so you can actually get it up on Xbox, then there's all sorts of other problems. You couldn't do a free-to-play game. You can't update your game with any frequency. *Minecraft* might be a good example. If you wanted to do *Minecraft* like *Minecraft* was done on the PC on the Xbox 360, you couldn't possibly do it. The only reason *Minecraft*'s available on Xbox now is because it was already so popular on the PC that they convinced Microsoft to take it as a first-party title. But they couldn't have followed the same strategy of releasing the game in a beta build and then having the audience continue to refine it and improve it, since they wouldn't have had that power.

Ouya is just sort of a "what if?" console. What if the TV world was different? What if the TV world was more like the phone world, where anybody who wants can very easily make a game for iPhone and put it out there and see what happens? That's the core idea behind Ouya that got me excited about the platform and the reason that I wanted to support it. As far as Kickstarter goes, it fits with the vibe of the console in the sense that this is going to be an open community–driven console. I wasn't surprised that it did well in Kickstarter because I think it speaks to the right community with the right language and with the right offer. Some people think Kickstarter is like a charity, but really it's a place where you can buy things that you want that just don't exist yet (and you have to wait a little longer to get them). You can actually make these things exist by buying them. In the case of Ouya, you're paying $99 to buy a console. It's like you're preordering it; you're buying it in advance.

HEINEMAN: What significant ways do you think the consumer market itself has changed for purchasing game console hardware in the decade since the Xbox launch? Is the Ouya something that, despite the possibilities of an open platform and all the things you mention, is being launched at a risky time to sell gaming hardware? There has been a lot of debate about whether or not the next console generation will be able to compete with smartphones and tablets.

FRIES: I think that's the $64,000 question right now, and I don't think anybody really knows the answer. I was at a meeting yesterday at San Francisco where Alex St. John gave a presentation. He was the early guy at Microsoft who really promoted DirectX and went on to start Wild Tangent and was the CEO of Hi5 and some other things. He gave an hour-long talk about the game business. He's a very self-confident guy, and a lot of his speech is about how "I was right about this, and I was right about that, and blah-blah-blah," but at the end he suggested that he's never seen the game industry be more confusing to figure out and expressed that he didn't really know what was going to happen next. I had never heard Alex say that before. There are a lot of things that people agree on, like that free-to-play is really important or that we are getting to the end of the ability to make pixels smaller and smaller and have that matter. But will the next generation of consoles fall on its face? If I had to guess, I'd say no.

Gamasutra had a great article about this not too long ago, and in it they said that the forecast for this year's sales for the United States in the console business is about $14.5 billion, which is down quite a bit from the peak at 2008, which was like $21-plus billion. But $14 billion is still higher than the peak of the last generation. So, this generation of consoles will make quite a bit more money than the last generation of consoles did, and so maybe this generation is the peak and next generation will go down some, but there's still a huge amount of money to be made in games, and the percentage of that money is significantly bigger in the console business than in any other part of the gaming business ecosystem.

My personal opinion is that another generation of consoles will launch, that people will go out and buy them because they're conditioned to buy new consoles, and that game developers are going to show cool new things that are possible on these consoles that weren't possible on the last consoles. We are going to have at least another generation of consoles that sell well and are important. That's my opinion, but I would certainly agree that there's never been more uncertainty in the market than there is right now.

HEINEMAN: Having an open platform potentially opens up the Ouya to piracy in a way that we haven't really seen in a console market. Do you think that that's a legitimate concern?

FRIES: I don't.

HEINEMAN: No?

FRIES: The reason I don't is because I think the kind of title that's going to end up being important on Ouya is going to be a different kind of game. I think it's going to be more a client-server model, more of a free-to-play design. In the client-server world, piracy is a good thing, not a bad thing. "Please steal my client." That's why it developed in Asia, where there was a lot of piracy. I just think the content itself will adapt to the environment.

HEINEMAN: If we're shifting to a model that's more client-server or free-to-play, does that hurt the possibility of things like retail sales? Is retail important?

FRIES: Yes, but I want to ask it a different way. I'm going to change your question around a little. I want to say, "Are some things, like retail holdings, going to hold back the next generation of mainstream consoles?"

So, you know [*sighs*], Microsoft doesn't support free-to-play right now. It turns out they announced their first free-to-play game last week, but it's only a first-party title. I know many people have tried to pitch them third-party titles, and they haven't been able to do it. Will the next console support a free-to-play model? I don't know. To date, they've not supported that idea at all, and part of the reason may have to do with retail because they don't want to be seen as supporting a pure digital product. Part of it has to do with data security around their data center and not wanting to expose the data center to outside groups. Part of it has to do with dynamic pricing and how that affects retail. You can go and you can make an Xbox Live indie game right now, but you can't price it the way you want.

Part of it has to do with certification. Consoles have this long-standing idea that any game has to be certified, and you can see that causing problems right now. There's been some very vocal complaints about the Xbox certification process that costs thirty thousand dollars every time they try to certify something. Microsoft won't even let you certify a title and then recertify it in a certain amount of time, which is a model that is very anti the free-to-play world. In the free-to-play world, you put something out quickly, you get customer feedback, and then you respond to that feedback. I think the question is "Will retail, will certification, will a lot of these old ideas (many of which date back to the crash in 1984 and the way Nintendo rebuilt the console business after that crash), will they hold back the new world when it comes to consoles?" And to the extent that they do is really where they create a market opportunity for Ouya or Apple or other people to step in who just simply don't have that baggage. They don't have the relationships with the retailers they have to worry about. They don't have the relationships with publishers who have the relationships with retailers they have to worry about. It could end up being that the real vulnerability for those platforms is just the fact that they come from this sort of older world and that their world is changing around them.

HEINEMAN: So what's the incentive for a large studio to create a multimillion-dollar game (e.g., *Halo* or *Skyrim*) if there's not that certainty in the retail sector where they make a lot of their money? Could you see something as big budget as a *Halo* game being released exclusively for an open platform like the Ouya?

FRIES: So here's why I think that thinking is old and backwards. How much money has Mojang (the makers of *Minecraft*) made so far? More than one hundred million dollars? How much money is *World of Tanks* making? I just came from a lunch meeting with a guy who told me they're making thirty million dollars a month on that product. So, there's clearly huge opportunity for games that don't fit the old model. Right now they don't look very good because people haven't made big bets on them, but sooner or later, the same competition that drove the old crappy games to get better and better and look better and better, the same thing's going to happen in the free-to-play space. The question is just whether it's going to be the traditional big publishers who are going to do it or whether it's going to be newcomers like Mojang and Wargaming .net and other people who actually "get" the free-to-play world and why it's important. They're going to make more money than any of those other studios. I mean, look at EA: they bought PopCap for over a billion dollars, and the entire market cap of EA is now about four billion dollars. Would you believe that PopCap is worth a quarter of EA? A few years ago, that would have been laughable.

HEINEMAN: What kinds of economic policies tend to be favorable to game companies when launching new hardware? Is there anything that you've been able to notice that "if this protection or regulation is in place, there's more likely to be success; if it's not, there's not"?

FRIES: I live in the Seattle area, and we try to cultivate a developer-friendly culture here. There's a group here called Win Washington Interactive Network, and it's sponsored out of a group called Enterprise Seattle, which is a public-private group that tries to promote business in the region. They did a survey in the region about three years ago, and there were 150 game companies. In the most recent survey, there were 350. So we have a very vibrant culture here. It's not particularly supported at the state level. In fact, the state has a film board that provides incentives for movies to be made in the state, but it doesn't have the equivalent for video games, which I think is silly because we're much more of a video game state than we are a movie state and it's much more important to the local economy.

There are more than ten thousand jobs in the Seattle region around video games, and it brings in billions of dollars to the local economy. But you can look at the kinds of incentives that Canada's put in place that's really built huge centers in Montreal and other places around game development. Game development is a fantastic business. It's a high-tech, high-paying business that is the kind of business that is not polluting; it's the kind of business that you want in your community. I guess I'm probably surprised that there isn't more understanding of that at the state level or even the federal level and that there isn't more competition to get game development or game development–related businesses in the region.

Louisiana is a state that's been very aggressive in promoting development in their state, and a lot of testing, actually, has moved to Louisiana. Big test centers have been opened up there because of the incentives that they've provided. So it is happening piecemeal here and there, but I'm surprised more of it isn't happening.

HEINEMAN: Do you think what happened with 38 Studios and their highly publicized government loan has anything to do with putting a chill on the future for state-funded game development?

FRIES: I think that that deal raised a lot of eyebrows when it happened and when the deal was first announced that the state was going to insure one individual company to such a large degree. I mean, any of us who work in the game business know that it's a risky business, like all entertainment businesses are, that most things fail and the few that succeed tend to succeed spectacularly. Usually, when that's the economics of the situation, the smart approach is to take a portfolio approach. That's what venture capitalists do: they invest a little across a bunch of different businesses, all of which are risky, and really you make your money on the few that pay off. I would think that the same kind of approach would make more sense for a city or a state than to put all their eggs in one basket. Politics and making sense don't always go hand in hand.

HEINEMAN: When you look at the history of dedicated gaming consoles, a high percentage of them have been unsuccessful. Apple tried the console market once. Panasonic didn't have much success with the 3DO. Even Atari and Sega, which had success, eventually didn't have success with console hardware. A lot of different companies have had to bow out or immediately ran into problems. Do you think, looking at that history, that there are particular factors that might cause a console to be successful or to fail?

FRIES: I think one really important piece is that you have to have a strong software component to it. It's not just about the hardware, and that really means you have to have a strong first-party software

group. I'm biased, since that's what I used to run, but all you're
going to get from third party is what everyone else has, and it's
still going to cost you a bunch of money to get that. The unique
differentiating content is going to be the first-party content.
Microsoft was lucky in a sense that they already had a successful
PC game publishing business. It wasn't like we were trying to build
a console and build a game publishing business from scratch. I
think that would have been very hard; that was the situation in
some of the examples you gave. Others, like Atari, you have to go
back and look at the crash of '84 and what happened there, which
is a different discussion. In the case of Sega, they ended up being a
better software company than they were a hardware company, and
so they decided to focus on being a software company. That was
probably the right decision when they were up against the likes
of Sony and Microsoft, huge multinational companies that could
afford to outspend them. So to get the right answer, you probably
have to look at each of the cases that you gave and say, "How are
they different?" But certainly one of the things you have to have is
great original content that's only available on that platform.

HEINEMAN: Sega did have that, though. Do you think it was just that
they could be outspent? Is it spending, then, that's more important
than the titles?

FRIES: You are asking a good question, and I guess I would have to
go back and look at what went wrong with the Dreamcast. I think
there were some financial issues. You should talk to Peter Moore.
Ask him why Sega ultimately did what they did and why. My
impression is that Sony came in and was not only powerful enough
to knock out Nintendo, which was the number one, but since Sega
was already having trouble fighting Nintendo, it was hard to be
number three.

HEINEMAN: I mentioned, when we started talking, that this project
is an attempt to bring together people who study the economics
of games, or games as cultural artifacts, or as art (and so on) with
people who are active in the industry in some particular capacity,
or who are part of game culture (and so on). What do you think
is important about those relationships moving forward? Do you

think that you'd like to see certain kinds of work done in game studies? Are there certain topics that you'd like to see researched? Do you think that there needs to be more academic influence in the gaming industry in any way?

FRIES: To me, game studies is a really new thing. I don't understand it very well. I'm not very close to it. I'm not very involved with it. And so it's really hard for me to comment on it.

I think the business has evolved. In the past, people mostly learned it on the job. If you compare games to film or something similar, people could go to film school and actually learn a lot about how to make movies and what had been learned over a long period of time before they went out and tried to make their own, whereas in the game business, it's more like a trade skill. You apprentice under some people, and maybe eventually you get your shot. I think that's still true in film and other things as well, but at least you have this sort of college experience where you learn a lot about what's happened before and, hopefully, a bit about where things are headed. So, that all makes sense to me. I'm on the curriculum committee for DigiPen around their RTIS program, which is the programming side of what they do. To that extent, I'm involved, but that has nothing to do with game studies. They just started a design degree, though, which is a little more interesting.

HEINEMAN: One of the things that at least some game studies scholars would like to see as one of the effects of their work would be a game industry that is, as a whole, more conscientious of the impact of their games on the people who play them. Not just in terms of "Are they having fun?" but something closer to how great directors might think about the ways in which their films touch on different hot topics in the culture. Does there need to be more of that, from your point of view, in the industry?

FRIES: I gave a speech in 1997 or 1998 where I said that our goal had to be to create not just entertainment, but art. I was trying to say kind of what you're just saying, that we need to have more impact and that we should. I was talking to a good, very talented, reasonably young designer not too long ago, and he was talking about how he thinks these sort of movie-oriented games are really the wrong track and that games should really be more toy-like (and he had made some very good toy-like games). I agreed with him that that spectrum existed, but I also told him that what was interesting about the movie-like games is that they have a human element to them. I think once people are involved, the game has an op-portunity to be more relevant to us and our lives in the way a great movie or a great book can be relevant and change the way we think about the world, whereas a toy is something that you use to pass the time. Is game studies the way to get there or not? I don't know. Maybe.

We're in the middle of a transition from the first generation of game designers who were really all programmer. If you look at Peter Molyneaux or Sid Meir or a lot of those guys, they're all programmers. We're in the middle of a transition to these people becoming much more artists than programmers, and even that is a very slow, generational change. You get companies like thatgame-company where they're doing new and interesting things that are much more art driven than technology driven. What's happening to game consoles, I think, is a good thing. In a way, we've been lazy that we could rely on technology getting better and better and better and pixels getting smaller and smaller; it makes us lazy about improving our art. I'm referring to art in the big sense, not art in the sense of what our game models look like. We're getting to the end of that period, and so if we want to keep our customers engaged and interested and keep our business relevant, we need to do things that are more about how people feel than what they see on the screen or what the technology is. All those forces are happening.

SIX

Kellee Santiago

INDEPENDENT GAME DEVELOPMENT

THE LAST DECADE OF VIDEO GAMING HAS BEEN MARKED BY THE rise of the "independent," or "indie," game. Enabled by the broader penetration of broadband into homes and by the creation of digital distribution networks on major gaming platforms (for example, Valve's Steam on the PC, Sony's PlayStation Network, Microsoft's Xbox Live Arcade, Nintendo's eShop, and others), game developers who work alone or in small teams have found new audiences and revenue sources for their work. Though most of these games have been relatively modest in their origins, some of them have found widespread commercial and critical success, success that has often prompted large publishers to scoop up promising or proven independent studios.[1] Such was the case with thatgamecompany, a studio founded by USC alums Jenova Chen and Kellee Santiago that was contracted with Sony Computer Entertainment to develop games exclusively for their platform.

In Santiago's time with the studio (she left in 2012), the game that was probably thatgamecompany's crowning achievement was *Journey,* a PlayStation Network title that received widespread critical acclaim (winning multiple "game of the year" awards from various press outlets and industry panels) and offered an emotional experience that many found both compelling and novel. In fact, in a brief review of the game I wrote for a game-related webzine, I suggested that the game "stands as a testament to the potential of the medium of gaming to produce something remarkable, artistic, universal, and beautiful." Like many other commentators on the game, I attributed its success in large part to the creative freedom that came from developing a game with a small, independent team.

Santiago's current role is one of fostering independent game development for the Ouya, an open-source, Android os–based game console. In the past few years, she has been promoting a number of ideas about the possibilities of new models of game design.[2] Given her particular background, her words carry weight for those looking to understand what makes the independent model a vibrant and viable one for the future of video games.

Despite its increased significance to the medium, the independent game phenomenon as such has largely been ignored by game studies scholars.[3] There have been essays and book chapters that focus on particular titles as part of a larger argument, but for the most part their unique economic position and their role in exploring new possibilities for the medium have been largely neglected. When one considers that many independent games have been developed in classroom settings or by recent university graduates, this oversight seems especially problematic.

The interview with Santiago in this chapter begins by exploring some of the characteristics of independent game development, focusing at points on its potential relationships to pedagogy and to independent work done in other fields. She also discusses her thoughts on gender issues that the game industry faces, the relationship between critical theory and game design, and the state of games journalism.

—⚏—

HEINEMAN: Some of the games that you have been associated with have won a number of industry awards as "indie" titles, and you've also been involved in several projects designed to foster independent game development. Given that this term has followed you around a lot, what does the word *independent* mean to you (when it comes to gaming in particular)?

SANTIAGO: It was a term that both Jenova Chen and I felt like we had to define for ourselves early on, since, technically, thatgamecompany was not an independent studio and we were fully financed by Sony Computer Entertainment. What we came to was that it felt like "indie" referred to making games that had unique content that

couldn't be made within the existing paradigms of game development, or that you were making them in a different way, or that your
business model was different. For example, the fact that you were
creating a game with a small team was different from the standard
model. In some cases, "indie" meant you were doing several things
simultaneously (as with projects like *World of Goo* or *Braid*).

HEINEMAN: Do you find that the other people who consider themselves independent game developers might disagree in any way
with that definition? For example, in the music and film industries,
"indie" artists will often speak about "indie" being defined as
something like "art for noncommercial purposes," yet other people
will disagree and argue that "indie" just means that you are not
signed on to a major label or that you are not working for a major
studio. Does that kind of debate find its way into independent
game development, and, if so, how does that play out?

SANTIAGO: The discussion, it definitely happens. In general, the feeling is that "indie" is just any development that happens outside of
the large studio model. This year only two of the Game Developer
Choice Awards went to AAA studios, so this year has been really
huge for independent developers, but that's not the norm. It is
still a totally different paradigm operating within a big studio
system. So I'm fine with continuing with that definition, but there
definitely are the conversations around what "responsibility" we
have to push new boundaries in game development or express new
messages, as indie artists do in other mediums.

When you are independent, the idea is that you are afforded a
freedom to make games about whatever you want and make them
in whatever way you want. The question of "Are we as an independent community really leveraging the freedom that we have?" I
think is a conversation that persists each year and can manifest
itself especially around award season. I remember a couple of years
ago that the *Pixel Junk Eden* game by Q Games was up for an award
or two in the Independent Games Summit [IGS] at the Game
Developers Choice Awards. A lot of people really questioned their
inclusion as a nominee because they were financially independent but were distributed through Sony and thus had this huge

platform through Sony. The question was asked, "Did they really need the awareness that IGS was going to bring?" Is the purpose of an independent award show to raise awareness around games that couldn't get that awareness otherwise? So that's one category of conversation that really manifests itself.

HEINEMAN: Is there a model in another entertainment industry or in another field for independent work that you think the game industry should model?

SANTIAGO: What has made independent game development so prevalent today is the success and plethora of digital distribution channels and players becoming more comfortable with getting their content in that way. The fact is that the game industry was accepting of digital distribution from relatively early on, and so it has just folded into the entire industry's business model very well as opposed to creating friction between an old distribution model. The film industry has struggled with theater attendance versus digital distribution, and the music industry has struggled with selling CDs and concert tickets versus digital distribution. In games, digital distribution has really electrified the independent world; they've really taken to it well.

That model will continue to support independent game development and foster diversity in game development. The continued growth and success of these channels will allow for gamers to discover content that's relevant to them. The other way it could go is that the digital distribution channels turn into digital versions of GameStop or Best Buy, where you have, visually, a very limited shelf space, now that EA and Activision and Ubisoft, and also the store owners, they're putting their own games on these "virtual shelves." It could lead to a place where, yet again, just like what happened in physical retail, independent developers get shoved off of the shelves and it becomes not viable as a business anymore.

HEINEMAN: Is there a point at which you think the market could reach a saturation of independent games, and it would make sense for someone who's working on an independent title to take their talents to a major studio environment instead of competing in a crowded market?

SANTIAGO: I can see a certain point at which it would make sense for various independent developers to partner together and create almost a new publisher in that way. That idea has been floating around the zeitgeist there for a while, but it takes someone to champion it and takes someone to find the right business model for it. Where we're at with distribution now I think is okay, and especially in the pay-to-play market (as opposed to the premium market) the sense is still that if you make a really high-quality game, you will get enough exposure to do fairly well off of it. You need some business savvy too, but there are a lot of resources and tools available right now for people and communities that can give support to you and give you advice on how to go about promoting your own game.

So I don't think it has reached that point; we are far from saturation. One of the challenges we face as a development community is the fact that we are so saturated with one another that we can lose sight of the fact that players en masse may not be that aware of these fantastic games. There's a challenge to meet in figuring out how to push that awareness and that discoverability further outward. There is a whole lot of room to grow there, and that's where the next business opportunities for distribution and discovery are.

HEINEMAN: It is well known that you got your start in the industry at USC in the master's program there. Given the time you spent there and given what you've seen in the industry since, what do you see right now as the role for higher education in the game industry? What is the relationship like now, and what do you think it can be?

SANTIAGO: Fundamentally, with any entertainment field, pursuing entertainment or communication or art in academia gives you that opportunity to create an experience within a safe environment that doesn't exist when you are forced to only make games for profit and you have to earn a living off of it. Already we're seeing huge shifts in what kind of games are getting made because of these programs. There's no way Jenova Chen and I would have ever made a game like *Cloud* had we instead spent three years going the typical route at the time, which was to go into a large studio and learn how to make commercially successful games for three years within a large company. Instead, we were given an opportunity where he was creative director of a game; that wouldn't have happened for many, many years going into a different route.

So, fundamentally, there's that aspect, and then there's the opportunity to really hone in on specific skills that a student may be in need of in order to succeed in the industry. For me, one thing that always comes up is collaboration. There are many softer skills like collaboration and leadership and communication that aren't taught through any sort of mentoring system in a game studio. That's seen as "fair enough," because chances are you are being brought on because there is a job to do and you have to get it done. By contrast, a university provides that opportunity to focus on skills that will allow students to really succeed and thrive within the industry but that they may or may not get exposed to. Sometimes it can be random, a roll of the dice depending on who happened to be your mentor at your first job.

HEINEMAN: Did you develop an appreciation for games as a medium for artistic expression when you were a student, or was that something that was external to your education? Is it a sensibility that can be fostered in a curriculum for students who are studying games?

SANTIAGO: Yes, yes, yes. Absolutely. I came from an art background personally. I studied theater as an undergraduate, and I had played video games my whole life, but it wasn't until I was at USC that I saw the craft of game design as another form of expression and art. Really, that is what attracted me to games to begin with. It was the art form I had always been looking for, but I just never thought about the process by which they were made or how one might communicate ideas through video game design. Yes, absolutely it is something that can be taught.

HEINEMAN: In a recent article in the journal *Game Studies*, Michael Burden and Sean Gouglas talk about the "games as art" debate because they are interested in that debate's impact on academia. They explain that "the debate about games as art has 'trickled' into the academic discourse as some seek to convince their somewhat skeptical colleagues and administrators of the intellectual authenticity of their object of study," as well as also noting that "the debate itself creates a discourse of head space for game study. Other forms have made this journey before, film, graphic novels, pornography, et cetera. Each has traveled the road in a slightly different manner negotiating and altering as appropriate to the medium's affordances, the various critical tools needed for effective engagement."

Do you think people who write about games have developed the tools needed for effective engagement? Have you read criticism, of your own work, for example, which you thought analyzed that work with the same kind of critical sophistication that one might expect in good academic work that deals with music, art, theater, or some of these other fields that have had a longer time to grow?

SANTIAGO: It is evolving. One of the things that I was especially proud of with our last game, *Journey*, was that a number of reviewers commented that they felt that the game itself forced them to review the game differently than they would any other game and to talk about it differently. For instance, on *Penny Arcade* the review opens with a section from the T. S. Eliot poem "Wasteland," and it goes on to critically compare the experiences in that particular hero's journey to the one that the game reflects.

So it seemed like maybe *Journey* was the right game at the right time. A lot of people were ready to shift the way that they were writing about their games, and there are a number of outlets like *Kill Screen* and *Venus Patrol* that very explicitly are trying to push game criticism and journalism in that direction. So it's happening.

HEINEMAN: Have you seen instances of that happening for games that don't get thrown into that "games as art" debate? Have you seen the lessons learned from critiquing something like *Journey* in a more sophisticated way applied to studying *Madden 2013* or other blockbuster games that you wouldn't necessarily think of through that frame?

SANTIAGO: Other than the times when the outlets I've mentioned have reviewed those games, I would say no. People definitely still cover traditional games in a traditional way.

HEINEMAN: Do you think there's a way that that can change? What do you think would have to happen for an outlet to transition into applying the same kind of that same editorial oversight or critical acumen to looking at a game that's seen as more popular fare?

SANTIAGO: You are conducting these interviews at a really interesting time, as it seems like this shift has just started to happen. At the last E3 [2012], where you typically see *Madden* and every game with a number at the end of the title, for whatever reason many journalists were commenting on that as a problem. "Yep, it's the same as it ever was! Isn't there something else? Why aren't they showing new stuff? Why is this the same every year?" The truth is I don't know why it's happening now. It feels like there are those of us who have seen that for a while ("Yep, E3 is pretty much the same show every year"), but now it seems like there's a desire to talk about other types of games and other ways of making games. Maybe the larger public, due to the proliferation of casual games, are just more aware of video games as a whole and of that standard vocabulary, and so they are ready to talk about something else.

HEINEMAN: Part of me wonders if maybe that's something that we see toward the end of any particular console generation: a kind of fatigue with the same franchises and the same types of titles.

SANTIAGO: There are a few examples, but they're far between, of writers that discuss the mechanics of *Madden* the way that they would other "highbrow" games. That kind of writing was something that we had to do as part of our writing assignments in academia. As more people go through these programs and take in a critical study perspective, we'll see more writing like this.

HEINEMAN: What do you think of the "serious game," as sometimes it's been called? Do you think there is potential for "serious games" that deal with sociopolitical issues to find commercial success, or to find publishers? Do they have a place in the market? Do you think the growth of indie gaming more generally gives them a place that they may not have had five years ago?

SANTIAGO: What I've seen is that there are more and more developers in the "serious game" space that have gained experience through being able to develop on various digital distribution platforms.

This is great to see because it is what for so long was really missing in that field. Previously, you maybe had educators or something like "idea lobbyists" who wanted to reach new audiences through games, but they didn't know how to make a game or communicate through a game. On the game-development side, there was a struggle with "Okay, how do you communicate these different kinds of concepts through games?"

There's been a lot of work in the last few years that has really propelled that whole scene forward. It is interesting what the studio, Robin Hunicke's studio, Funonema, is doing right now. They are a commercial, independent development studio, but they have taken on, through a grant, a 20 percent project, which is a serious games project that deals with getting kids to exercise more in the Sacramento area. We're even seeing companies like Zynga launch Zynga.org, and EA is working with a not-for-profit. That model is interesting: not trying to necessarily convince commercial studios to go 100 percent toward a serious game, but to diversify their portfolio and consider a new type of serious game as part of that.

I'm definitely interested in how you can use game design and interactive design to create compelling systems that people engage in. I am intrigued by the question of "How can we use game design to get people more active in local politics?" But, even in my own work, I compartmentalize those questions into "one or the other." I believe in the power of entertainment and art to affect our collective consciousness, and therefore in all my work I desire to create games that I think can impact people in a positive way or help them through something. But then there's the other component of it, of "How else can you use that knowledge as a game designer in nondirectly game systems?"

HEINEMAN: How did you translate certain parts of Mihaly Csikszentmihalyi's theory of flow into the development of both *Cloud* and *Flow*?

SANTIAGO: Fundamentally, being in the state of flow is being in this perfect state of engagement where you are not so challenged that you get frustrated and the challenge is not so easy that you're bored. You want this perfect balance of the challenge in front of you and your ability to meet that (you can see that a lot of video games have tried to address this through offering different modes of easy, medium, and hard difficulties). These ideas were in Jenova's thesis, and we then applied them to our work by figuring that we could create systems within the game that allowed the player to choose the kind of experience they wanted to have, leaving the game open to satisfying a wide variety of players. By doing so, we thereby were expressing a different emotion in a video game but still creating a compelling experience where you are getting someone to play your game who might not have otherwise played it. We did so by simply creating this embedded system of play that allowed them to find their own level of engagement within it.

HEINEMAN: Ian Bogost wrote in *How to Do Things with Videogames* that with both *Flow* and *Cloud*, each game "embraces relaxation" while sometimes using "sensations and themes that also defy it," and ultimately they offer "movements that strain rather than calm" [90–91]. I'm curious whether you concur with that somewhat unique assessment of the work.

SANTIAGO: From that quote, taken out of context, if I understand what it's referring to, I would definitely agree. One of the main takeaways from *Cloud* that led Jenova to his *Flow* thesis project was the fact that, because we were making *Cloud* with the explicit intent of creating a game that extracts a different emotion that could appeal to anyone, we attempted to create a control scheme that would be more accessible than the average keyboard-mouse control system. But what ended up happening was that we alienated most people, because most people that were players were familiar with mouse and keyboard control, and we confused them because we had changed it a lot. For the new players, there were too many buttons, and it was confusing for them.

The application of flow into the game itself was to try to figure out how to create systems of engagement that would still get this wide variety of people feeling comfortable within a game. With *Flow* on the PS3, we were a new studio and we were playing around with the accessibility of the motion control, and, for many reasons, we wanted to keep the game very, very simple. We did not want to give the player the option of inverted or noninverted controls. One of the fundamental things in that game is that you tilt the controller forward to go up and back to go down on the screen. For some people, that was confusing, and the implementation of the controls was not too sophisticated (I think because of our state as new developers). When I go back and play that game, I can definitely understand the frustrations that can happen, although it was meant to be a calming experience.

HEINEMAN: With *Flow* it sounds like at least a considerable part of the design process began with a consideration of theory. Have you approached other games from similar starting points? Have you considered design theory or maybe even psychological theory, philosophy, etc.? Do you incorporate aspects of theory into the early stages of designing a blueprint for the game you want to create?

SANTIAGO: Yes, definitely – especially the games of thatgamecompany. We were really inspired by a lot of psychological theory and storytelling books. We read a lot of books on happiness that were extensions, in many ways, of flow theory. For *Journey,* Joseph Campbell's *Hero's Journey* model was a huge inspiration point.

HEINEMAN: You have been named one of the most influential women in gaming, a historically male-dominated industry. Gender representation in the game industry has been an increasingly considered topic as the industry grows. Do you think about gender much as you go about your day-to-day work? Is it a palpable consideration in the kinds of things that you find yourself doing, or is it more a subject that's worth considering and analyzing but not "felt" on a regular basis?

SANTIAGO: In the development environment, I thought about gender in my sort of day-to-day work by just wondering how much gender played into the overall dynamic of the team. It was hard because of the predominance of a kind of alpha-male personality within the game industry. I would find that there would be struggles whenever that personality, whether it came from a man or a woman, came up against another kind of personality because it leads into how you work (especially with creative pursuits), how you find inspiration, how you manifest it, and how you work with it. Those are very different things depending on different personalities. So I thought about it then. Again, this is an interesting question this year, because it feels like, with the Anita Sarkeesian backlash and a couple of other incidents (like the *Tomb Raider* promo at E3), where women are speaking more about the representation of women at events or within games, it feels like the bullying around those incidents (in both the online world and in the real world) led a lot of us women in the industry over a tipping point. It's just like "Wow, we can't even mention it? That's kind of ridiculous." It is like we can't even have an adult conversation about women in the industry.

HEINEMAN: So you're suggesting that in the last year, the game industry has reached a tipping point on gender?

SANTIAGO: The public discourse that has come about over the last year has come about, and this is somewhat sad to say, because it's not just coming from a small group of women within the industry. First of all, like I mentioned, there are many more women now who have been kind of sent over the tipping point and are speaking publicly about it. But then also it seems like there are more even male leaders in the industry. Cliff Bleszinski recently had a blog post that I thought was really great, and that kind of thing helps too (having leadership in the industry as a whole). Journalists as well who have set a tone for a professional discourse on the subject to marginalize the haters (so to speak) is a big step toward that.

HEINEMAN: Are those kinds of things enough to dramatically shift either the industry's culture or gamers' behaviors (or both)?

SANTIAGO: It can go a long way. Shifting the dynamic of online competitive multiplayer games is a really tall order, and it's something that it is hard to say if it needs to be done or should be done. People should have and feel the freedom to play the way they want to play, but it also makes me think of discourse around professional sports about the way women are represented during an NBA game, during the Super Bowl, and during boxing matches. There have been ongoing debates about those representations, where the question is asked about how much people who participate in those games get to dictate how they want to watch them and play them and how much need there might be to impose some civility or code that allows the game to be more open to a wider audience. It's not a clear line.

HEINEMAN: When you look at students who are interested in going into fields like game design (or into STEM fields in general), there tends to be a largely disproportionate amount of men involved in those fields. Are there steps that you think universities should incorporate into their curriculum to address this discrepancy?

SANTIAGO: This goes to teaching students codes of conduct and not just accepting the default culture of game development due to the subset of people that have been attracted to it or that are the ones that have historically been most often encouraged to go into it. I have had a poly-male engineer tell me that if a female engineer were to show up for work or on a project, dressed up or having put makeup on, it would be assumed that she was not as hardworking or as smart because she had done those things. And that goes back to school; it goes back to the culture of how you do these initial projects, and what's acceptable then, and what's not. It is an opportunity to have conversations around this issue that would open up the field more to a wider diversity of people.

SEVEN

Chris Grant

GAMES AND PRESS

ALONG WITH FORECASTS OF INCREASED DIRECT DEMOCRACY
and a migration to virtual global currencies, one of the frequent predictions made by many of the early Internet prognosticators was that narrowly targeted news feeds would become the standard form of gaining information for those connected to the Internet. Specifically, many of them suggested that people would be able to find news that was specific to (and exclusionary from) particular geographic locations, particular ideological interests, or particular hobbyist pursuits. These targeted audiences would form communities and cultures around the news sites that appealed to them, creating a kind of feedback loop that kept the audience fixed and isolated. In the past twenty years of online journalism, some of this has indeed taken place. One of the best case studies for how it has occurred is unquestionably that of video game journalism.

Gaming journalism, popularized in the 1980s and early 1990s by thinly veiled adverti-zines such as *Nintendo Power* and *Sega Visions* and in youth-focused publications such as *Gamepro* (and, to a lesser extent, *Electronic Gaming Monthly*) joined much of the rest of the magazine industry in undergoing a significant sea change when the Internet gained in popularity in the mid- to late 1990s. In many ways, games journalism grew up with the medium it covered. As game publishers started creating more games meant to retain their aging player base, introduced a ratings system to make the content more palatable to parents, and started pushing toward multimedia, gaming journalism followed suit with more organized and focused writing, more objective and regular reviews, and more features that responded to the rapid pace of change in the industry.

In the present time, video game journalism is dealing with a variety of concerns that seem especially appropriate for a maturing field. They are grappling with issues of how they choose to represent the interests and varied politics of an expanding gaming demographic, of how and what to critique in their reviews of particular titles, and in how to maintain interest and profitability in an era when there is an abundance of free content (much of it very good). These are the issues that Chris Grant, editor in chief of the games journalism website Polygon, considers on a regular basis. In the interview in this chapter, Grant discusses these issues as well as the relationship of his field to academia, to game culture, and to game publishers. He also offers some thoughts on the future of games journalism.

Grant is in an especially advantageous position to weigh in on these concerns. As the former editor in chief of the influential game news blog Joystiq, he learned to navigate the industry and publish content about it in a way that attracted a large following. Some of that following left Joystiq with him when, in 2011, he joined several other well-known gaming journalists and editors to form Polygon, a website whose founding members formed something like a "supergroup" of gaming-press figures. In its relatively short time publishing game-related articles, Polygon has developed a reputation for games journalism that pushes the envelope, and its editor has curated a site with discernible, nuanced approaches to the medium it covers (and all that is related to it).

—⁓—

HEINEMAN: How would you characterize the "landscape" of games journalism? Are there outlets more or less all doing the same thing, or are there some differences between them?

GRANT: There is not a formula for success anymore, so that's gone. We used to have magazines, and there was a clear business model. There was scarcity at the newsstand, but now with the Internet you have an infinite number of possible outlets. You have an increasingly small number of business models that work and a huge density of people who want to write about and talk about video games. And they'll gladly do it for nothing.

You have a huge audience that wants to read this stuff, and you have a medium that is still so nascent that we don't know how to properly talk about it all the time. We don't know what is interesting or uninteresting sometimes, and you find all these niche focus areas of coverage because it's such a big industry with so many unique audiences. I'll give you an example: the fighting-game community. Not a lot of professional outlets cover fighting games. It's too dense. It's too complicated. It's actually not really about games at that point; it's about competition and sportsmanship. That's more like sports journalism than games journalism, so how do you cover that? Who covers it? There are outlets like Shoryuken that focus on just that, and that's all they do, and they're not hugely commercialized, but there's this huge audience that wants to read about this stuff. Video games' popularity and diversity create a massive opportunity on the Web to provide coverage. It really comes down to how you want do it; it's virtually limitless at this point.

HEINEMAN: What differences would you say exist between online games journalism and other online journalism outlets that focus on different entertainment media (e.g., Pitchfork)?

GRANT: Gaming is bigger. Pitchfork's not that big, but they have a massive amount of credibility. The CEO of Pitchfork just said in an interview something along the lines of "We don't have a hundred million passionate music fans in America, but for Pitchfork it's on a scale play. Maybe we have five million, and all we need to do is be the best outlet for those five million people." That was Pitchfork's strategy.

But look at IGN. They've got a comScore around nine million, and internal numbers for them are probably double that (including international and everything else). Gaming is a much bigger market for journalism than music. Movies are different, because movies have celebrity culture, and so now you've got TMZ and everything else tied in there.

I think a big difference with gaming journalism is focus. Music's and movies' coverage both tend to focus on people (e.g., bands or actors). Games have not enjoyed that. We tend to focus a lot on product. So we talk about what's new with *Call of Duty* and how many guns it has, how many maps, how long it is, how many levels there are, all that dumb stuff. One of our big objectives at Polygon is to write about people, to try to bring the focus back around to something that everyone universally finds interesting, which is a focus on the creative decision making that happens even on games like *Call of Duty*. I think that's been historically the big difference.

You now see the rise of the name-brand developer (your Cliffy Bs and Kellee Santiagos of the world), people who have a reputation that's been earned over a long time in a flash of inspiration, like Phil Fish. That phenomenon is much different and really unique; it also presents a challenge for the gaming press to learn and do a different kind of job, one that doesn't look much like what it used to do. It's also challenging those people to occupy a spotlight that maybe, as evidenced by Phil Fish's recent resignation, they are not accustomed to or maybe not even capable or desirous of handling. I think that's one of the biggest changes that's happening now, and it's going to get more complicated.

The exciting thing about it is that the gaming audience themselves are coming to terms with the role of these people who aren't maybe nice all the time and who can be arrogant, but I think that's a role we are comfortable with by those who occupy the spotlight in other media industries. Nobody accused Stanley Kubrick of being nice, and we celebrate that. But then Jonathan Blow is a little arrogant, and people say, "Man, that guy is really arrogant. What a dick." Well, he's probably smarter than you . . .

In my role, I'm excited about developers looking and acting more like traditional artists, whether mainstream or otherwise, where they have a lot of opinions and big ideas and thoughts and they don't have a PR handler telling them to say something or that "that's not nice." After doing years of interviews with people where

my interview literally has the same quotes as somebody else's,
it's nice to have people that actually talk to you and have actual
thoughts.

HEINEMAN: How would you say games journalism in the United
States compares to games journalism more globally?

GRANT: My caveat is that I have never worked as a member of the
press in Japan or Europe, but from my vantage point I find a couple
things to be true.

For one, I find the Japanese press to be pretty inscrutable.
There are long-ago-published and long-standing allegations about
the inappropriate relationships entered into between much of
the Japanese gaming press and the Japanese gaming companies
(the publishers). For example, a very large, very notable Japanese
developer, one of their "rock star" developers, told the publisher
for their game at the Tokyo Game Show that they didn't want to
do interviews with Joystiq about the game because "we ask hard
questions." I hate saying this, as a person who will adamantly push
back on the focus and emphasis on scores, but we've heard this
kind of thing several times, that the questions we ask in the United
States or even in the Western press are sometimes viewed as inappropriate to Japanese developers. I think for the most part that has
begun to change, but some people still have that expectation and a
historical context for that expectation.

Europe is interesting. We hear from PR people and developers
here all the time that the European press can be really hard to
deal with because there are so many countries, and each of those
countries has different cultural expectations for how the press
is going to behave. For example, the UK has a publishing model
that looks way different from ours. Magazines are still a viable
product there because it's a small country and distribution costs
are low. Look at *Edge* magazine's subscription numbers. That's a
magazine I still subscribe to at the pretty penny of $120 a year. It's a
great magazine, but the magazine would never, not even for a mil-
lisecond, survive here. But it survives there. I think the publishing
industry there is a lot more boutique and a lot less complicated
from a logistics standpoint than it is here, which is why our biggest

games magazine [*Game Informer*] is owned by a gaming retailer [Gamestop]. It solves a logistics problem: distribution's built in.

I think a lot of the global press has grown up very fast. You see outlets like Rock, Paper, Shotgun taking a real dominant voice in the UK gaming press, and that voice is very different from a lot of the stuff that preceded it. I also think the UK press was maybe late to get online. We saw the rise of something like Euro Gamer because they had a strong and healthy magazine ecosystem longer than we did.

HEINEMAN: When you encounter game studies researchers, or faculty who teach in journalism departments at different universities, or other interested academics who hang around this periphery of gaming, what are some of the common misunderstandings that you find they have about your profession?

GRANT: For journalism professors, it's myriad. With all due respect to journalism professors, when students ask me what they should study in college if they want to do what I do or to get into the games press in some way, or if they tell me they're in journalism school and are thinking about going to graduate school, I'm super quick to say that they should not go to college.

I'm very comfortable recommending to a young student that they not go to college for journalism because every student I know that's graduated from journalism programs, with the exception of a couple (like those from NYU's journalism technology program), are people who could tell you what lineages are. They don't need to know that; they should have never learned that – it is so meaningless and worthless. It's a workman-like job. I think studying a lot of craft and history sometimes gets in the way. By going to school, you are not learning what it actually takes to make money doing this skill.

So I often don't see eye to eye with the world of journalism academia. I think kids will get a lot more experience and actually make money by, instead of spending thirty thousand dollars a year, just going out and doing it, making a Tumblr, and starting their writing. I think most faculty are training kids to write for the *New York Times*, but the *New York Times* has a certain number of staff positions. Or maybe they are training them to write for their local newspaper, which, if it still exists, probably won't for much longer. So they are training kids in a quickly anachronistic tool set that they won't need anymore, and they are training them to do a certain kind of journalism that audiences don't even want anymore.

I still subscribe to a lot of magazines. I still read a lot of real news. I just think that if you're in a journalism program, that program isn't teaching you the real nature of the Web and what it's doing and where we're going. It doesn't teach you to be entrepreneurial, which is the biggest thing, I think. If you're going out there, you're going to have to make a lot of your opportunities for yourself; they don't exist. To me, what is valuable is finding ways to make new models work. With the exception of a few programs, I haven't heard of journalism programs embracing that kind of thinking and that kind of product- and user-focused teaching because it all changes so rapidly. You can get a job now, but in two years it's a different job, and what good was your degree?

I have a team of twenty-five people. I don't even know who's been to college. I have no idea. I don't look at it. I don't care. I didn't look at it at Joystiq. I've probably hired a hundred people in my career. I don't know who's been to college. It's meaningless to me. It's simply "Can you do the job?" It's a vocation.

HEINEMAN: I would guess that training in good writing is still important, but not necessarily to a particular model.

GRANT: I usually say it's a writing job, not a gaming job. It is important to be a good writer. We have people on our staff that don't play a lot of games at all and don't care about it really. They're journalists and they really like the industry, and they like covering it.

College can help a lot of people. I went to college, and I think it helped me a lot in that I got a base in liberal studies, in humanities, in literature and history: I think all of these are a little different from going to school for journalism, which is very vocational. So if a student wanted to go study English, sure. If you can afford it and you're not worried about the money, it's a great background for anything you're going to do, but for journalism it makes a lot more sense to me to just start doing it. You'll save a lot of money, and you'll probably have a paycheck, even if it's small. At the end of four years, you are going to have more experience than anybody graduating from college. If you are a good writer, I'll hire you much faster than I would somebody who has a degree and no experience.

HEINEMAN: When you left Joystiq in 2011, you wrote that, "weaned on innovation and excellence, video game players are practically bred to be the most critical, passionate, and invested audience imaginable. There is no harsher critic or stronger supporter and that investment will continue to lead to great things." Considering that almost everyone plays some kind of video game, what specific audience were you referring to in this statement? Was it all gamers, or was it a definable subset?

GRANT: I would think the "core" gamers, the ones that were likely to be reading that. In a lot of ways, a lot of people genuinely misunderstand gaming and what value it has. If somebody wants to place a [negative] value judgment on the time people spend playing games, they're usually missing what games teach people to do or teach them to be, which is critical thinkers and problem solvers.

You learn in high school how to read a text and how to read closely. I think gamers have a honed skill set for reading closely that, unfortunately, many never learn to acknowledge. I've had discussions about why we don't teach gaming in schools, when much of what they do there is learn to read, solve problems, and find patterns. I think gaming is overwhelmingly attractive to people who might have different pockets of energy or focus than others. If you look at a kid who can't sit still, part of the issue is probably because they're used to being challenged over and over again with new things that they can't solve. When they know how to solve a puzzle and it's the same puzzle twice in a row, it's boring; they need fresh blood. I think that hyperactivity leads to a reader that is super demanding and highly nomadic. If you don't give them something fresh, they will leave. They'll go somewhere else. They have an infinite number of choices with where to spend their time, and if you're going to ask for it twice in a row, you've got to earn it.

Every year we lose readers who get older and stop playing games and stop reading about them, or we get new readers who are young and, for the first time, have thought, "I'm interested. I like *Minecraft*. Maybe there are other video games that exist that I'll read about." I feel that in some ways we are like a school, where we're fixed in place and the audience goes through us in the timeline. At Polygon, comScore data suggests we have the oldest audience out there and the highest earning, which tells you a couple of things about who's reading our site. But I still feel like we have a magnifying glass that's fixed on one part of time, and the audience moves through it, and we keep seeing the same group moving through the glass. That's the audience I'm thinking about, but I think it increasingly means there are people outside of our core audience that exhibit these same traits.

HEINEMAN: So Polygon is an example of a site that often delves into what can be considered "game culture." How would you define that term, and what is the relationship (or, maybe, an ideal relationship) between games journalism and game culture? Is it part of it? Does it report on it? Does it define it?

GRANT: In some ways it defines it, because the press often (knowingly or not) codifies and validates things that exist. That responsibility is often very abstract, where something that seems cute and simple to you can be quickly picked up, extrapolated, and then lead to assumptions.

I'll give you an example. The fighting-game community got upset at Kotaku, a site that does a really good job, pretty much all of the time, on a lot of the stuff they do. They published a story about a competitor at a fighting-game event that got arrested for hitting his girlfriend. A lot of people in the fighting-game community were like, "Why is this a story? This guy wasn't a name-brand player. He was a nobody. Even if he won something at the event, you wouldn't have covered it. Most of us in the industry don't know who he is. The guy hits his girlfriend. What does that have to do with the fighting-game community? It doesn't. He was looking for a juicy headline."

Kotaku, on the other hand, saw it as a story that has to do with an event in the fighting-game community and that saw it as newsworthy because of surrounding things like discussion of it by others at the event and previous accusations of misogyny levied at the fighting-game community. But for the fighting-game community, it was a validation from the press that those things happen, that this is okay to report them, that when it happens again we should report on it, and that other outlets are going to report on that same story. After the report is published, people are going to Tweet it, Tumble it, and share it until it spreads and becomes a media narrative that was created based on an initial decision to run a story that, by their criteria, is newsworthy.

So, yes, I definitely think we do help create gaming culture for better or worse. What is it?

There's so many games. I grew up with punk music. I went to a lot of shows and bought a lot of seven inches and records. Back then we didn't have MP3s; we didn't have the Internet. The way that you found out about new music or new bands was that you went to shows, and you'd hear an opening band. They would tour, and they made no money, and they lived in vans. You bought a seven-inch for five dollars and you listened to that, and then some band you hadn't heard would be on a B-side, and then you'd go see that band. It was very weblike. Then the Internet happened. The indie bands are global, and there's a different strata of how we define music now, and that punk culture is a lot different. There's a lot that's changed, and those people aren't necessarily outsiders anymore because they can find like-minded people online and talk to them.

For game culture, a lot of it is an "outsider" status. The mainstream media doesn't cover you, your teachers think you're wasting your time, your parents hate those stupid, infernal games that you're playing, but it's a culture that you grew up with that you feel very strongly about that, in a lot of ways, helped sculpt and shape who you are as a person, even if it happened in isolation by yourself.

Then when you find people who share those same experiences, it turns out there's a lot of them. The Internet and sites like ours show you that some goofy kids in Seattle made a fuckin' YouTube video about Mario. You find out there's a lot of like-minded people, and there are conventions like PAX. There are other people that like the stuff you like when, for a lot of your existence, you might have been told that it was bad for you or stupid. For me it lines up a lot with punk rock. There is a reactiveness there. You want to push back, and then you want to even further embrace this thing that you care about. That might mean the way you dress. It means the friends you hang out with. It means what you spend your time doing. What you think is artistically valid. So you define yourself that way.

I think in gaming culture, there are a lot of people that play games. Not everyone associates with that part of gaming culture that comes with a triforce tattoo. I think the people that do engage that part of game culture are doing it in a very similar way to punk rock. Perhaps, like with punk rock, people in high school that felt disaffected can find it. I think with games, increasingly we're going to see the other role of scene culture, which is that people that like certain types of games, or certain types of art styles, or certain creators will follow them and then share them with other people.

Then the press has a curatorial role that we haven't had for a long time. There are fifty AAA games a year, and though maybe you can remember all fifty, when there are five hundred or five thousand, now all of a sudden you couldn't possibly pay attention to all this. As curators, it's our job to listen to the taste makers, to have our ear to the ground, to identify what's interesting or unique for you, and then to present it to you in the same way the music press would present, "Here's a crazy punk rock band from the UK that you've never heard of and you've never seen in your life. We're going to tell you it's valuable, and then you're going to go buy it." We are right now inheriting some of that responsibility in the press, which is really exciting.

HEINEMAN: In her 2007 book, *Cheating: Gaining Advantage in Video Games,* Mia Consalvo talks about magazines like EGM and *Nintendo Power,* especially in the 1980s and 1990s, serving as "paratexts" for gamers. By this, she means that the magazines could "alter the meaning" of games, "further enhance meanings, or provide challenges to sedimented readings," or even "shape players' expectations of what it means to play a game properly or improperly." Today, sites like Polygon increasingly serve this function. When you're choosing stories to cover, when you're choosing games to highlight and focus on, is that consequence a concern?

GRANT: It's very much gut based. We're here looking at the things that we think are likely to be successful, and we think our readers will like it because it's fun, it looks pretty, it has a certain sound, people who made it have made other great games that we know did well, etc. So we can use a lot of different criteria that for us is relatively easy to assemble. There's a lot of experience being called upon to make that evaluation. So I think a lot of our role is like that. Just like the music critics that identified the Sex Pistols as important: they weren't doing it in a vacuum.

HEINEMAN: I guess another way of thinking of the question would be, since you mentioned it doesn't happen in a vacuum, is there a fear that it becomes an echo chamber?

GRANT: Yes.

HEINEMAN: When do you notice that it's becoming that? Do you try to consciously avoid it?

GRANT: There are hip developers, and there are scene developers. They talk to certain people, they go to the right event, and they know how to talk to the press.

Then you've got another developer who's a shy, nervous guy. He's a great programmer, and great designer, and supercreative, but he doesn't like to talk to people, doesn't like to leave his house, and he's making a game quietly by himself. Maybe that's a great game, but we never learn about it; we never see it. Maybe it gets put up onto the Apple App Store quietly one day along with a hundred or more other games in a week.

At a certain point, scale wise, it would be literally impossible for us to discover it. If it is a great game and takes off, we will discover it later. We've gone back and done stories on games that came out six months ago that just took off, and we wonder how we missed it. The entire gaming press was like that with *Minecraft*. But that's the great thing about the plurality of the Internet: if we're not covering it, there are probably thirty Tumblrs and a dozen WordPress blogs that are. They might not be the most well written, and maybe they're a little overenthusiastic . . .

HEINEMAN: They have the same role.

GRANT: They have the same role. We can use those things to say, "Hey, there's a lot of talk about this game! Why? Who's talking about it, and are those people credible? Did they talk about other games that ended up being good? What is the context for this celebration?" We can just go for a hunch. For us, a lot of times those hunches are more interesting from both a journalistic perspective and from an audience standpoint, in that the audience don't usually know about these kinds of titles, so there's some actual curiosity there. People already know if they want to buy *Gears of War 6*. It's really interesting when you can go to something that's completely unknown and then evaluate it and put it in front of an audience for consideration.

Is there an echo chamber? Absolutely. I think you're only going to see that happen more with more games and fewer people who are paid who exist in an ecosystem where payment isn't even an option that are able to do that work. Leigh Alexander published something in *Gamasutra* just recently where she said, "Hey, indie developers, here's how you get us to cover your games: do not ask us to help; we're not here to help you. Don't ask us to cover your Kickstarter because we don't really care about that. We care about the game: is the game interesting or cool?"

That said, developers who are Kickstarting projects have to learn how to use the press. If you look at the Kickstarter numbers, there is a direct correlation between projects that get press and money versus ones that don't. It's direct: if you get more press, you will have a better Kickstart. I think the press is going to get better, but I think a lot of it is also going to be that developers have to get better, and, if you want to find success, it means knowing who to talk to and finding the right people.

So I definitely can see the paranoia or anxiety about the role of the press in that respect and how it might be funneling attention, but I think our role is going to be relatively fixed, and there are a lot of opportunities for games to be discovered.

HEINEMAN: Samantha Allen, a student at Emory University, published an essay wherein she asked for sites like yours and others to publish a highly visible reference statement explaining your site's stance on sexism, racism, classicism, ableism, homophobia, and transphobia. She feels that's such an important statement to make in the contemporary game-culture climate. Do you feel that, in general, editors recognize these concerns as legitimate problems, and, if they do, do you think they're working to address them meaningfully?

GRANT: I think if you look at the feedback some of the other outlets gave to her open letter, IGN addressed it and said that they were going to start actively monitoring the comments, which they had not been doing. Kotaku addressed it. I think she had a couple other in there who also addressed it.

My response to it was that, at Polygon at least, there were certain instances that she rightfully calls out. For example, when we broke the secret and announced the site, it was a reveal featuring a website run by a bunch of white dudes. We've already explained why that was and also said that we don't insist that it was above reproach.

There are reasons it was that way. I could make a bunch of excuses. Those were all people I knew. It had to be secret. I still had a job. They still had jobs. There are only a handful of professional female video game editors in the industry. If we're hiring all people of long careers, there are only a handful to go to and I went to them. So anyway: excuses.

At the end of the day, it comes down to, for me, what you do. Editorially, we were already doing all this stuff before she wrote that letter. We already had active moderation policies. Go and try to drop an ableist slur in our comments field, and it will be gone in maybe a couple minutes. It's all human moderated, not software moderated. We literally did it at launch, and it was an important part of why we even have comments. It was not that way at Joystiq, where we didn't have anywhere near the money or staff to do it.

In terms of editorial coverage, we don't have a manifesto about the nature of our coverage and our ideology behind who we cover, how, and why. Instead, we just cover the topics that we think are interesting, a lot of which includes stuff like an article about a gender gaming summit or a twenty-five-hundred-word feature on the queer gaming scene in the Bay Area. We've done articles on disabled gamers and the different technologies and companies that are helping them play games.

HEINEMAN: Maybe the larger related question would be to what extent does criticism from readers shape the direction of the site in general?

GRANT: I think it happens in a huge way. We've already taken a lot of criticism at Polygon for some of our policies or how we do things, and we use that criticism a lot. Obviously, we knew it going in, but it certainly wasn't as strong as postlaunch criticism about not having enough female writers. Our challenge when we were starting the site was finding women and recruiting them, and doing it in secret.

Postlaunch, for every fifty applications we would get from a man, we would get one female applicant. So it was hard to find a lot of talented female writers in the space without also hiring the first woman who applied and saying, "Here's a job." The point being is it takes time to build it up. What we've found is as we've hired more women, when we have open casting calls, we now have more women applicants. It's related. When people who read the site recognize a lot of the female names on the site, they are likely to recognize it as a place or opportunity that may also be available to them. Just those simple changes of having content that also is respectful of women and criticizing and challenging games that were not respectful of women give readers female names on the site that they can see and even treat as role models. For me, that was really eye-opening – that some of those little changes could result in having more female applicants, especially since gaming journalism has not been traditionally seen as a welcoming environment.

HEINEMAN: Does the field of games journalism face a substantial conflict of interest between who pays the bills and what gets covered?

GRANT: I can tell you with all honesty that I've never heard a story of a game getting explicitly different coverage or a different specific score, which tends to be what they're upset about because of an advertiser. It just doesn't happen. I understand the paranoia for it, but I don't think it happens.

HEINEMAN: I am referring more to the closeness between the coverage of the industry and the money in the industry that pays for advertising in those places where coverage occurs.

GRANT: I think the big thing I would look at would be press events. For me, the advertisers on the site don't mean much. We rarely even know who they are until they're up on the site. One of the biggest reasons we have an ethics policy and one of the times that our ethics policy has had to be publicized is when companies put on big events. Those events are usually very fancy, and they can often be in exotic locations like Hawaii. The publishers pay for press to go there because we're not going to pay for expensive travel to one event to cover a game or two.

So we have an ethics policy. I had it at Joystiq, too. It says very clearly (and it's a very simple one to have and to enforce) that we will not accept travel, hotel, or airfare accommodations. If we go and you see us at an event, it's because we paid to get there. I'm a little sensitive about events. A lot of times, because of the way we work them out, PR people will hate us. Sometimes we'll work with them to manufacture a mini event for us. "We'll skip the junket where we take a tour around the city in full period regalia, and we'll play the hour of the game you have for us and we'll be on the train home. Can you arrange that?" So a lot of times, we'll negotiate those types of things so that we can get in and get out, making it as unexciting as possible for the person going.

A lot of the big outlets, you'll see skipping them more and more, which I think is great.

HEINEMAN: Reviews are often seen as "bread and butter" for a lot of game websites. Do reviews promote consumerism and

consumption, and could you envision a successful model of games
journalism that doesn't do reviews?

GRANT: Reviews for us are not our biggest traffic generator by far.

HEINEMAN: So that adage is maybe . . .

GRANT: Antiquated. It is certainly the biggest market for Gamespot
and IGN – it's their biggest product by far.

So what are reviews? Here's the secret of how reviews work
and why they're such huge traffic generators: because when you
search for a game's review the day it came out, you click on the first
link. That gets the traffic, and that traffic on review day is a lot. If I
can receive over a million page views a day on a big review, I'll take
it. But I can't always get it because I don't have a page ranking of
seven or eight or whatever IGN is at with twelve years of links and
with Google knowing that the word *review* means IGN. There is an
algorithmic bias there that we can't dent. So, reviews for us are really for our audience. They do well. Our audience absolutely wants
to read reviews, but as a result they take a long time, they're expensive to make (you have to buy the whole game), and you need to
edit it, review it, and write it. Getting the game itself is hard to do
and requires a lot more negotiating than you'd even imagine. You
could be the biggest outlet, and you're still negotiating for every
game. The publishers are treating it like they're doing you a favor,
like "Here's a free game!" We don't give any fucks about the free-
ness of it; we want it early so we can finish it in time, so our readers
get the best products when they go to buy something. If they're
curious about it, if they've been excited about it for a long time
or whatever, they want to know what we think. Besides, we don't
keep the games anyway.

So if you don't get review games early, you might as well not do
reviews. You might as well not write. So it's this vicious circle.

Metacritic is owned by one of our competitors. We could just
say, "Hey, don't put our reviews up. Thanks. Stop doing that." It
enforces this sort of binary-ness that I don't think is very helpful
for reviews. But I'm also saying, in defense of reviews, there's what
we call a "service journalism" role to it. Consumers understand
the nature of service journalism: we've been doing movie reviews

for decades. We gave out a Pulitzer to a guy named Roger Ebert in the '70s. He put stars on his reviews. He also invented the most popular review system we've ever had [thumbs up or down]. Reviews and scoring aren't the problem that people want to say it is. As much as academics say, "We really need a Roger Ebert for game reviews," I am inclined to ask, "Oh, you mean the guy who popularized scoring?"

So that's not the problem. There are a lot of other problems, though, like the focus on the numeric score in a review that a lot of our audience has. That is weird. It's the focus on that number relative to other numbers that's especially weird. "This game's a seven. That game's an eight. How dare you." They're trying to chart the world with a perfect system that is perfectly valid relative to everything, including itself. It's absolute fucking insanity. It's complete insanity. So I don't like to get caught up in numbers because I think it's insane. I think the fixation in our industry on numbers is so bizarre.

So most outlets don't put a huge focus on reviews because it's hard to get that nomadic traffic that is just using Google to find the review in the first place. That said, I think there's a lot of value for them. Readers really like them and care about them. I think there are ways to do them better. I think there are interesting things to be done in reviews. We have a big focus right now on video reviews and showing footage of what we're talking about, making it contextual. I don't like to apologize for reviews a lot. I think there's a lot of self-flagellation in our industry. In the academic industry, I think reviews are the one thing that they look at most often when they criticize the press and say, "That's bad." I think, again, their relative ignorance is that they radically overevaluate the worth of reviews to outlets, with the exception of the two big guys [IGN and Gamespot].

HEINEMAN: What do you see as the future of your profession over the next console generation?

GRANT: I think more than with the last one, you're going to see more niche approaches happening with the meteoric rise of e-sports. Blizzard bought IPL off IGN, so now they're into the sports tournament business. There's obviously Major League Gaming. Valve is getting into it with *DOTA 2*. So when you've got all these giant companies all going after something and putting tons of money into it, watch out. It's already huge; it's going to get much larger. It is a market that the traditional gaming press almost doesn't cover at all, and doing so is more sports coverage.

The fighting-game community's a little different. I think it's big, and it will probably stay big and maybe get bigger. It doesn't have the money and other big games tied up in it. The market tends to be more niche, but I think also you'll see more outlets growing to cover it and more people learning to enjoy watching it because of the accessibility of streaming programs, which has enabled all of this to happen. You will go to some bars now that are playing *Starcraft* games instead of football games. It's like, "That's weird."

So you have these approaches that are just really different and new and were not possible a few years ago. Either the games weren't there or the audience wasn't there or the technology to connect those two wasn't there. Now it is.

Also, both new next-gen consoles from Sony and Microsoft have built-in game streaming. Microsoft has the added benefit of having an actual Windows layer platform on it that I think is a little more hospitable to development, but the point being is you've got a button on the controller to stream. You're just broadcasting.

At the beginning of the last console generation, the most exciting launch game was *Geometry Wars.* The most exciting thing about it was seeing YouTube videos and somebody holding up a shaky cam recording gameplay, showing them beating a crazy high score. That was insane back then, and we covered it at Joystiq. We were so excited about it. Now that's going to be built into every box on launch day.

User streaming, I think, will be really transformative for how people learn about games, the type of people they interact with, how they see games, and how publishers put out new games. Self-publishing, on that model, is when the curation of content becomes of even bigger importance. I don't know whether there are good games on this new XboxOne indie platform. "There are so many – how do I find good ones?" "Well, I went on Twitch, and I just searched, and I found a guy who just goes through every week and streams twenty games and talks about them, and this one looked funny."

So I think that will further democratization. Writing can be hard and reading can be laborious and searching can be tough, and video games are made out of video. Getting and removing pretty much all friction for that stuff is going to be huge, and it will further complicate and confuse the economics of what we think of as traditional games journalism, and so we'll all have to lean back and think, "Well, now what?"

So that's all changing, and that's really exciting. It's exciting working in the context of an industry that no longer has rules, no longer has an established way of doing things, and where everything's up for grabs. That's only going to accelerate. I think people get worried or nervous about the way the press works or whether it might "become stagnant the way this industry is." It's like, "Stagnant? It changes every month!" We can't stop changing; we can't stop inventing new stuff, inventing new types of games or new types of places for people to play games. It seems hyperfast to me, not the opposite.

Granted, we are still making *Call of Duty.*

EIGHT

Edward Castronova

GAMES, ECONOMICS, AND POLICIES

EDWARD CASTRONOVA BEGINS HIS BOOK *EXODUS TO THE Virtual World* with a discussion of *Star Trek*'s holodeck that, at first glance, seems very similar to Eugene Jarvis's discussion of that fictional technology in chapter 3 of this book. Castronova explains that it is a "perfect simulation room" that "allows users to enter into a deeply accurate simulation of any environment, from the Wild West to the surface of Pluto" (3). He begins that book with a discussion of the holodeck because, like Jarvis, he sees in it a model for where games might go and what they might do to and for the people who play them. Castronova's perspective, however, offers a kind of cautionary reply to Jarvis's enthusiasm. If the holodeck was ubiquitous, he offers, "no starship would do anything at all" (3). Instead, there would be a dramatic shift in what people did with their time, where they did these things, and what the value of that time was considered to be. Simulation, in the form of games, would introduce dramatic social change.

More than a decade ago, Castronova posed the questions "Will multiplayer online games become an important part of the social life of humans? What does the market for games look like? What kind of market structures can we anticipate in the future?" and "How would a large emigration of work and play time to these virtual worlds affect the economy of the real world?" Since then, he has engaged in a number of research projects meant to address these questions by grafting economic theory as a frame of analysis onto games. Castronova's writing about the economics of games is not, primarily, about the way that studios or the industry more broadly might best reap larger profits. Instead, Castronova is interested in what the logics of economics have to teach us about game design, about the kinds of interactions that players have in games, and about the effect of these choices on real-world attention, economy, and social change.

Beyond the specific focus of his research on particular kinds of games, Castronova has developed a thoroughly informed perspective of the place of video game research in academia and, most interesting, the relation of that research to the video game industry. In the interview in this chapter, for example, Castronova suggests an uncertainty that game studies might even be considered a field at all, citing his experiences with various faculty and administrators at a large land-grant institution. Castronova is critical of the territorial relationships that exist between researchers from different fields; the disconnect in perspective that exists between professors, students, and administrators; and the lack of productive discussion that occurs between academia and the game industry, discussion that he believes could yield fruitful collaborations.

In this chapter, Castronova discusses these ideas as well as offers further perspective on the concepts he's confronted in his work. Specifically, he sheds light on the continued relevance of his previous predictions about the relationship between virtual economies and real-world social changes, on the productive connections that can be found between an economic view of games and stagnant theories of public policy creation, and on the ideal functions of game research. The interview also offers some insight into comments made elsewhere in this book concerning the value of a college education for a career related to games and the popularity of and ideological rationale behind "artistic" games.

—⁓—

HEINEMAN: In *Exodus to the Virtual World*, you talk about game design as a model for public policy making. Ideally, how would policy makers learn to adopt that model, and how might public policy education change?

CASTRONOVA: The larger question is how public policy should respond, and then there's kind of this implicit thought that you would have to also change public policy education. What needs to happen is governments have to build reasonable simulations of the society under their control. They should be willing to put quite a lot of money into those simulations, and, to the extent possible, they should have them populated with real people. I think those things are technically feasible. I think they're artistically feasible, simulations like that.

So I would start by having governments have those things. Then you would need to have a cadre of people in the government who are comfortable implementing policy suggestions in those simulated environments, kind of like the way the Congressional Budget Office has become adept at forecasting future deficits by making assumptions about a simulated model of the US economy. They're good at doing something like that, and I don't see any reason that couldn't be extended to a full-blown simulationist approach.

In terms of the education part of it, I would have virtual worlds be a part of public policy education so that when a student was doing some sort of an analysis, they actually could have a little Tinker Toy world to play with (e.g., "If we did this to the sugar price-support payment, what would change?"). That would be my recommendation: build Tinker Toy worlds for policy makers and students to work with.

HEINEMAN: Have you seen models of that approach in academia? Have you seen some promise for more academic programs doing that kind of thing?

CASTRONOVA: Not really, no. I think the roots of it are there in that most policy analysis students, they have to spend a little time playing around with economic models, and it's not that big a leap to go from that sort of abstract economic model to some sort of breathing simulation. It's kind of the same mind-set. You change a parameter and see what happens. The roots are there, but I haven't seen anybody that I know of trying to do it.

But what if, and I don't know this, but there's probably some policy people who have simulations of climate and global temperature, where you could sit down and say, "Oh, what if we did this with CO_2? And what if we did that?" and it sort of models it. So, there may be things like that out there – I just don't know.

HEINEMAN: You write about the concept of governance in *Synthetic Worlds* and discuss several different approaches to managing governance within game worlds both for designers and for players. But in all cases, it seems like governance is at least partially influenced by real-world rules, its regulations, morals, ethics, and, in particular, its laws. You point out as much when you discuss how important laws are to things like end-user license agreements and terms-of-service agreements. Is this an obstacle that has to be overcome for virtual worlds to best function as useful prototypes for new public policy? In other words, if game design is ultimately still subject to approval by game-company lawyers, from where is the possibility for change coming?

CASTRONOVA: The state of the law is still uncertain enough that we're not forced to proceed on the assumption that the laws of the real world will operate with 100 percent force in virtual worlds. "There's plenty of wiggle room" is just a quick way to say it.

There are some possibilities for building an economy that doesn't completely follow the laws of the real-world economy, yet it provides a teaching moment to everyone (like "Wow, if we do it that way, look at what happens"). So, I think there's enough wiggle room, although I think that with what you're saying, there is a concern. There is a concern that maybe the time of innovation may end up being limited, that soon enough the real and the virtual will fade together so completely that it will be impossible to imagine anything other than the way we do it in daily life.

HEINEMAN: Is a theory of social change that's grounded, in part, on a theory of self-satisfaction and fun inherently taking a view of humanity as somewhat selfish and hedonistic? Yours seems to be a theory of social change that's more out of step with what we tend to think of as collectivist or progressive politics, which are understood to be about lifting up others more than necessarily about fulfilling oneself.

CASTRONOVA: Yeah, that's really a question for psychologists, and this is a point in my career where I wish I also had a PhD in psychology. As you know, in economics, we tend to assume that what people want to do is up to them. We don't try to crawl inside the brain. We just say, "Well, given that they want to do this, here are some predictions we can make about the social forces that emerge." That model really starts to have problem in conditions like you mentioned where the well-being of others is a part of an individual's motivation (or the well-being of society is part of an individual's motivation). Economic reasoning becomes circular at that point, and there really isn't any way out. I haven't figured out what the solution to that is.

All that is by way of sort of general comments. Specifically to the question of a model of social change based on selfishness, I'm still pretty comfortable with that because betting against altruism is generally not a losing bet. That's the cynic's point of view, I suppose. If you build your model of the future, your prediction of the future, by saying, "By and large, when people have the chance to take advantage of this thing, they will," those predictions end up being pretty accurate, and it seems like it's the exceptions that prove the rule.

I do talk about hedonism, but we have to be really careful when we talk about what's in somebody's self-interest. A large part of the problem we have today is that people have goals that don't necessarily align with their self-interests. This whole discussion is about people selfishly pursuing their goals, but there could be a change where people become aware that their goals really aren't making them happy. I'll give you the classic examples of the business executive that gets a job offer in a different city and says, "That's what I should do." He goes there and he and his family are miserable, because it turns out happiness depends on having long-run relationships in a single place (all the research shows that). So, we've got all these people moving all over the place, and they never find a sufficient level of happiness. They're just making themselves sad.

Well, what if awareness of that changed? What if all of a sudden people said, "You know, I'm now aware that making a move for a 10 percent salary increase is not a good idea." Well, then it can be different. So, even though my discussions of social change are based on self-interest, there is always this possibility that our perceptions of self-interest could change.

HEINEMAN: The example you just gave of the businessperson who moves for more money seems strikingly similar to the examples you write about of people migrating to and then between virtual worlds. Do you think that in virtual environments, where even though things might get static in a particular world or where there's often a shinier new technology elsewhere, users will stay where they are currently having fun?

CASTRONOVA: This is speculation, but I have this feeling that the world might be taking a turn against the material. I don't know how well that lines up with your question, but I get this sense that with their interest in virtual items and in being online, people are buying fewer cars. The sophistication of society does increase over time. It is true that, generally speaking, people stop believing things that they believed before, and they come to new insights. It is completely possible that we might be in some sort of a postmaterialist moment, and if we are there would be definite consequences for the economy. It might well be that when you see behavior in virtual worlds, it is sort of a harbinger of that.

To give an example: You're in a video game, and people are talking about their jobs or their apartments and so on. They're sort of laughingly saying, "Well, I don't care about that. I've got a level 80 guy in here," and blah, blah, blah. You know, maybe that could be a moment – sort of a leading-edge moment – where some people are just saying, "You know, really I don't care if I have nice clothes and diamond earrings. I don't care. I do care about my online connectivity and my entertainment experiences. But I don't care about too much other than that." That could be a leading-edge phenomenon.

HEINEMAN: It seems that, currently, the virtual world seems to amplify a lot of the power differentials that exist in the real world, whether those are based on gender or (maybe even more so) on race and class. Most virtual worlds tend to be created by and created for either Caucasian or Asian men. From your perspective, is this a problem, and, if so, is there a solution that you can see?

CASTRONOVA: I see this in my classes. I'm just another professor at this university, and I don't feel that I'm particularly different from other professors on this. Like every other guy, I'm like, "I'm not sexist. And, in fact, I took my wife's last name." Yet I teach video game classes, and out of fifty students, I'll have two females. I've talked to some people, and the industry says that it's a problem. For them, just in terms of raw resources, they're upset because they feel like there's half a nation out there that they can't sell to. There's that view that it's just a lost market, and that's why it's a problem.

But setting aside that sort of crass reason, I don't have an explanation for why that is. We all know women who like to play games. What I don't understand is why the percentage is so much lower. I've had some professors say to me, "You know, this isn't really our problem, because we're teaching students who are twenty-two and twenty-three." By extension, the industry can say, "Well, it's not our problem. We're hiring people when they're twenty-four and twenty-five." And they all just sort of say, "The problem starts when girls are twelve, so that's when things have to change."

This is the flavor of the discussion I've seen, and all I can say is that I don't do anything in my view to discourage women gamers, and they generally do not select this kind of a class from all the class offerings.

HEINEMAN: Your work on emerging virtual economies has coincided with a time when the real-world economy has been going through a lot of turmoil globally. Do you see any connection between these phenomena? Are they linked in any way, or is it just kind of coincidental?

CASTRONOVA: Again, it's speculation, but I have this thought in the back of my head that the reason the real economy is staying so stagnant is because people are moving to the Internet. I don't mean that they are spending every waking hour there, but just a little bit more of their attention is focused on virtual items and they're a little less interested in things like houses, cars, and clothes. Virtual items don't show up in the GDP, and all it takes is a couple of percent decline in aggregate demand, and then it starts to feel like the economy is in a funk.

It is surprising to me that we're now five years past the financial crash, and we're still feeling that we're in a recessing economy and in an economy that's not completely healthy. So yes, I have a feeling there may be a connection there, but it's speculation. I can't say.

HEINEMAN: Ed Fries said something that made me think a little bit of some of your work. He explained that he's seen game development shifting from an activity that was prompted primarily by new technology (e.g., graphics advancements) to one that is instead prompted by a need for artistic expression. How does thinking about "games as art" mesh with what you talk about as the trajectory of game development? You talk about development as being a series of innovations pushing us closer to something like the holodeck, an attempted reproduction of an immersive and realistic experience that's more about an adept technological simulation and less about the artistic expression of the developer.

CASTRONOVA: Well, actually, I agree. I think the technology of game production is getting so much cheaper, and the sophistication of people in dealing with a piece of software is growing so rapidly, that I anticipate that we're entering a time when we can expect lots of people to be making lots of games for lots of other people. I certainly do think that's going to happen or is happening already. As that happens, it won't be such a commercial thing. Just as there are people now who write poetry in their little books, there will be people who write games in their free time. I see that as a healthy development, but I also think it contains with it the seeds for a lot of social change. If we're making virtual worlds for one another or we're making entertainment experiences for one another that can be immersive (and they don't have to be virtual worlds), then it seems likely that the number of places to escape to will rise, due to the sheer manufacturing economics of it.

HEINEMAN: So then the central idea driving development is one of escapism, regardless of how "authentic" that experience is or how well it blurs the distinction between the virtual and the real? As long as it's an escape, it doesn't matter?

CASTRONOVA: I don't think people, even now, are concerned about whether their time on Facebook is real or not. I don't think they really are particularly concerned about if they spend lots of hours watching a movie versus lots of hours watching YouTube videos, or

lots of time on Tumblr versus lots of hours playing a game. What's
real and what isn't gets a little funky there.

The original question was really about artistic expression.
Here's a caveat, something that's changed in my own mind. I'm
not as persuaded as I once was that this was always going to be
going in the direction of immersive 3-D. I've kind of given up on
that. I think immersive 3-D and virtual worlds seem to be for a
fairly small percentage of fantasists and role-playing enthusiasts.
It seems like most people want to escape not by doing that, but
by engaging in largely athletic activities. It feels like sports: they
are playing these games, and they are trying to maximize their
dominance and understanding of a system, rather than immersing
themselves in an alternate reality.

I'm getting the feeling that the immersive part is increasingly
less significant than we thought ten years ago and that it's more
just "streams of sensation" with or without any kind of overarching narrative. That can occupy lots of time too, when you are in a
completely unimmersed moment just using the tools of a system
to combat somebody else. I think these are all forms of escapism,
of spending time on the Internet, that are sort of equally valid.

HEINEMAN: You write a lot about the notion of fun, the economy
of fun, the theory of fun, and so forth. You explain that "fun" is
often found in a state of play where one's action is deemed to be
not serious or, perhaps, not having real-world consequences. I
wanted to ask you about games that people often talk about as
not being fun. In games like *Dear Esther, Papo & Yo,* or *To the
Moon,* the end result of encountering the game, for many players,
is introspection, sadness, and melancholy. It's certainly not the
shot of dopamine and escapism we associate with "fun." Based on
reported responses to these games, it seems like they enter into a
realm of seriousness that fun, as you've defined it, doesn't entail.
What do you make of these games in your larger framework for
games as "fun"?

CASTRONOVA: They would probably slide over into the same sort of
artistic category as tragedy. No one would describe *Hamlet* as a
fun experience, yet somehow it engages us. The answers here are

in the emerging studies around the psychology of media engagement, which is just right on the research frontier at the moment when people are starting to make distinctions between attention, which is "I look at something," and engagement, which is "I look at something and I want to interact with it," and then there's a state beyond just interacting with something where one actually tries to adopt parts of it. Something that's "fun" gets our attention; it can get the engagement part, but it may not be "joy," because maybe it causes more introspection. We really don't have any solid answers on those things, but I think it's a research frontier right now.

Right now, in terms of research about psychology and media, all we really have are measures of attention (e.g., "Are you looking at it?"). What we're missing is "What's the content of that attention?" The games you are bringing up are excellent examples of where these categories break down. Yeah, I paid attention to *Papo & Yo*, but I wasn't laughing and jumping up and down and talking about how excited I was.

HEINEMAN: Your approach to doing game studies scholarship is shaped in very large part by your academic background in economics. Other scholars that I've talked to concerning this have been working in game studies in ways that are shaped by their own disciplinary training in fields like history or literature, and they take those theories and methods and bring them to bear on the study of games.

But it seems that in your work, even though you're coming from an economic background, you're kind of advocating for a reversal of analysis. You are suggesting, instead, that people use their time playing games and their subsequent understanding of things like game design to then go and address other fields of knowledge. This is a very different role for game studies. How, then, do you understand the current relationship of game studies to other disciplines in the academy?

CASTRONOVA: Right now [at my institution] we are merging several departments to create a new school of communication. I can see coming down the pike a desire on the part of the administrators to create some kind of a new department, and they're fighting over "Is it emergent media or new media?" and whenever somebody asks what those terms mean, they always say, "Well, you know, like Ted and his game stuff!"

So is game studies something that should be its own department? Should it be the core of a new media department? It's tough for me to answer that because I'm not really sure that game studies is a field. I don't know what I would do if I was to create a curriculum in which you would learn a lot about games and then that would be sort of broadly applicable to the study of some important issues.

It's more like something like architecture, I would think. To the extent that architecture is its own field, I think that game design can be its own field. We think about architecture's relationship to other things. It has a strong scientific component: if you build games and they fall down, or build buildings and they fall down, it doesn't work. With games you have to rely on the role of play, so we have to build things that people like to play, and there are these scientific limits. Also, there's the technological aspect of making computer games: you have to know how to code. But at the same time, we all know that architecture is a canvas on which artists paint. So, there's that part of it as well, and I think it has this sort of hybrid art-science role to play.

Now, all that having been said, I do think that using virtual worlds as a resource for doing experiments has a lot to say to basically all of the social sciences. It's just a much better way of doing rigorous empirical work than what we do right now. But I think that's a temporary phenomenon: we happened to discover test tubes first, and now everybody's using test tubes, but it's nothing inherent in game design. It just happens to be here.

HEINEMAN: Then do you think that game studies will continue to be well served by having people who were trained in other academic disciplines bring their attention to games as opposed to it being its own field?

CASTRONOVA: This may be a little bit of a blunt thing to say, but a background in the humanities hasn't, to my mind, proved particularly helpful in the understanding of games. The reason is that the humanities don't operate with the concept of the formal model that you get in science. And games are formal models. That's what they are. There are a set of structures with benefits and costs to doing things, and there are effects, and there are all kinds of quantification that can go on. So a background where basically what you do is just sort of look at things and talk about them doesn't seem all that helpful to me. It starts to sound like people writing journals ("I played this game, and here's what I think"). I feel like to truly understand what's going on in a game, you really ought to know what the supply-and-demand model does. You really ought to understand the concept of equilibrium. You should know what a complex system is. You should know what dynamic equilibrium theory is. These are all things that come out of economics and sociology and formal anthropology and cognitive science that are really important for understanding all kinds of social systems, whether it's markets in economics or governments in political science. I find that lots of people in game studies don't have any of that. They've had lots of literature, but they haven't had any social science.

At the current moment, if I was to set up a curriculum it would be totally different, because in the first year our students take economics. They'd take statistics and topics like that. I think, at the moment, what we understand game studies to be is much more oriented toward the humanities than I would be comfortable with. That doesn't mean that a future game studies program shouldn't do its own economics class. I kind of want to write the book of hard-core social science for game designers, where some of it's from econ and some is from sociology and some is from political science. So maybe it does have to be that way: you have to have a game-design curriculum that involves some humanities and a bunch of social science as well. But, really, we don't know right now.

HEINEMAN: Most departments or universities don't mix those things well. They have students who do game design who never spend time sort of thinking of the humanities side, and they have students who are on the humanities side who don't understand game design or the way that the social sciences might think about those same problems.

CASTRONOVA: I feel like everybody in game design is either a digital artist, a programmer, or a cultural theorist. What I hear from people in the industry is they're dying for people who can design entire social systems, which is a skill you're only going to learn in public policy analysis, in econ, and in political science.

HEINEMAN: Have you seen improvements in institutional gatekeeping processes, like IRB [institutional review board] approval, for example, that make doing good work in virtual worlds easier, more attainable, more feasible?

CASTRONOVA: Not really. [*Laughs*]

HEINEMAN: What needs to happen?

CASTRONOVA: I'm convinced right now that institutional review boards don't even understand the Internet at this point. They're built on a medical model, and they're not really up on the kind of threats that exist online. So, they tend to view every application for human-subjects approval from the same sort of lens, which is based on a model of injecting a drug into people to see what happens. So, I haven't found it to be particularly effective to begin with, in that the researchers are really actually left to their own ethical guidelines. In other words, you can get IRB approved and do all kinds of unethical things, even with the approval of the IRB, because the IRB doesn't know what to tell you not to do.

Meanwhile, companies remain as xenophobic as ever. The real block with getting company data is that the companies don't collect the data in any way that they should. Companies still have not figured out how to collect data sets that are immediately useful to someone asking the kind of questions that, for example, social scientists would want to ask (e.g., "What's the average number of people who did this in the last version?"). You can go to a game company who happens to open their doors and ask something like, "What's the average price spent for all forms of cloth in the game over the last month?" and their response is typically something like, "We're going to have three people work on that for a week to get that number." That information should have been built into their database.

HEINEMAN: Well, they didn't take economics.

CASTRONOVA: Exactly. They decided at some point, "It's important to have an economy in here," and then they just sort of record everything. Then, when then I go in and I say, "Can I look at the difference in prices across servers?" they tell me that they didn't collect that kind of data. That's the problem: there's this real disconnect; all the data is recorded, but they are not thinking in a sort of social scientific way about the data they're collecting, and it's generally not too useful.

HEINEMAN: Are there logistical roadblocks that they encounter trying to do that, or is it just they haven't put systems in place?

CASTRONOVA: It is not so much that something's in the way; it is that they are distracted by the waterfall of money that, generally, is falling down on them. They have a bucket that has holes in it, and we professors are standing there saying, "Hey, give us that bucket. We can patch up the holes." They respond, "We're too busy collecting the money!" And then, on the other hand, if they aren't collecting from a waterfall of money, they don't want to worry about your problem right now. They have a game to make and will worry about those problems later.

That's why I still think the best thing is, eventually, university PhD students will start making their own virtual worlds, and then the IRB probably won't be there because we'll just put in the terms of service that "you're part of an experimental environment," the people will check off on that, and that'll be fine. The data sets and the databases will be built from the beginning so that they're easy to use.

HEINEMAN: How have you been able to successfully describe your work to people in the game industry who might not think that they'd be interested in public policy or economics?

CASTRONOVA: I'm not sure that I am going to accept the premise that I have been able to successfully explain my work. Every once in a while, I will get a phone call from someone in the industry asking me some "top-level" question like "Should we charge for storage?" If you go back to 2002, in a lot of games, you'd have a "closet" built in your character in that you would have a backpack, and it would be of unlimited size. You could store an unlimited number of shirts. So, I would say things like, "Don't do that."

But beyond that, I think every time people in the game industry have reached out to an economist, they get stuff that's so theoretical that they think that they're not learning anything. So, instead, what they do is they pretty much do trial and error; they figure out little policies that get the economy to be where they want it to be.

My coauthor Vili Lehdonvirta gives talks at the Game Developers Conference that present a series of "baby steps" about how to build different markets. It is very, very simple stuff, and I think the reason for this is that there isn't a literature yet; that hypothetical book I was referring to hasn't been written (although Vili and I are writing a book about designing virtual economics that presents the importance of economics to people in the game-design industry).

HEINEMAN: Are those lessons just as useful for people who aren't designing games with large social worlds with microtransactions and the like? Is there instruction for those who are designing single-player experiences or games that don't have any economy?

CASTRONOVA: Well, my belief is that even single-player games are more entertaining if you work on the economy and make it so that it's entertaining, even though a lot of people would say, "Well, a single-player game, why would that have any particular need for an economy?" But even in single-player games, you'll notice that you always go to the store, you collect coins, and you pick up things. So I think economic lessons are appropriate even if it's a single-player game. There are hardly any games that have a character in it that don't have another character, and a lot of times that other character is some kind of merchant.

HEINEMAN: When I spoke to Chris Grant, who is the editor of Polygon, he told me that he doesn't know which of the people he's hired over the years had a college education because he doesn't even look at that line on their résumé. He said that was because the vast majority of degree programs, even if they talk about games, don't produce students who are dynamic enough and who know how to cover, write about, or think about games in an engaging and adaptive way. This is a common complaint about academia: it is slow in responding to what happens in the game industry, and this is detrimental to its usefulness for that industry.

CASTRONOVA: One defense of academia is that it is our job to "get it right," not to get it "right away." However, we're in charge of this vocational tract; we're supposed to be preparing people for these careers. What you've found dovetails exactly with everything that I said and that I've encountered, which is that people in the industry say they don't care where anybody went to school. They don't care what degree they have, what grades they got, or who they worked with. They don't care. All they care about is "What have you done?"

As we were building our program here, I looked at the writing on the wall and said, "I'm not going to care too much about the classes. Instead, I'm going to tell the students, 'You guys have to have your own game-development studio and you have to make games, because that's the only thing people in the industry respect.'" So we've done that: we have a student game studio, and we're starting to make small amounts of money, enough to maybe send a couple of students to GDC. My hope is that, in the matter of a decade, people will say, "Oh, that's that Hoosier Game Studio. Those are the Indiana University students. They make games. You came out of that studio? Great!" in the same way as if somebody said, "Oh, he worked for Blizzard North, and he was on this project. Good!"

It does upset me the way the academy is so out of touch. I'm involved with many efforts to get professors to connect to their students better. Professors generally don't realize that they're not teaching to themselves: "'I wish I were at Harvard.' You're not. You're at Indiana University. The people sitting here are Indiana kids. They're not inherently interested in philosophy. You've got to translate; you've got to express."

Everybody knows that the future of education is going to be two kinds of places. One kind of place is where it is really hands-on, with one professor mentoring seven to ten students. The other kind of place is going to be one professor entertaining millions with his YouTube feed, and, otherwise, students read content and take multiple-choice tests. Those are kind of the two future outcomes for education from where I'm sitting. And so the game industry is sort of shrugging at the way education is right now and just saying, "We demand people who know how to work in teams." How much teamwork is taught at the contemporary university? Virtually none. "We need people who can do a lot of different things on a project." What do we do at the university? We tell people, "Take a major and basically read books and listen to lectures and do tests in that major," which doesn't prepare them at all for that kind of work.

I'm very sympathetic with the game designers on this, and I'm trying to make sure that our particular curriculum, to the extent possible, meets what they need.

HEINEMAN: Have you encountered much in the way of "institutional blowback" from administrators when you've tried to institute things like this game-design program?

CASTRONOVA: You wouldn't believe it: it's the opposite. Everybody at the presidential and vice presidential level is jumping up and down, screaming and yelling, and pulling out their hair and saying, "Make education more interactive. Make it more digital. Stop lecturing so much. Here's a new classroom. Here's a new thing. Here's another." And the professors say, "I made my class more digital. I e-mailed my students yesterday."

The professoriate is thoroughly and completely out of touch, so much so that when I talk to faculty members, I say, "Don't even try to make your class into a game right now, because your game literacy is pathetic." We all know people who do nothing but play golf their whole lives, and they watch football on TV (I love football). But when you ask that person, "Do you know what *Dungeons & Dragons* is?" "No, what's that?" or "Oh, my kids will play that thing sometimes." It's like, "What the hell are you doing saying you want to gamify something?"

I feel like I'm sitting in my office and I'm an architect, and people come in and say, "I've heard about buildings. We have to have more buildings on this campus. Buildings are going to save the world. I've never been in a building, but I'm going to be involved in telling you exactly how this building should be made." The people who are watching the progress of the educational establishment are well aware of the threats and opportunities, and it's professors who are just married to the idea that "I'm Einstein. I publish two papers a year. I lecture to a hundred students. What's the problem?" All of those people are going to be out of a job.

HEINEMAN: In *Exodus* you make a number of predictions about long-term migration and some of these things we talked about, like retention in virtual environments. But in the time since you've published, a lot of MMOs have launched and very few have succeeded and persisted. Many others, such as *World of Warcraft* and *Second Life*, have seen decreases in usage over many of the past years. Now, some years after writing that book, do you think the predictions you made there will still come true?

CASTRONOVA: I would say the prediction about people spending time in immersive 3-D worlds was off. I think there will be a solid core of the population, maybe 5 percent, who will go into places like that and kind of never come out. At one time I thought that the percentage was going to be a lot higher. I'm pretty sure now that it's not. However, I think there will be a larger percentage of people, not so much in immersive 3-D, but in immersive competitive situations. The number of people who seem to be able to get interested in being in a community of folks who are trying to flex their muscles around a bit of software – that seems to me like it could potentially become very large, an e-sports phenomenon.

Even that is not going to be as big as what we seem to see with people disappearing into the Internet more generally and just picking up little bits of entertainment everywhere. It is like the Internet itself is the immersive world, and the avatar is the

Facebook profile. Many of the predictions still hold; it's just that the Internet itself is a format that I didn't really expect. That it would be this, this conglomeration of disparate, small, hedonic moments rather than, like, spending time in a particular world is a surprise. It is much more fluid.

I do think that as long as this stagnation in the economy persists, I'm sticking to my gut feeling that the Internet has something to do with it. There might be a change under way in terms of the amount of time people spend buying and selling things in the material economy as opposed to just surfing, and that's having an economic impact.

To me, those were the big things in the idea of *Exodus:* that more and more people would be spending their time in some sort of fantasy environment (which seems to me to be true) and also that that shift would have economic consequences. Unless somebody comes up with a better explanation, that's what I'm putting on the table, that the exodus is starting. For all I know, next year the economy will take off. But that's what my gut is telling me.

HEINEMAN: Will that exodus have the same public policy implications that you predicted it would, if now a much smaller percentage are going to be involved in those worlds where there's a lot more policy?

CASTRONOVA: I think there are some really strong political and policy effects already visible. Even someone as jaded as me is shocked at how disconnected politics is becoming from any kind of reality, how little time in politics is spent in reasonable discussion, and how much is spent in creating competing constructions of an alternate reality.

Here's a moment that really struck me. I had a line from a Rolling Stones song in my head, and so I went and looked into this Rolling Stones song. You know how a lot of times a YouTube video will have an advertisement? I found a political advertisement. All of a sudden, I'm wanting to watch the Rolling Stones in the '60s, and here's the president talking about some initiative he's got. They're so desperate to have people pay attention to them that they're running ads on old Rolling Stones videos on YouTube.

To a large extent, people are turtling up and putting their heads in the sand and really not caring anymore. I think that might have huge political implications. If that's really what's going on, then, my goodness, people being in a virtual world and learning about different ways of running the economy are not going to be able to compete with a general apathy that seems to be growing. I think the apathy is kind of growing on my radar a little bit more than the idea that people will spent time online and then say, "This is how we'll change the world." Instead, they're just turning away. It's almost like the 1960s drug that doesn't kill you, and everybody's taking it now. That has different political implications for sure.

Games and Culture

THE FINAL SECTION OF THIS BOOK IS CONCERNED WITH culture that takes video games as its starting place. Video games are, of course, firmly embedded in contemporary popular and media culture globally; the industry's rising financial successes have correlated with a wider demographic range of more players playing more types of games in more contexts. Indeed, one of the reasons game studies has found a foothold in many universities is that video games have become more or less ubiquitous, and there are ample opportunities to study many academic topics (for example, human behavior and communication, principles of artistic creation and design, and more) through the lens of video games and to direct students toward a variety of careers related to the medium. In some sense, then, it is difficult to consider "games and culture" without opening up a very broad discussion about the relationship between video games and the popular culture at large (and previous sections of this book have done just that, to some extent).

Instead, through three different interviews, this section spotlights what it means to consider video games as the foundation for a particular kind of cultural experience. That is, the three primary subjects discussed in this section – a community coming together for a cause, a designer fostering a real-world community through virtual-world design choices, and a scholar who thinks about the analysis of games as a mode through which to understand shifts in human communication – all take video games as a kind of origin point for doing something larger. Reflecting on this process, they discuss both the role of video games in public culture at large as well as their thoughts about specific video game–related subcultures linked to their personal areas of interest.

What this section cannot be is exhaustive: there are many kinds of unique cultural experiences and many varied cultures and subcultures that are related to video games in some form or fashion. To provide some context and suggest future areas of inquiry, this introduction offers a broad overview of much of this culture, a discussion of some shared concerns found within cultures associated with video games both historically and today, and some direction for considering the questions raised in the subsequent interviews.

GAMER CULTURE AND GAME-RELATED SUBCULTURES

The term *gamer culture* is one that is regularly used to describe a collective of individuals who are especially enthusiastic about video games and, as Chris Grant suggested in chapter 7, usually consider themselves to be involved in a set of practices and interests that are misunderstood and underrepresented in the larger cultural and media landscape. As hinted in that previous discussion, though, there is an increasingly wide spectrum of interests that are today subsumed into this larger label. The original definitions of the term *gamer*, as Kirkpatrick (2013) points out, emerged out of a specific series of usages of the word in magazines in the early 1980s that, in many ways, cannot fully encapsulate the breadth of practices that are affiliated with the label today. For example, the bestselling magazine *Game Informer* recently published an essay by Matt Helgeson (2014) that addressed how the term's regular historical association with "real" or "core" gaming is itself problematic and suggests that the range of games played today means that holding on to an old definition smacks of "snobbery and resistance to change." Rather than try to solve this intractable problem of definition, it is perhaps more useful to consider the range of contemporary game-related subcultures that exist today. These can be grouped into three major categories (in which membership will often overlap):

1. *People who play specific video games or specific types of video games.* This is probably the broadest category of game-related subculture, as there are numerous communities formed around a strong interest in specific genres and subgenres or around

specific games. Beyond this, there are people who play games from a particular era, people who play games for a particular platform, or people who play games in particular settings. The defining characteristic of participation in these subcultures is playing (and usually communicating about) some delimited set of games. People who play *World of Warcraft* or *EVE Online* exclusively would fall into this category, as would groups of players focused on retro games, on Bioware-developed intellectual properties, on Japanese role-playing games (RPGS), on first-person shooters, on fighting games, and so on. One's identity within these subculture is tied, in part, to his or her knowledge of, communication about, and performance in an identified, specific game, genre, or other community-defined grouping of games.

2. *People who play video games to achieve specific goals.* Everyone who plays games does so for some reason or another, but this category is meant to identify those individuals who play games to reach a particular kind of goal and, importantly, form a community and culture around those goals. Professional gaming leagues would be a prominent example, as would groups who collaborate on completing speed runs, boosting their Xbox Gamerscore or PlayStation Trophy count, or working through their backlog. These goals are above and beyond those suggested by the game itself and can be considered an additional challenge that emerges and is delineated through various group communication and playing practices. One's identity in these subcultures is often closely tied to his or her skill in accomplishing or moving toward defined goals, and thus competition is often a significant factor in the community's interactions.

3. *People who incorporate games into new forms of representation.* These individuals use games as a jumping-off point for creating something new, usually within or for a community of people with shared interests. This can include working on new ideas outside of game worlds themselves, such as creating game-related artifacts (for example, podcasts, videos, journal articles,

paintings, books, modified consoles), engaging in cosplay and
LARPing (live-action role playing) related to games, performing
music related to games (for example, chiptune artists), or even
curating exhibits or other forms of public engagements with
video games. Beyond this, some subcultures form around
modifying or creating within and for game worlds; *Minecraft*
has a large community surrounding this kind of activity, for
example, but many modding and level-creating communities
also collaborate across multiple games.

These three categories capture much of the activity that exists in contemporary video game–related subcultures, but they cannot by themselves
provide much insight into the various community dynamics at play in
each instance. This is where existing (and future) research into game-
related subcultures plays an important role.[1]

Across these categories are also a number of shared concerns about
how various game-related subcultures are or are not adapting to larger
changes in player demographics, communication technologies, and increased attention. That is, as the membership of these various groups
becomes less white, less male, and more public, there have been a host of
controversies surrounding most game-related subcultures, and, increasingly, these controversies play out online in websites, forums, and social
media. As was discussed in some of the previous interviews, controversy
and video games have a long history, and that legacy persists today.

CULTURE AND CONTROVERSY

Background

From the start, video games and the subcultures surrounding them have
been the subject of public debate and controversy. From the late 1970s to
the early 1980s, video game arcades were one of the most popular amuse-
ment diversions for adolescents. In the United States, players could be
found in arcades engaged in games such as *Space Invaders, Pac-Man, Ga-
laga,* and *Satan's Hollow.* National arcade tournaments were held, news

publications such as *Life* and the *New York Times* published features on the gaming craze, and game-themed music, movies, and clothing all found popular success. The popularity of video games during the arcade craze was not limited to the United States – sales of arcade machines in Japan and much of Europe also skyrocketed during this period and became the financial foundation for companies such as Sega, Nintendo, and Atari.

Worth noting, however, is that this golden age of the arcade almost passed by the children living in certain cities and towns in the United States. Citing concerns over drug sales, truancy, and the perceived effects of gaming violence, worried parents and legislators in towns such as Oakland (California), Durham (New Hampshire), and Mesquite (Texas) passed laws barring children from entering arcades without parental supervision. A 1982 "Issue and Debate" article in the *New York Times* covered these laws and explained that the rise of gaming popularity had brought about an increase in parental concern. Setting the stage for a conflict that continues to this day, the author explained:

> [Parents], whose children spend hours peering into the games' multicolored screens, express concern about long-term psychological damage. Some even contend that the highly competitive and warlike nature of many games could cause increased hostility and violence among those who play them. The manufacturers and operators of coin-operated games, however, maintain that there is nothing harmful about this form of entertainment. They argue further that laws that forbid young people from playing the games violate both the operators' and the players' constitutional rights.

Elland Archer, the city attorney representing Mesquite in a court case against arcade operating company Aladdin's Castle, Inc., explained the city's rationale for censoring adolescent access to the machines: "You can carry the First Amendment to a ridiculous extreme," Archer said. "This is not art. Kids are just going in there to put money into a machine" (Kerr). The people of Mesquite, like those in other cities around the country, had decided they had a moral obligation to protect their youth by restricting access to video games.

Mesquite's law was overturned in 1980 by the Fifth Circuit U.S. Court of Appeals, and an appeal to the U.S. Supreme Court in 1982 went unheard. The judge's opinion following the court's ruling included an admonition that "on the seventeen year old age requirement of the ordinance, we reverse, holding that it is constitutionally offensive" (*City of Mesquite v. Aladdin's Castle, Inc.*). Though this particular case was thrown out, a series of antiarcade ordinances passed throughout the "golden age" of the arcade.

These laws marked the origins of what would soon become an even larger conflict between the video game industry and those concerned about the negative effects of games when home gaming consoles gained widespread success in the late 1980s and early 1990s. As video game playing moved from local hangouts to private homes, the settings for these clashes were increasingly global. Countries where games were popular, such as Germany, Australia, Japan, and England, all saw game-related controversies play out on a national stage. Indeed, after the attempts at arcade legislation in the late 1970s and early 1980s, most of the debate around restricted access to and censorship of video games in the United States surrounded home consoles.

Published reports of parental concern started with the first widely popular home console, the Atari 2600. In a 1983 article for *Videogaming and Computergaming Illustrated,* Tim Moriarty wrote about the controversy surrounding *Custer's Revenge,* the first X-rated video game for home consoles, and explained that the game prompted public protests and picketing, angry letters, a lawsuit, and a lack of retailer support. A few years later, parents concerned about the influence of the occult in the media and in role-playing games like *Dungeons & Dragons* would point to many of the games available on the Nintendo Entertainment System as potential negative influences on their children and pushed for boycotts of the console.

Parental concerns over sexual themes and the occult notwithstanding, the production and sale of video games remained relatively free from any kind of federal intervention until a series of congressional hearings in the early 1990s. Specifically, at hearings in December 1993 and March 1994, Congress listened to arguments about violence in video games as part of its deliberations in considering a bill proposed by Senator Joe Lieberman to require the industry to place ratings on its products. Fearing censorship or banning of popular games like *Mortal Kombat* or *Night Trap,* the industry formed the Entertainment Software Ratings Board, which continues to rate games based on their "objectionable" content today.

In the decades that followed, public controversy around video games tended to focus on particular franchises known for their themes of violence or sex or both (for example, *Grand Theft Auto, Leisure Suit Larry, Doom, Manhunt, Mass Effect*), though games with "addictive" qualities (*World of Warcraft, Everquest, Starcraft, League of Legends*) also generated headlines when players neglected some important real-life problems, such as the well-being of themselves or others, to continue playing a game. By and large, though, in recent years public debates surrounding video games have shifted from a mainstream media focus on supposed cultural fears about particular games to more localized scrutiny of the relationship between video games and behaviors in various game-related subcultures.

Today

Due in large part to the maturing and increasingly diverse demographics of video game players, many of the contemporary debates surrounding video games and their related subcultures have been centered on issues of race, class, and gender. Like most tech-related industries, the video game industry has long been populated primarily by men. With notable exceptions such as the *King's Quest* series (Roberta Williams) or *Wizardry* (Brenda Braithwaite), the vast majority of "classic" video games were designed by men, from a male perspective, primarily for a male audience. Additionally, and also reflective of the industry's hiring practices, video games have largely featured playable characters that are Caucasian or Asian, heterosexual, cisgendered, and conforming to traditional gender norms. Furthermore, some have suggested that the representation of male and female characters across the history of games has contributed directly to some of the hypercompetitiveness, misogyny, bullying, and other abusive behaviors found among gamers and in many of the game-related cultures mentioned above.

A number of critics, many of them women, have recently engaged this history and its implications for women's relationship to video games in the present. A notable example would be Anita Sarkeesian, who produces a Kickstarter-backed video series entitled "Tropes vs. Women in Video Games" that aims to "explore, analyze and deconstruct some of the most common tropes and stereotypes of female characters in games . . . highlight[ing] the larger recurring patterns and conventions used within the gaming industry rather than just focusing on the worst offenders." Though reception has been largely positive to her series, Sarkeesian has also received death threats and regular harassment for what some perceive as an "attack" on men and on video games as a medium ("The Mirror"). Leigh Alexander, who regularly writes about video games and video game culture for *Gamasutra* and other video game–related websites, has covered topics such as game developers who are mothers (2014) and the plight of women in game culture (for example, "Grunge, Grrrls and Video Games: Turning the Dial for a More Meaningful Culture" [2013]). As Chris Grant indicated in chapter 7, many of the popular gaming-related websites also feature articles and stories tied to race, class, and gender in gaming culture (for example, Harris O'Malley's "Nerds and Male Privilege" on Kotaku [2011] and Polygon's coverage of the "#1reasonwhy" Twitter campaign to raise awareness of misogyny in the game industry and related subcultures [Sarkar, 2014]). While the debate about gender and games has received the most attention in popular gaming media outlets, issues of race and class have also been covered with increased frequency.[2] These identity-focused areas of debate are increasingly relevant to video game–related subcultures, especially as the dynamics that play out in online spaces extend to physical meeting spaces such as conventions and competitions.

SUMMARY

The interviews in this final section of the book are connected by each interviewee's shared interest in engaging video game–related culture(s); each of the chapters highlights a different way of doing that (through community organizing and formal structure, through design and communication, and through education and research). The relationship between video games and popular culture more broadly has largely been defined by media coverage of games and gamers; as mass media has ceded coverage of both to specialized and social media, gamers have increasingly interrogated the specific dynamics of their various subcultures and the industry with which they are affiliated. Though the history of public controversy and debate around issues such as violence and sexuality continues to have some relevance in contemporary discussions about games, there has been a radical shift toward a prolonged consideration of identity-related issues in both popular and academic analysis of relationships that exist between video games and various cultural practices.

NINE

Jamie Dillion

GAMERS, COMMUNITY, AND CHARITY

SINCE 2003, THE CHILD'S PLAY CHARITY HAS RAISED MORE than twenty-five million dollars in efforts to purchase new video games, game consoles, and other toys for patients in children's hospitals. The organization was founded by Jerry Holkins and Mike Krahulik, the creators of the wildly popular *Penny Arcade* webcomic, a three-day-a-week strip that is primarily based on skewering tabletop and video games, game culture, and related topics. The organization's press kit explains its origins: "In response to the media's negative portrayal of gamers, the pair called for the gaming community to donate to Seattle Children's Hospital during the holiday season" (Child's Play). The charity's program coordinator and developer is Jamie Dillion, who oversees many of the day-to-day operations for the organization and often represents it in the press.

Though Child's Play is not the first charitable organization created primarily for gamers, it is certainly the most successful. Every year the organization engages in Web-based holiday-season fund-raising efforts, holds memorabilia auctions and other fund-raising events, offers workshops and presentations at the various Penny Arcade Expos, and otherwise raises the profile of the charity through efforts at publicity. The 501(c)(3) organization is relatively small in its actual staffing and organization, but it has a large amount of leaders in hundreds of "local" game communities (mostly online instead of geographically situated) that it works with to best coordinate fund-raising efforts. This means that Dillion is in a somewhat unique position of being able to observe the similarities and differences in how various pockets of game culture (and various gaming communities) approach a similar objective: fund-raising.

The interview with Dillion in this chapter covers her interactions with various gaming communities, the novel considerations that go into working with them to do fund-raising, the criticisms that the charity has sometimes faced, and her understanding of the causes for its overall success. It is worth noting that, due to scheduling conflicts, this interview differs from the rest of those in the book in that it was conducted at Dillion's request via e-mail.

—m—

HEINEMAN: You've talked about how Child's Play offers an offset to the negative perception of gamers as violent, uncaring, and apathetic – and in fact this was part of the motivation for its founding. Can you point to some examples of how you've seen this perception change among the general public?

DILLION: Video games as a media are very young, but growing rapidly. That means society as a whole is becoming more exposed to games and, ideally, more comfortable with them. The technology associated with video games is becoming more useful in a huge number of ways. For example, the Microsoft Kinect is now being used to help stroke victims regain movement.

HEINEMAN: What do you think accounts for the success of the charity? Are there important lessons you've learned along the way that might be unique to working with a charity surrounding gaming?

DILLION: The community is absolutely the driving force of what makes Child's Play successful; there's no question about that. Child's Play is very much a grassroots organization – everyone who works at Child's Play is a gamer, so when we talk about "the community," we're talking about our friends, coworkers, and gaming buddies and ourselves. Identifying with our core support group makes it easier to understand what's important to gamers, how we consume media, how we can connect with the community as a whole. You'll never see us send physical newsletters – instead, we engage via Twitter, Facebook, and our website.

HEINEMAN: Have there been any ongoing failures or shortcomings that you have had difficulty addressing? How have you tried to so far?

DILLION: I think we've been pretty effective at addressing issues as they come up – part of this is endeavoring to grow at a sustainable rate regarding expansion and ensuring we keep both the hospitals and children and the community in mind whenever decisions are made.

HEINEMAN: There's been a proliferation of game-related charity events and organizations since Child's Play's founding. What do you see as the long-term future for your organization and for others that may have been inspired by it?

DILLION: I often describe game marathons to nongamers as a type of walk-a-thon. It's a clever but natural evolution of traditional fund-raising, and I think as technology continues to grow in both expected and unexpected ways, it will have both expected and unexpected outcomes. A long-term goal of ours is to continue to grow – not just to expand, but to adapt and adjust to the changing environment as games and technology change with us.

HEINEMAN: Much has been written in game studies about the nuances of gaming culture compared to fan culture in general and especially compared to those communities that form around other forms of mediated entertainment. What characterizes the community surrounding Child's Play? Are these characteristics in any way tied to the broader gaming culture itself as you understand it?

DILLION: The Child's Play community, to me, is really characterized by generosity, enthusiasm, and commitment to the cause. The same passion that gamers apply to games (whether they be tabletop, video games, or even larger "geek culture") carries over to Child's Play, and we see a very high number of supporters who go above and beyond a simple donation to support the cause. Many spread the word to families and friends, encourage their employers to donation match, organize fund-raisers of their own, and donate year after year.

HEINEMAN: Much of gaming culture is marked by competitiveness, something that has also been a part of the fund-raising campaigns surrounding each year's drive. Has this competiveness been a strictly positive force for Child's Play and its community, or has it caused any of the problems sometimes associated with hypercompetitiveness (cheating, physical or mental anguish, overexertion, bullying, etc.)?

DILLION: I think, on the whole, competitiveness has been positive for Child's Play. There are certainly times where it can put a lot of pressure on fund-raisers or us – essentially the idea that if the current event or drive doesn't exceed earlier years, it is considered a failure. We really don't see it that way – if a single kid is able to take their mind off being sick for a few minutes with a game or toy, we consider it a success.

HEINEMAN: What techniques have you found to be effective for growing the Child's Play community without alienating or marginalizing existing members?

DILLION: The community does a lot of the heavy lifting in terms of growing itself – word spreads through specific niches fairly easily. For example, folks who play a specific game are likely to hear of a fund-raiser run by other folks who like that game. We essentially focus on supporting everyone who wants to hold a fund-raiser or support us in any way, big or small, year one or year seven. Existing members of the community are passionate and enthusiastic, and they all are happy to see Child's Play gain more support.

HEINEMAN: You are in an interesting position to see a "dispersed online community" collide in a very material way with "physical local communities" at the hospitals that benefit from your work. How would you describe that dynamic? Are there differences you try to bridge or similarities that you try to emphasize?

DILLION: We work almost entirely on the online community side, because that's where our expertise lies. We coordinate directly with hospital employees, which generally are directors or managers of Child Life. They know the best way to interact in their physical local communities and the best ways to distribute gifts, work with kids, and ensure that programs like ours impact their facility in the best ways possible. We just work to focus the incredible generosity of the online community into having an impact on physical communities that need help.

HEINEMAN: I want to address a few of the criticisms I've seen of the charity. They include statements like "Gamers should be donating food and medicine, not Xboxes and PlayStations. . . . They only care because it is about games and a comic strip"; concerns raised over the "political" uses of the charity, such as when gamers used donations to try to spur changes to *Mass Effect 3;* the use of the charity's name by groups who donate very small percentages of profits; the effectiveness of games themselves as a rehab tool; etc. How are these criticisms usually handled within the organization?

DILLION: If the mission of Child's Play doesn't resonate with a member of the community, that isn't offensive to us – we hope that they find a charity that they identify with and send their money and support there. We have found that the demand for what we do is high, and that's reflected in the testimonials we receive both from families and from doctors and medical personnel alike (you can see them on our website, www.childsplaycharity.org /testimonials).

In terms of "political" uses of Child's Play, we've implemented policies to help prevent that as much as possible. Jerry Holkins, one of the founders, elaborated on this issue (and my role in it).

As the main point of contact for Child's Play, Jamie has been buried under mail about this situation. Apparently some of the people giving to the cause seemed to think that they were paying for a new ending to Mass Effect. She's been asked what the goal is, and how much they need to raise in order to get the ending produced. We've also been contacted by PayPal due to a high number of people asking for their donations back. This is in addition to readers who simply couldn't understand how this was connected to Child's Play's mission. We were dealing with a lot of very confused people, more every day, and that told us we had a problem.

We have policies in place to deal with direct abuse: we don't allow companies to use Child's Play in order to sell more stuff. To that end we do not allow deals like "1 cent of every dollar goes to Child's Play!" or whatever. But this isn't anywhere on that continuum! This is a passionate community that formed around one thing, and some of that passion was expressed in charitable giving. I actually support this cause, but I am a pessimist, and I'm thinking about the next time something like this happens – when someone attaches Child's Play to something we can't get behind, or leverages your history of generosity and fellow feeling for their own weird bullshit. So, we need to have something like a policy on this. This is the best way I can think to say it:

Child's Play cannot be a tool to draw attention to a cause. Child's Play must be the Cause.

Nothing like this has ever happened in the almost ten years the charity has been running, so it kind of threw me for a loop. Thanks for listening. (Holkins)

We work hard to ensure our policies and practices reflect the expectations of the community and what we believe is best for Child's Play and our beneficiaries in the long term.

HEINEMAN: Are there ways that you think other charity organizations might better tap into online communities, gaming or otherwise, to advocate their causes and raise awareness and donations?

DILLION: I think the biggest requirement of "tapping into" online communities is to understand them. If you want to connect with a digital community, you need to know how they want to be connected; otherwise, it can come across as insincere or heavy-handed. Public relations is changing drastically with the growth of social media, and for us the most successful and important approach has been to focus on staying true to our mission and transparent and sincere communication and support for our communities.

TEN

Casey Hudson

GAMES AND EMOTION

THOSE FAMILIAR WITH THE ONTOLOGICAL DEBATES AROUND what kind of medium video games might be, what they offer that is distinct from other mediums, and what their relationship is to other digital texts are likely familiar with the suggestion that a defining aspect of video games is their ability to create a more intense emotional response than other media due to their representational and interactive qualities. This oft-repeated argument, offered with varying degrees of sophistication in both academic analyses in video game media outlets and online discussion forums, essentially contends that games create a kind of physiological investment that cannot be found in other media, thus amplifying the body and mind's reaction.

Casey Hudson, former project director for Bioware's *Mass Effect* series, has long had a guiding role in producing titles that push the edges of how video games function to generate a range of emotional responses by players. Games like *Neverwinter Nights* and *Star Wars: Knights of the Old Republic* continue to be heralded for how they were able to bring together thoughtful science-fiction/fantasy writing with novel implementations of player-choice scenarios, believable relational interactions with NPCs, and, especially in the most recent *Mass Effect* games, believable animation and acting that take place in fully realized environments. Most recently, Bioware developed a strong reputation for fostering fan-based communities around their games and, importantly, forging ongoing dialogues with those communities to further improve the quality of the game components on which the studio built its reputation.

That reputation (and the studio's constant management of it) puts Hudson in a unique position to speak to a number of issues of relevance for both those interested in understanding game design (specifically as it relates to emotion) and those interested in gaining perspective on game-based communities (especially those surrounding a particular IP). That audience includes academic researchers who are invested in considering the links between gameplay experiences, player psychology, and "gamer culture" more broadly. For example, Adrienne Shaw's essay "What Is Gamer Culture?" argues that any productive consideration of the term *gamer culture* needs to be rooted in a critical analysis (as opposed to a description) of how those cultures are constructed, what kinds of hierarchies and communicative practices those structuring processes express, and how a particular culture's actions are related to the experiences found in the specific games around which they are focused. Bioware, from that perspective, provides a case study that offers a kind of publicness and transparency into a number of complex community relations (both within communities and between community members and game developers).

In the interview found in this chapter, Hudson discusses these elements – emotion, narrative, choice, systems design, and community – as they relate to the recent *Mass Effect* series and to his ongoing projects. Furthermore, he provides thoughts on topics addressed elsewhere in this book, including the relationship of the video game industry to the video game press and the economic considerations behind certain design choices (specifically, Bioware's use of downloadable content).

—⁓—

HEINEMAN: Many of the games that you're credited with – for example, those in the recent *Mass Effect* series – have been noted for their ability to create strong emotional responses by players. It would seem that there are most likely a number of factors that come together, including design of gameplay, narrative creation, and art direction, that have to work in a particular mixture in order to facilitate this. What have you learned about creating emotion in games?

HUDSON: I think it goes back to when we working on *Stars Wars: Knights of the Old Republic.* We had previously done games, like the *Baldur's Gate* series, where you would adventure with a team, or a party. Part of the fun of that was that you've got these interesting personalities around you, and they add to the narrative texture of the story, and that's kind of an interesting part of the experience. As we started to move into a more realistic or cinematic kind of experience, one thing that occurred to me is that part of what's nice about having other characters with you as you adventure is that it creates a sense of shared experience. That's one thing that's fairly unique to the kind of games we make at Bioware, beyond the fact that we make role-playing games and they have story and whatnot.

If you look at most video games, a good proportion of them involve your character as a player adventuring in a world pretty much by yourself; though you come across characters, they may come and go in the story. It's not really about kind of a shared experience with you and several friends going out and doing something. But, if you think about what you do in real life, it's so much less fun to go out by yourself and do something. Going by yourself to a movie, to sit in a restaurant, to go hiking: people bring their friends. They'll beg their friends to come with them just so that it's interesting and there's a shared experience.

When you're on a holiday by yourself and you walk around an interesting town, or you go see an amazing location, what you end up constantly doing is thinking about "Oh, I wish my friend was here," or "I wish my wife was here; she would love this," and you're constantly thinking these things. But when you're there with your friend and people that you know, part of what makes it a memorable experience is looking to them for their reaction. You look for the way that the situation reflects off of their personality, and it becomes flavored by that. Those are the things that you end up remembering; it's not just the thing that happened, but what your friends thought about it.

So it became really important to try to capture that sense of shared experience as we tried to make our games connect in a more memorable way through emotions. That was kind of the first thing that we really started to try to develop is a sense of shared experience. One thing that I liked about KOTOR, the *Star Wars* game, is that wherever you were, you could have a conversation with your party members and your squad members. So you could turn to someone no matter where you were and have a conversation and say, "Hey, what do you think about this world?" That kind of moment, which we have done in different ways in our games, that's really special, and I think it adds a lot of humanity back into an experience that would otherwise be kind of strangely solitary.

As we moved into the *Mass Effect* series, I think the next frontier for us at that time was realizing that we had a new level of fidelity that we could bring to the screen and to our characters. We didn't know how far we'd be able to go, because when you start a project, that one in particular, it was in advance of that next console generation of the Xbox 360. So we didn't know what we'd be able to do, but it felt like we would be able to get pretty close to realistic and compelling digital actors that could have expressions. They could cry, and have tears, and so we knew we could do something in that area, and we made a conscious decision to really push toward that and create digital actors that could convey emotion.

We didn't know if we could do it, but that was what we tried to do, and *Mass Effect* was really built around an experience that kind of lives in the eyes of the characters around you. So we put a lot of work into the eyes, and the motion, the way that the eyes track you as a player, especially in conversation. And in there is a lot of life, you know? It's true that the eyes are the windows to the soul. You look deeply into someone's eyes to try to figure out how they're feeling, or what they mean, and if you can put that life into a digital actor, then you can get away from so much of that uncanny feeling.

With every game we'd refocus on the life that's portrayed by the eyes of the characters, and then on out through facial expressions, and wrinkles, and larger gesture acting, stuff like that. That being a focus for *Mass Effect* allowed us to then have characters that do things that we didn't know at the start that we could do, but were part of our goals. For example, previous games required us to write everything that we wanted to happen into the words spoken by the characters, because we didn't have acting, and we didn't have a lot of other stuff that you have when you shoot a movie, for example: the unspoken stuff. Everything was written, or everything was spoken, but in *Mass Effect,* right in some of the opening moments of the game, you're able to see Ashley, for example, if you as a player scold Ashley for causing a situation where you got injured, her response is (I think) the first line that we'd ever done that has no voice-over. She just looks at you, but by the look on her face, you can tell that you've hurt her feelings, and that surprised a lot of people. I remember reading it in a review that, for that reviewer, getting to that moment and realizing that he felt bad because he hurt her feelings, and she didn't say anything, that showed that we do have access to this other new language of interactive storytelling. Then we tried to play with that and expand on it more throughout the *Mass Effect* series.

HEINEMAN: Are there certain kinds of facial expressions and emotions that it might not make sense for Commander Shepherd [the avatar the player assumes] to show because doing so could infringe on the audience emoting on their own? Is there concern that if they see a response on the character model that they will mimic it or that the character's response might stand in for a response that they might have?

HUDSON: A question that we're constantly asking ourselves is how much can we infuse the player/character with reactions and emotions that are appropriate, but are kind of authored to help tell the story? Where does that cross a line into taking away the ownership of that character? We do ask that constantly, and it's something that the writers are conscious of as they build the basic story and write in what the decision and the lines are. When that starts to move on to a point where the cinematic designers and artists are actually bringing those moments to life with expressions and reactions, they're thinking about that as well. It's something that we review constantly.

We have an interesting process where it's sort of like dailies in the movies, where you will get everybody together, and we will play through a section of the game, and we'll all talk about it. We just talk about everything that's happening on the screen, and it's a really good way for us to, first of all, develop a common language and common values and principles about how we believe we should be doing things. The other thing that it does is it allows us, as we develop each portion of the game, to bring everybody's diverse talents to make everything better.

One of the things that we end up talking about, as we get to a certain choice, is whether that scenario is giving you enough agency. In *Mass Effect 3*, for example, one of my favorites was the way that the plot leads into Mordin's possible death. In *Mass Effect 3*, this was really interesting because I think it's the only one that we've done where the player lies and then has to constantly decide whether to continue keeping up the lie or to come clean. It was a really interesting situation to put the player in, but for us it was something that we had reviewed over and over again in these sort of dailies. We would talk about things like "Okay, at this point I need an option to explore this other feeling that I'm having, and currently we're not offering that" or "What if I wanted to ask a question here?" or "What if I wanted to come clean at this point?"

It ends up getting quite complicated in terms of leaning toward Mordin's death, and you're feeling responsible, and you're perpetuating this lie. As you lead toward that, we give you moments to interact with Mordin and explore what you think is right or wrong in terms of the morality of that situation. We only arrive at the end point by putting ourselves in that situation and talking as a group about how we feel about what you would want to do and then trying to give the player those options.

That is also all in balance with the fact that we're still trying to get you somewhere. There is still some sort of backbone of an authored story that is going to end up somewhere. We'd never put the player in a situation where they're perpetuating a lie against a friend for potentially the greater good. That's very unique, and so there's no common rule that we can apply to that. It's a conversation that we have about the actual content that we're seeing on the screen.

HEINEMAN: Some of the emotional response that players have to the game is credited to the implementation of romantic elements in Bioware games, including courtship and sex. Rob Gallagher recently wrote a piece for the journal *Games and Culture* wherein he argued that a reason that most games choose to shun sex is that "as a digital medium, games themselves operate not according to a logic of reproduction, but one of replication, iteration, and modulation. They remind us of the fundamental otherness of digital technologies" (415). He goes on to suggest that whatever games might have to say about sex will necessarily be different from what every other medium has been able to say. So, for example, books excel in a particular way in discussing or portraying sex. Film does it in another way. What aspects of sex and romance do you think games are able to address better, or perhaps differently, than other media?

HUDSON: Well, I think we're still in the very beginnings of exploring how to approach it and what it means. I think one thing that's really interesting about developing an interactive story is that it is really different from any other medium. The big difference between interactive storytelling and everything else is that if there's an element that is not interactive – you can't modulate it, change it, or control it – then to the player it doesn't really matter.

An example of that would a movie where you show a character that has a dog, and then the villain shows up and hurts the dog. Now you feel empathy for the main character, and you're angry at the villain. But if in a game we say, "Okay, here's your dog, and now the villain hurts your dog," it's a different reaction because the player hasn't learned yet, in an interactive way, that in fact it is their dog. They don't buy into it, and so they would respond, "Well, no, that's not my dog." They're just not as concerned about it. You're telling a more static story, so you can't rely on empathy, But what you could do is you could have the player spend some time. You give them a dog, the player plays with the dog, goes on an adventure, the dog has a little bit of personality, you have some fun, and you're able to pet it. If you have a little bit of interactivity, and you develop that bond through interaction, and then someone hurts your dog, not only will it have an emotional effect on you, but it will probably have a stronger emotional effect on you than the empathy that you feel in a noninteractive medium.

That's the challenge, but also the power, of interactive story-telling. I think that's true with aspects of what we try to do with relationships and interactivity. If we were to say that you are this very specific character, and this other character becomes your girl-friend, and there's a romance, and we show love scenes and things like that, if it's not interactive as part of an interactive media, then you probably won't care that much about it. What makes that interesting in other aspects of relationships and friendships are the things that you do to bond with characters that are memorable moments outside of romances. All of those things become interesting *if* they're optional, and because you chose to do them, and because you chose to pursue a relationship, and a friendship, and you kind of tease open these moments. That's where they feel like they have something that starts to emulate the uncertainty, the nervousness, the unpredictability, and the excitement of relationships in real life.

HEINEMAN: Is that one way of saying that games teach us something about the play that's inherent in a relationship, which is a lesson that we might not get from other mediums?

HUDSON: Yeah, I think so, if it's done right. We're still trying to learn how to do that. I think a game can allow you to explore how you feel, not only about different situations and different characters as part of a relationship, but also about how you might do things that you can't do in real life (e.g., to role-play a character of a different gender). It's amazing to me how many times people play our games from beginning to end because they want to see what would have happened differently.

There's the electricity of not knowing what's going to happen when you make certain decisions or say certain things as part of a relationship that's unfolding in real time in an interactive way. But then there's the curiosity of what would have happened if you would have done something different, and you can explore that as well.

HEINEMAN: The games you've worked on often feature morality choices that shape the progression of the character. One criticism that I've seen in game studies scholarship is that, because the paragon and renegade scales slide independently, a player can potentially play the game in a way that nothing is closed off – there are no direct penalties on gameplay for the choices, only penalties on certain narrative arcs (Schulzke, 2009). First, is this a fair criticism, and, second, what kind of discussion goes into determining "what is moral" and how to reward/punish players for choices?

HUDSON: Because of the terminology and the symbology around our paragon and renegade scales, it is very easy to associate them with good and evil. There's an assumption that that's what they are, but they weren't meant to be that, and I think if you look at the actual things that you're able to do in the game that contribute to either paragon or renegade, you will see that they are meant to be more of a morality scale that is not aligned with good and evil; it's kind of 90 degrees from that. The idea is supposed to be that you are out to do things for good, one way or another.

Then there is a more brutal short-term-sacrifice/long-term-gain version of that, which is what renegade is. Then there's the approach that you're trying to be more gentle, you're trying to balance things out and be more peaceful. But you may not actually get further along with that; there might be longer-term sacrifices that you're making there, and so it's a little bit different in terms of the scale.

It's sort of like if you imagine some of the things that Jack Bauer would do. Jack Bauer's always trying to save the world, but in the moment, as he is interrogating someone, he may decide to knife the guy in the kneecap to get an answer, which is one way to handle that situation, and there might be a different way to handle it where he doesn't have to do that. Obviously, it's a brutal action to take, but in either case he's trying to do the right thing that is going to save the world. But is he going about it in a brutal way, or is he going to try to find something else? There are advantages in that immediate sacrifice as well.

Those are the things that we tried to write into those decisions, and that's why the scale works the way that it does. It is always a challenge in terms of providing people with the ability to make agonizing decisions, which was always a focus for us on

Mass Effect. We would try to write those things in. Then, because it is a game and you want ways to see how you've done and how that contributes to things, ultimately you need systems. You transition from the analog creative side (writing a good story) to working on things that become systems, and then systems ultimately rely on numbers. As a player, you want to see what those numbers are so that you can figure out how to make the game do the things that you want. We have to represent those somehow, and so you end up seeing scales and seeing numbers. We're always looking for ways to do that better, or to circumvent the gamification of the analog creative side.

HEINEMAN: As you have that discussion about how to make those adjustments and both meet expectations of "This is a game – let's move the numbers in a particular direction," as well as those of particular story needs, does the discussion ever turn philosophical? Is there debate about the question of morality itself? Do you ever find that, around the planning table, people will argue for particular philosophical or religious or psychological understandings of morality?

HUDSON: It absolutely does happen, and it really depends on the content we're looking at and the story that we're trying to tell. It ranges from looking at certain situations, the question of whether a certain action is considered renegade or paragon, and you'll have people arguing the case for it being one versus the other. When you do come to a resolution on it, you come out of it with some kind of agreement on the principles behind why you would choose one for that situation versus the other. It especially comes up as something that we would talk about if you're doing something that is really, really rough and violent, but it results in something good. Sometimes people would see that as the paragon thing to do, the right thing. But we would keep going back to the definitions and try to find what we meant with that.

Players would later talk about how they would be in a certain situation in the game and really agonize about what they should do. They would put the controller down and really think about what they would want to do. They're not trying to think, "Am I a paragon or renegade player?" In those moments, they're thinking about the story, and they're thinking about the fact that they really like a certain character, but they also feel like the right thing to do is an action that may hurt that character.

And it's those situations that I think are where the interest is in the story. But then, like I said, as it sort of moves along into the interface and the systems and numbers, that's where the representation of it, and its effect on the game systems, becomes more crude. But I think the actual experience is a lot more analog and textured, and that's where the interesting things happen in terms of the moral dilemma. Ideally, what we're trying to do is not to invent the "right way" to label decisions with morality, but rather allow players to explore how they feel when placed in different situations.

HEINEMAN: Both academic and popular audiences have tried to psychologize certain points in the *Mass Effect* games or tried to figure out what philosophies are at work in the story and choices. These pieces will often cite well-known philosophers, or talk about Freud, or do these kind of "scholarly" things as they discuss the game. Does any of that level of discussion actually take place, where you're citing theory and so on, at any point in the creation of the game? Or is it all after the fact?

HUDSON: Everyone brings what they know and their experience or their education to their process. So the writers and designers were all bringing these things in as inspiration or as ideas or things that we want to explore as part of our story. Then those things maybe become part of the discussions and the debates that we have. But for the most part, I think what we're trying to find is truth in the experience and more as it relates to our real-life experiences. How do you feel about things? What would you do in different situations? What kind of "rings true" as the way that this would play out? That ends up being more of the source of what the content is initially and the discussions that we have around it.

HEINEMAN: One of the things that Bioware over the years has become known for is fostering community around your games, whether that be at conferences, whether that be online through forums and efforts of community managers, or other kinds of things.

It seems that there's a lot of obvious advantages to this: greater involvement with games, a constant interest with an audience, feedback mechanisms, etc.

What are the less obvious drawbacks, if any, that you've encountered by fostering this culture? Does, for example, paying close attention to what a fan base might want ever risk compromising a team's artistic vision? Can fandom end up hurting certain things that you're trying to work toward instead of helping them get realized? What are some of the drawbacks of that kind of culture?

HUDSON: I think building a stronger connection with fans and the gaming community would only have drawbacks if you misused it. It's all about getting more data and better data, ultimately, in terms of the game-design side. Outside of that it is just about building relationships and trying to understand better the people that play our games.

In terms of whether it could have a negative effect, well, I think I see what you're getting at in terms of the question. But it ultimately comes down to what you do with the information that you get. So, for example, we do go to many conferences throughout the year, and one thing that we're doing more and more is finding new ways to actually sit down with players from our community and ask them questions and show them some of the things that we're working on that nobody else has seen yet and ask them questions about it. The reason that is really good for us is because it helps us, sort of like the way that we learn internally by having a shared discussion about values and what we're building. Bringing fans into that discussion is really valuable, because ultimately that's who we're building our games for, and it's very hard for us. We love games, we play games, and we feel like we understand what it's like to play our games, but we really can't know. So to show people things, ask them questions, and build that shared set of values and language is really valuable for us because it does help inform what we should be doing in our games.

But that's different from asking fans what our games should be and then designing exactly that. You do want the ability to

create something that surprises and delights people and delivers
something that they've never seen or thought about before. So
the benefit is being able to use the information and be inspired by
the things that they're excited about, or that they want, but then
to try to make something out of that that is able to still surprise
and delight. I love to look at fan art, for example, because I know,
for myself, the things that I've loved most in games, and movies
are the things that I've re-created in art and projects that I did.
So if I look through fan art, it's the characters, it's the scenes that
they re-create, or scenes that they wish would have happened that
they're depicting. That tells us so much about what's working and
what was memorable and what their values are. That helps us understand that if that is what is really connecting with people, then
"How can we draw that out more in our games?" The answer to
that is something that we can come up with, we can try it, and then
it ends up surprising and entertaining people. Hopefully.

HEINEMAN: One of the things that is true for a lot of series that have
iterations or sequels is that, when changes are made, some in the
existing community or fan base will respond very positively and
some will respond negatively. So, for example, changing the inven-
tory system between *Mass Effect* and *Mass Effect 2* might make
some people who consider themselves the core audience take
pause. On the other hand, a change like that can be a device that's
useful for the studio to draw in a new audience.

Ryan Milner (2013), another game studies researcher who
has written about the politics of gameplay and specifically about
questions of audience convergence, discusses how communities
get divided over these decisions and the complications that ensue
when new audiences are converging with the old.

Do you think about the politics behind these choices and the
kinds of repercussions that they might have? Are they vetted in
particular ways? Do you announce them with particular strategies
to try to best bring together old and new audiences?

HUDSON: A lot of that discussion makes the assumption that there are
certain segments of players and that those segmentations are fairly

absolute in terms of "casual players like X" and "hard-core gamers like Y." But I don't know that those assumptions are as valid as people sort of require them to be in order to follow the logic of why a game was designed in a certain way for a certain audience. I think players are more sophisticated and less easily categorized than that. I don't think it's that there are casual gamers that only play casual games in a casual way or hard-core gamers that only play the most hard-hitting, densest games for twenty hours a day. I think that if you actually talk to players about what they play and to many different kinds of people, you get something that is much more nuanced and sophisticated.

We break it down to something that's a lot more simple, which is that we're trying to make the best version of a game that we can. You don't really know how all your ambitions are going to turn out until you wrap it all up, you finish it, and then you release that game. We didn't really know what *Mass Effect* would be like until we finally finished that first game and then looking at it and listening to the feedback from people and the things that they thought were great, or the things that they thought were broken, or bad, or whatever. We would take those things and then try to figure out what the next improved, better version of the game is. Much of it was to solve issues that people had and also to bring back things that they liked. It's not so much about trying to identify a theoretical market segment that wanted something different. That hasn't really been proven to work; it doesn't seem to work in music, or games, or movies. If you have a group of people that like what you do, it doesn't seem likely that you can then do something different and bring all those people along and get a whole new audience. I don't think that actually works.

We're just trying to make the best version of the experience that we can, and part of that means that we have to have a central core of what that experience is supposed to be about. Those things would remain the same: the idea of story and character choice and progression and exploration. We're trying to make sure that the things we identify as the *Mass Effect* experience are there and constantly being improved. But we're trying to do it as informed by what our players are telling us as well, and that's also not always consistent.

So you have to take a very diverse and varied set of reactions and figure out how you can improve on what you've done before. But targeting it at a certain audience is not so much of a factor, partly because I just don't think that's a reliable approach.

HEINEMAN: What do you think the ideal relationship between the press and the other parts of the industry should be, and how have you seen that relationship change in the past decade or so?

HUDSON: It's hard to say what it should be. What us game developers are trying to do is not necessarily the same as what different kinds of journalists might want to do. Ideally, we're able to interact with the media and the press in a way that helps us to connect with our fans and helps us to reach a wider audience, thus showing people what we're doing, what our people are about, and what our games are about. That would be the ideal from my perspective, to be able to share that message with the broader gaming community.

All of gaming started out as very much a sort of a hobbyist or enthusiast kind of movement. With early PC games, it was just exciting to be able to play a game on a computer in the '80s at all. There was this excitement, and it's really interesting if you go back and read magazines from the '80s about computing and games – it's this almost hysteria about the most basic things that could happen on the screen. I remember doing my first programming, and just getting something, like being able to draw a pixel on the screen, was amazing. So it has moved from that very excited hobbyist thing into a gaming culture that, by the early 2000s, started to actually become critical of games.

I think what we have now is quite a mature economy of media where there are many different types of outlets and lots of different specialties. There are websites that are mainly trying to drive headlines and controversy, and then there are ones that are really interested in deeper analysis and sophisticated review of the artistic and technical aspects of games. There's some really in-depth sites in terms of exploring the industry, so I think it's kind of approaching where the rest of media is in the world, where it's quite diverse and there's a lot of stuff out there. From our perspective, we want to be able to just work through that and continue to broaden our relationship with people who play our games.

HEINEMAN: With the *Mass Effect* series in particular, you've received a lot of praise for high-quality downloadable content. That's obviously a relatively new phenomenon, at least the way it's been done in the last console generation. How do you, as a studio, think of downloadable content, in terms of both its place in a larger narrative as well as its function as a product to build a business?

HUDSON: First of all, it's something that allows us to tell other kinds of stories. That's one of the unique things about it for us, that we get a little bit more experimental. Another thing it allows us to do is, especially with *Mass Effect,* is really explore transmedia storytelling. There is really one story that the whole *Mass Effect* trilogy was about, yet some of the real estate of that story is in comic books, or novels, and the main characters weave into other media, and then back into the core games, and then into DLC. It is all canon, even though the games and the DLCs are interactive. One of the things that I'm really proud of in what we achieved with the *Mass Effect* trilogy is that we had a story that spanned many different kinds of media, yet it's all canon. It doesn't step on decisions that you might have made in the game. As much as possible, it doesn't contradict itself. That's the other thing that DLC allowed us to do is to tell parts of the story that weren't told in the main games. With something like a comic book, we can insert an idea into a gap that we had in the interactive story and tell the story that happened there.

In terms of a production level, one of the challenges that a game studio has is that you have very cyclical demands for staff. You might work on a game for two or three years (or more), and the first year or two requires so much time spent just figuring out what you're doing (What is the story? Where are you going? What are you going to need to build?). Then, the other thing is that you're building all the technology, the basic tools, and all the things that you're going to use once you get into production. So you're not in production for a year or more, sometimes, and in that time you have writers, you have artists, you have level designers, and, unless you have lots of other projects going on in your studio, there are periods where you have more staff than you can use. That is a very difficult problem to solve.

That's one thing that's really great about what DLC helps answer. In the period between games, you have a fan base that is interested in getting more content, and you have people who are there in the studio ready to make more content. So previously, without DLC, both of those remained a problem. It becomes kind of a conversation with our fan community about, now that they've played the game, what are they really interested to see, and what did they want to do? We can hear that and build that into what our downloadable content plan is. It becomes more of a conversation, and I think that's a really good thing that we can do more of in the future and maybe shorten the iteration on that.

It's interactive on a meta level as well, where, because it is an interactive story that you're telling, and it's an interactive experience, there is a dialogue going on between the authors of the content and the players. That can exist on higher and higher levels where you are actually designing new content, whether it's new downloadable content, or it's the next game, and you're doing that in conversation with the people that are playing it.

ELEVEN

Ian Bogost

ANXIETIES, PROCEDURES, AND GAME STUDIES

IN LATE 2012, IAN BOGOST PRESENTED A PUBLIC LECTURE AND exhibited some of his work at the University of North Florida's Museum of Contemporary Art. The museum's director, Marcelle Polednik, in a press release advertising the event, described Bogost as "one of the foremost scholars and designers of games and game theory.... [His work is used to] both reflect on and deploy the media of today to highlight timely topics and issues to a wider audience." Most who have had occasion to read Bogost's writing or listen to him speak would probably recognize that, in Polednik's description, there is a lot of truth. Bogost's work is widely read and cited both inside and outside academic circles, he is a coeditor of an influential series in game studies (MIT Press's Platform Studies series), and he has produced thought-provoking video games that model how we might think about design itself as a kind of critical practice.

Bogost often discusses the subjects he critiques – games, academia, business, and so on – with a pervasive cynicism and a seemingly entrenched skepticism. His work tends to favor clarity and directness over hyperbole and obfuscation, a characteristic that makes it hard to believe he would be comfortable accepting the kinds of accolades that Polednik's statement ascribes to him. In the interview in this chapter, for example, he is somewhat blasé about the success he has had in a relatively short period of time, suggesting that "someone would have made similar observations at that time if it hadn't been me."

Whether he would be willing to accept the moniker "foremost scholar and designer" or not, there is little question that Bogost's work has had a significant impact on the three groups of readers to which this book is itself targeted: video game players, makers, and researchers. For the first group, Bogost's most accessible work, such as *How to Do Things with Videogames,* offers a bridge of sorts between playing games and contemplating them. For the second group, Bogost's writing about and own programming within specific platforms (such as the Atari VCS) has proved to be both inspirational (see Ed Fries's *Halo 2600,* for example) and profitable (see Bogost's consulting work with PopCap Games). For the final group, Bogost's more academically oriented books, such as *Unit Operations,* offer a model of scholarship that connects various disciplinary canons in an effort to direct the work of game studies research toward more considered, cognizant, and critical endeavors.

In the interview found in this chapter, Bogost discusses the goals for and reactions to some of his past work, offers insight into some of the central concepts of his work on procedural rhetoric, provides thoughts about the future of games and of game studies, and considers the pedagogical implications of his research. Furthermore, Bogost comments on the kinds of relationships that exist between the game industry and academia, noting especially the problematic application of certain strands of game studies research in both.

—w—

HEINEMAN: You wrote in a 2009 DiGRA paper that participants in game studies needed to question their McLuhan-esque impulses to focus exclusively on the medium and, instead, pay more attention to games themselves in order to better understand what they have to tell us. Do you feel that this is the approach that you try to model in your work, especially with the Platform Studies series?

BOGOST: Yes. The Platform Studies series is definitely a part of this; maybe it's my main contribution to this effort. That work, which is not just mine, which is hopefully expanding (we have three books, and two more almost done, and more coming), was really about looking at machines and platforms, software platforms, and hardware platforms and to understand their implications. I guess another way of putting that observation is that we need even more focus on the medium and its properties, not just on its uses. So maybe we need more Kittler and less McLuhan in some way.

The Platform Studies project represents one model for really seriously looking at the construction of hardware and software platforms that are at the heart of, or at least involved in, every video game, whether we like it or not. It's not the only method, but it's one method, and I think that there's been an assumption, maybe, that it's a normative approach, that I think that this is the only way, or that this is the best way to investigate the hardware and software material to games. That's not necessarily the case at all, but it is *one* way.

It seems unlikely to me that I would have said exactly that about McLuhan, because I'm a big McLuhan fan. I think if anything, it's like we need to take that more seriously, the intervention of the object as a thing in the world, both connected to and separate from us, rather than simply as a plaything, as an instrument of the human player. That was four years ago, and it's only gotten worse since then. The DiGRA conference just took place again here in Atlanta, and it's become even more overrun by the social sciences and by something like "player theory." I think all that's great. I don't want to get rid of that. I just would like to see a greater balance of attention to players and social phenomena as well as to the construction and operation of hardware and software platforms in the games themselves.

HEINEMAN: Other than Platform Studies, then, have you seen recent work that you feel is taking a really interesting approach to the study of games?

BOGOST: One of the things that we're finally starting to see more of is just better and more games criticism. Interestingly, this is coming from the kind of new generation of scholars and writers, some of whom aren't working as scholars at all. So I think about projects like Brendan Keogh's book *Spec Ops: The Line* and his new publishing venture, Stolen Projects, which is an attempt to get people to write more seriously about individual specific games. There's another example of that kind of project called Object Books.

The interesting thing about those projects is that they believe that the problem is the avenues for publishing, which theoretically we already have in the scholarly world. You could write a book about a game, and you would get it published by one of the university presses that expressed interest and demonstrated that interest. But they're kind of establishing a culture of that practice that I would say is not missing, but is rare, is scarcer, in game studies. We spend a lot less time looking at and talking about specific titles than you would see in literary studies or in film studies or so forth. So that's one area that I think we're seeing more of that attention developing.

I also think that if you look at the intersection of game design and game studies, then it's impossible to ignore the ways in which that effort is forcing scholars to really pay attention to the stuff out of which games are made. That comes in two forms. One of them is the expansion of computer science–style approaches to games that treat games in earnest, rather than as instruments to carry out some ulterior motive (like "Oh, I've got this machine-learning project, and I guess it would be cool if I did a game thing with it" or "I'll put it in my grant, and that'll look good" or "It could be used for education or something!"), but rather to actually be doing game-technology research with an interest in changing and influencing game-design practice. The best examples of this kind of work are coming out of UC Santa Cruz, which, as it happens, also has an entire degree program devoted to this kind of focus on games technology. That would be one example.

Another is game design as an increasingly serious scholarly discipline. I think there's a long way to go, but something like NYU's establishment of a bachelor's and master's in fine arts program (and the presence there of Frank Lantz and Eric Zimmerman) that is a focused, serious effort to not necessarily formalize, but to spend all of one's time thinking about the process of improving game design. So that's another example.

When you make a game, you have to actually make something. When you talk about a game, you can effectively make anything up. I think those two forces have always been friendly with one another, but the influences haven't mixed quite so much.

HEINEMAN: As I've talked to various people who are on the industry side of games, they tend to feel that their needs are not met by academia, that most academic writing doesn't speak to them, and that most students coming to work on games for them aren't really drawing on things that they may have learned in the classroom. Do you think that the type of promising, emergent work that you're talking about addresses those problems, or are they going to persist?

BOGOST: There are two ways of looking at it. One is that they're not really a problem, that we shouldn't care about what the industry thinks they want, as they've already demonstrated that they're only interested in immediate short-term gains anyway. I'm not endorsing that. It would be one way to look at it, and it is a useful kind of dampening agent in that our job in game studies is not to service the game industry. That said, I think that we are seeing a tremendous amount of influence in the graduates of programs that are focused on game design or game development (or that are sort of "cousin" fields). We don't have any degrees that have "game" in the name, but I look at my alumni who work in the game industry, and they definitely are bringing the perspectives that they learned and experimented with as students into their work.

It's not like you have a hammer that you get (or some sort of special implement) that, when you graduate, you're given this "secret tool," and then you go and you hit things with it and produce results. These things are much squishier. Certainly, the focus in those programs is on creation. There are plenty of examples of the rise of successful, independent creators out of university programs. I think of Carnegie Mellon and USC as having had particular good fortune with this; both schools graduated students at all levels and are working nontrivial new kinds of roles within the industry. We have a PhD graduate from Georgia Tech who's working on analytics. There have been folks who went to Santa Cruz, who worked at Google, and who worked at other places in the industry, so the idea that this is sort of a problem on which no progress has been made is a myth.

What it comes down to is that the entire technology industry is fairly anti-intellectual and doesn't particularly care for the idea of the university in any way. We have this kind of tradition of conflict between technology as an industry and intellectualism. You've got the hero dropouts of Bill Gates and Steve Jobs and Mark Zuckerberg, so there's already this kind of underlying distaste for education as an institution. I think that some of that will dissipate over time, but some of it is deeply ingrained into the kind of ideology of technology.

There's certainly more that we scholars can do. I'm in a weird place because I sit on the fence between these worlds; maybe that's one of the answers. I spent a majority of my summer working with PopCap Games, and their R&D group, both seeing how they're thinking about new game-design problems and also giving them perspectives that they wouldn't have had otherwise, because there are only so many things you can think of when you do it with the same kinds of people day in and day out.

Having more of that overlap or interaction, that's more valuable than just a conversation at a conference where we exchanged e-mails or an interview or whatever, and we can't help but benefit from that. But the industry's mistaken in thinking, like so many industries and maybe culture in general these days, that what they deserve, what they are owed, is some sort of immediately fungible, predictably useful quality or utility guarantee out of the educational process.

HEINEMAN: In your work, you write different books for different audiences. Do you think that training about audience(s) is something that is lacking in game studies?

BOGOST: Well, I think this is true of any field in the academy, actually. We're terrible writers by and large, and we think we're very good and very fond of ourselves, particularly in the humanities and social sciences where things are the worst. We just engage in this obfuscationist dance, sort of a murky prose that uses jargon and name-dropping instead of insight. That's a bigger problem than game studies. The problem, and it's a particularly ironic problem, is that we are writing about video games. Like the rest of pop culture, this is kind of a low-culture popular form that's generally considered beneath everyone, yet we're still not able to get a general audience to attend to it in a meaningful way. That seems like a particular loss.

Game studies wants it both ways. It both wants to be its own thing, its own field, its own discipline, and within that discipline wants to converse with one another, but also with the world at large about games. But then it also wants to pledge fealty to these origin disciplines, whether those are film studies or sociology or computer science, and you see that in the way that the work gets carried out ("Oh, I really need this to be an ACM digital library article" or "These are the key figures in my discipline, and I need to make sure they get cited, and I need to make sure you cite them, or I'm going to be offended"). All of that sort of stuff is at odds with one another, and one of the things that we need to do is to just let go and allow our work on games to be about games. We need to stop thinking that our work is just for a tenure committee or just for a particular journal. Maybe, instead, that work should be for a different and, hopefully, a broader audience. I think that's hard to do for professional reasons that are obvious, but I think we need to do it anyway.

I am in the position of good fortune where I don't have to pay attention to what anyone wants of me, and that's let me push harder on talking to a wider variety of people with greater clarity, and it takes practice to do, and it's hard, and I'm still working on it. But I also think I've always been doing that. I've always been working on that progression, and though *Unit Operations* is intentionally scholarly, it is still clearer than most books of philosophy and theory (and I like that genre). I don't want us to give up on that kind of writing. I just don't think that's all that we should do.

We need to talk to the general public more. We need to be more public intellectuals and less private ones. Part of that is because games are misunderstood and demonized, so it becomes enjoyable and productive to talk to the world. If you just treat people as worthy of your attention, whether they're game developers, or our parents, or just anybody, those things usually pay dividends. So it is not this kind of pedagogical and moralistic approach of "Let me educate you about your ideology" or of "Here's what you don't see about your game-development practice, how wrong you are about the educational potential of games, or whatever." Instead, just talk. Just do the work. Then maybe we would earn more of that trust back.

I think there's another factor here that is maybe hidden, which is that it's actually really hard to find channels to the general public on games. I'm working on a trade nonfiction book now, which is not really about games, or at least not solely about games. Selling a book like that, a traditional kind of commercial nonfiction title in this field, is almost impossible. Publishers have all decided that this is a weird niche that nobody's interested in, and there's a kind of chicken-egg problem in disproving them, whereas if you notice, all of the nonfiction books about Internet culture, about Twitter, about whether the Internet is destroying or enhancing our lives, etc. – it's just exploded. Closing the distance between popular interest and the feasible channels for long-form nonfiction discourse to that audience, that's also something that we have to work on. It's just very hard to know how to make progress on it without simply trying some stuff out and seeing what sticks.

HEINEMAN: As an educator, how do you foster that in the students that you teach? How do you teach them to get out of that box of writing toward tenure or toward academic journals and, instead, to speak to a wider public?

BOGOST: I've started trying to get my undergraduates to write a lot more, to produce smaller-scale work that has the properties of the kind of conversational but insightful analysis that I think we need to see more of. This is an unfair characterization of my esteemed colleagues in the disciplines of composition and rhetoric, but it does seem to me that the way that something like writing and communication get valorized in an academic context focuses on a kind of formal academic writing. This is a kind of writing very few of us will end up doing, or need to do. Really, what we need to be able to do is to communicate effectively in a number of modes and to communicate with the right audiences at the right times.

One of the things that I've learned from writing more for smart general audiences (but general audiences nonetheless) is that that kind of writing is really the kind I want to see more of and I want to engender in my students. I'm having them do more of that. You could call it more "journalistic" writing. In some ways, I've folded in a lot of techniques from journalism education into my classes that would have never had it in the past, and I've asked students to write very short-form essays addressing immediately current events as a way of exercising their capacity to do this work. That's one example, but it's not the only one.

The other thing I've done more of at the graduate level is to work directly with my students more. Two of my PhD students and I wrote a book called *News Games* a few years ago, and, actually, one of them was a master's student at the time. We worked on it together, and they learned a lot about writing a smart nonfiction book that anybody can read. I don't know how I could have taught them that process in the abstract; I have no idea what it would have felt like. You have to just kind of do it. This is a tradition in the sciences and in engineering, to do collaborative research and writing with one's students, and I think that model has a lot of merit. Doing work with our students keeps us honest, but it also helps them learn in a way that they wouldn't be able to learn if you just send them off to do something in the abstract.

HEINEMAN: I've noted that you are critical of some of the "corporate-culture buzzwords" that are often affiliated with game studies (things like *gamification* or *flipped classrooms*). Why do you think these ideas catch on so readily with marketers or other people looking to find a use for them, and what kind of misunderstanding do you think that represents?

BOGOST: They are really very effective, the rhetorical terms. The reason they catch on is because they work; they are useful. Back in the early days of "serious games," there was a lot of conflict about whether this name "serious games" was good or bad. It was both: it is a stupid term, on the one hand, but it had a rhetorical function at that time and place. If you said "game" at that time, the reaction was that a "game" was not a thing that government organizations or corporations wanted to invest in. But the term *serious game* acknowledges that context and, in some cases, might allow the conversation to move forward.

Gamification has entered that door, and kind of upped the ante and said, "Not only are games welcome here, but it's easy. You don't have to worry about all the investment, all the difficulty, and everything you've been scared of with games. It's all going to be fine because we're just going to 'gamify' things – it's like a magic trick! We'll pull the curtain and then, voilà, it's all done!" Whether it works or not, whether it's even really possible, is sort of irrelevant when all you're doing is selling the service, which is my take on what gamification really is all about. The fact that we've seen it picked up in educational contexts is for the same reason: it feels easy. "I've heard about this game stuff. I don't really want to bother figuring out what it means and what it's all about, but there are these techniques, here's a set of recipes that I can follow, and so I'll just do that instead." Of course, nobody's thinking that in their head. That's the temptation.

HEINEMAN: They think they are being innovative?

BOGOST: Yeah. A lot of these changes that we've seen in education or in culture in general, they have to do with portraying and selling the facility of ideas. We are more and more focused on generating concepts rather than on carrying out those concepts. I think Kickstarter is an example of this, and then MOOCs and flipped classrooms are an example of this. It's a very complex world in which, in order to advance, especially in this new executive managerial class (which is increasingly larger), you don't necessarily have to do anything. You just have to appear to have done something innovative. Then, because it's a process of moving on rather than carrying a plan out, you do your thing and demonstrate results or impact; it doesn't even really matter if the impact is positive. Then you get your next gig, the next administrative post up the ladder, or the next faculty position, or the next executive position, or whatever. That may be a cynical way to look at things, but that logic is driving a lot of these decisions without us knowing it.

In the academy, it's partly because we have so divested the faculty of freedom, power, and, in many cases, compensation that the only way to move ahead is to get into one of these increasingly common administrative posts. Then, when you're in that world, you must demonstrate a certain kind of innovative action. In those sort of circumstances, I understand why experimenting in the classroom feels like a way to make progress on your newfound plan to advance your career. I don't think that this means that everyone's not earnest about their work, but I just think that these temptations lie in front of us, and so those interests are increasingly easy to cater to.

HEINEMAN: In *How to Do Things with Videogames,* you wrote about the inevitability of games eventually becoming domesticized and demystified, despite the attempts of people both in the game industry and in game studies to argue otherwise. In that future, what is the field of game studies? If game studies now is largely announcing, "Hey, games are ubiquitous. Games are important," once that's understood widely, what is the task of game studies at that moment?

BOGOST: If we imagine a future in which we mattered as a field, then presumably there'd be all sorts of just ordinary work to do. It's just that nobody likes to think about doing ordinary work, modest work, or work that is not as gratifying. The work of the critic, or the work of the inventor, or the work of the ethnographer: all of these things would persist; it's just that they wouldn't be so sexy. We wouldn't be able to just kind of barf anything out onto paper and get a bunch of press attention for it not because of what it says, but for what it is. If you look at other mature fields, this is sort of what happens.

You do the work of being a chemical engineer, or of being a historian, or of being whatever, and it becomes increasingly difficult to find low-hanging fruit, and so you have to dig deeper and deeper and deeper, and then can justify some of the esotericism of specialization. It makes sense that you would have to look at a very particular problem, because now you know that that problem exists and is worth investigating.

This is a really difficult reality to come to terms with when you've become accustomed to being special. If you look at areas in which this has happened or is happening at a faster rate than it's happening in game studies, you can see that anxiety. I have appointments in the Liberal Arts College and in the College of Computing at Georgia Tech, and in computing as a field, this is happening. Computing is becoming a domain that everyone does, no matter their field. Of course you use computers – they're interesting, useful tools that we can use to carry out different kinds of work. This is one of the external pressures that's exerting in the field of computing and making them less special in some way, making the principal kind of first-order research in computing more scarce, maybe even more difficult, and making more casual second-order access to computing as a discipline more desirable.

For example, we've seen a massive increase in the interest in computer science minors this year. I think that one of the reasons is "Well, I want to do this other thing, this thing that I'm really interested in. Obviously, computing might be useful as a part of that, and so I want to get some computing along with it."

So we have to come to terms with that anxiety. That's one of the first observations I would make. Then we need to take the invitation to the next stage of serious work and realize that it's no longer going to be enough to just point at things and say, "Oh, look. People who play multiplayer games are engaging in some kind of social interaction." Those sorts of first-order observations are not valueless, but they're not going to be enough anymore. They shouldn't be enough for us anymore. We should move on to great detail.

The other thing this means is that the gold rush ends, to some extent. I was very fortunate to be in the right place at the right time with the right ideas phrased in the right way, I guess, to get a lot of attention around my work. I think a lot of the things that I've said in print are obvious in some way. Someone would have made similar observations at that time if it hadn't been me. It was just an explosion of interest and a vacuum of materials, and as we have more and more of those materials already present, then it will simply be harder to find new white space in the research domain. There's still tons and tons to do. I'm not saying that the work has really ended, but it will slowly end, and we'll have to face the reality that it's going to be harder to find justifiable problems. But then new problems open.

So this question about interactions between industry and academia that you brought up earlier, one of the reasons I'm interested in that is because the question of how you do game-design research seems like one that really hasn't been tackled at all in game studies. Are there processes from other R&D field that we can draw on, other fields of design that we can learn from? Is there something truly unique about game design, or is it, in fact, more like other fields than we'd like to think? What are the dynamics of innovation as those relate to marketplace changes in the industry?

I don't know that I've read any theories of game-design research that answer these questions, let alone a dozen of them, because there are certainly a dozen possible answers. That's just one example of something off the top of my head that we can work on.

The anxiety of domestication is that of ordinariness and coming to terms with being ordinary. I think at that stage we may realize that, gosh, trying to start a new field of X studies in the late twentieth century may have been the worst possible time to try to do such a thing, and, perhaps, it's impossible for there to be X studies anymore, given the state of the academy. In light of that, we may find ourselves facing a secondary question, which is "Where does this stuff live?" There are very few, if any, real departments of game research, and so I think that fact, coupled with this domestication issue, coupled with the economic austerity in the academy (especially in North America), is going to be a challenge that we have to overcome.

HEINEMAN: In *Persuasive Games*, you suggest that "procedural rhetoric" might be understood, at least in part, as an alternative to what's been referred to as "digital rhetoric." This is scholarship that, in your view, fails to account for the centrality of computational processes in persuasion via digital media. Would you say that's a fair characterization of how you understand the relationship of "procedural rhetoric" to "digital rhetoric"?

BOGOST: I think so. I think it's fair.

HEINEMAN: So given that the term *rhetoric* itself has lots of different field-dependent canons (because rhetoric is important to composition, to literature, to communication, to political science, etc.), is there a "disciplinary home" that you think is best equipped to begin moving toward a procedural sensibility?

BOGOST: Short answer: no, there doesn't seem to be. I don't know if that's good or bad. If you look at the literature in computer science on procedural literacy, much of which I discuss in *Persuasive Games,* it goes back to the 1960s, this question of how you become literate with processes. Even in those early days of computer science, becoming literate in processes was considered not to be the same as becoming literate in programming. We have that tradition in computer science and computer science education (although I think it's fallen out of favor in computer science education), so that would be one candidate for a "disciplinary home."

Rhetoric is sort of this utility field. It's a chameleon in a lot of ways, and it is a very pragmatic field, too, that faces the reality of trying to find a place to situate individuals in groups so that they can actually get work done, rather than resigning themselves to the corners of obscurity. But rhetoricians traditionally aren't procedurally literate or aren't computationally literate. That's changing, but it's one of the reasons there was that chasm in the first place and why "digital rhetoric" rose to flourish in the traditional rhetoric and composition community, whereas a more computationally inspired version of rhetoric was harder to grasp.

I could have done a lot more to advance procedural rhetoric in the rhetoric community. It's been picked up to some extent, but I don't hang out in that world enough, and I don't evangelize it enough to those groups to have made as much of a dent as maybe I could. Otherwise, where would you try to situate a domain that is general enough that it could apply to anything? You can interpret procedural rhetoric as a way of making arguments for expressing ideas with processes and models, whether or not those processes and models are made out of computers.

You could do it with wood. It could be a design field, in other words. It doesn't necessarily even have to be related to computing or rhetoric at all. In that respect, I have a hard time feeling at home in any field, and so I pawn off this feeling of "out-of-placeness" onto my own theories and ideas. I assume that if they were animate, they would also feel ill at ease in any particular context, and it would rather be a case of flitting between them, looking for possible connections.

So maybe it's a little silly to say, but maybe with theories like this, we need to let them be postdisciplinary. We need to let them potentially connect with a lot of different disciplines, but not in a way that then returns favors back to a home base.

I think one of the things I like about rhetoric as a field is that it's deeply and earnestly committed to actually doing things, rather than just talking about them. But then at the end of the day, it is its own very large community, and it has its own language, and people go to the big conference of rhetoricians and composition-ists and so forth. Anytime you have something like that, it's just too easy to get comfortable and to think, "Well, my ideas are well known in my field, and that makes me pat myself on the back and feel like I've been gratified!" I would rather not have that result, whether it's rhetoric or computer science or design or anything, but we kind of have the concept float and resist reincorporation into a single field.

That said, I think it's way bigger than games. If I have any regrets about the procedural rhetoric stuff, it's that it's been so intimately connected to game studies just by accident by virtue of the fact that I discuss games as my primarily examples. But I think it's really much bigger. It's a much bigger concept than just that.

HEINEMAN: One of the reasons you justify talking games as pro-cedural rhetoric is because games are one of the more complex, interesting expressions of it, right?

BOGOST: Yeah. That's true. I'd say that.

HEINEMAN: If you think of rhetoric in the composition field, you're
absolutely right that there's this big community who has to cite
certain persons when they do their work and use rhetoric in a very
specific disciplinary way in their writing and so on. But to get to
the practical component, they can still say, "But these ideas are
distilled, and they are presented in an accessible way in a class
like Writing 101" (or in my field, communication studies, in public
speaking). All this writing we do in *Quarterly Journal of Speech*
and so forth, a lot of those ideas we can distill into a very practical
classroom application for students, which isn't in service of an
industry need or academic posturing; it's about teaching people
how to express themselves in a meaningful way.

BOGOST: Yeah.

HEINEMAN: So does procedural rhetoric have some kind of a
classroom analog to those other understandings of rhetoric? You
mentioned a context like a shop class, or something similar, as a
possibility. What would be the way to think about that?

BOGOST: That's a great question. I'd love to hear more answers to that
question from anyone, especially from the rhetoric community.
I'm not even sure that I'm the right person to answer that. I do
think that if I sat down and I worked up a design, or programmed a
course, or wrote a book on procedural rhetoric in the abstract and
tried to focus its specific influence, I would look at it as a series of
different materials, and I would imagine this process of constructing models in a variety of material circumstances. I think comput-
erists would have to be one of them because they are important in
the present moment and also abstract enough that you can model
almost anything with them.

   Even in writing, you are doing procedural rhetoric when you
adopt the five-paragraph essay or the inverted pyramid. You are
saying, "Here's a model. This is a model for the communication of
ideas." Let's forget about even writing. Let's just design models for
the expression of writing or look at the ways that models for the
expression of writing have been carried out. In public speech the
same is true.

So you could consider procedural rhetoric partly a kind of metadiscourse around communication. That would be one way to look at it. But I would hate for that to be the only way to look at it – in other words, that they're just rising to the next level and then talking about all of these other disciplines as kind of puppeteers. I would also imagine that the construction of things out of materials, and the way that those materials change and push back and resist, this kind of platform studies work or kind of material-history sort of thing, that would also be important.

The way that the tools and the materials that we work with influence and alter our conception of what is even possible, that sort of work I think we could do with wood. Seriously. I have a colleague who does this. He gets his building construction students together, and they make Thoreau's hut, and they do so by using traditional tools and methods, and so they experience the first reality of that construction method as it relates its expressive ends. That kind of work has almost been completely eviscerated in contemporary education. We removed vocational training of any kind. Nobody can take shop class or these sorts of things. All of that sort of stuff, that ability to recognize and work with the different materials in our world, and to understand the different ways in which they structure our perception of reality, I think that's related enough to procedural rhetoric that I can imagine justifying a series of those kinds of exercises.

The problem, of course, is that this is an almost infeasible idea. If you imagine an actual classroom environment, would you really go out and saw wood? Then, the next week, you would do public speaking in front of an audience? How would you even make it work? It feels like such a kind of pipe dream, really. I guess the question there might be, well, is that the case? Is the idea of a structured procedural rhetoric fundamentally incompatible with educational practice, or is it just a matter of using the constraints of educational practice to let it speak in more voices?

Every time I talk about this subject, I'm tempted to work on it more, but I still haven't, and I don't know what to say about that.

I'm really interested in it, and I've thought about it a lot, the idea of how would we abstract procedural rhetoric and allow it to work on a number of different materials beyond computing with this idea of the construction and evaluation of models at its heart. But I do think these practical concerns, they have to be resolved for it to work. Otherwise, you can just talk about the idea like you would read a book or something. "Hey, imagine if we could do this," and it would be kind of a joke.

HEINEMAN: I interviewed Edward Castronova as part of this project, and he suggested to me that in his experience, a background in the humanities hasn't proved particularly helpful in the understanding of games. He credits this in part to a lack of a familiarity with the formal models that informed games from their creation and design through to their being played. Do you think this criticism is fair? Does procedural rhetoric address that concern in the way that might make him see more value in the humanities?

BOGOST: I think it's a nice provocation. The humanities is obsessed with systems and processes; it just doesn't admit it. I always laugh when humanists talk about how difficult it would be to grasp the systemic behavior of computers in order to learn programming or procedural literacy, when then they go and adopt these complex, deep understandings of incredibly arbitrary theoretical systems, such as Jacques Lacan's theory of the unconscious, which are completely absurdist in their level of detail and specificity and arbitrariness compared to the way that a computer works.

So I don't know that it's not there in the humanities. I think that it's just that we don't talk about it in the same way, and maybe that's because of structuralism and poststructuralism. It's as if in the humanities, we've trained ourselves to believe that any kind of formal description of something is violent, and we distrust it. So the moment someone starts to fix anything, then the next voice he'll hear is someone saying, "Ah! I see you attempting to apply fixity to these ideas, and that is dangerous and violent, and I am going to call you out on it by using this theoretical apparatus that is my favorite tool to use!"

Enough of that kind of metadiscourse, and you become exhausted with showing people your formal models anymore, even though you're also using them. So you just kind of use them in the background and don't talk about it anymore. Then, ironically, all of these so-called liberalizing theoretical apparatuses are just as formalized as structuralism was; it's just that they do so from within the context of recognizing that, "well, of course, my model is completely arbitrary, and you can choose your own."

If we harnessed that, or at least if we acknowledged it, then maybe we could reintroduce some of the material structures of games and computation into the conversation. That's one of the reasons I've had such a hard time selling this idea of platform studies or procedural rhetoric in the humanities, where there's a distrust of material analysis and a temptation to call it determinism at the very first breath.

So I think in some ways, I agree with Ed, but for different reasons. It's not because of something intrinsic to the practice of humanistic research. It's rather because of the way that those traditions have established their own professionalization and their own conversations, and their resistances, and also their neuroses about colonization, and dismantling, and things that are real.

The answer is maybe just to somehow stop worrying about all that stuff and to instead let in the voices and the tools that seem useful and to be aware that at some point, they're all going to have their limits. We should also discuss their limits, but let's not discuss their limits with the very first sentence out of our mouth; let's see what they're good for. It requires an opening up of method and a trust that no one is trying to dupe anyone else.

I think the irony, though, is that Ed's an economist, and economists get to just kind of piss everybody off. That's kind of what economists do. But within the social sciences, this is just as bad, if not worse. I don't know what we call economics these days, but sometimes it's situated somewhere in between the sciences, the social sciences, and the humanities, and they make these claims toward being scientific, but, of course, they aren't, really. Then they destroy the global economy in the process, and everyone's like, "Well, we'll just pretend that didn't happen."

So the idea that the economics have it right seems to be deeply wrong to me. But at the same time, I think the truth in that observation is that when we build these tools that we can use, we have to take them more seriously than we have been. We are paying the price now in the humanities for more than a half century of free-for-all. It's almost like the real estate bubble of theory, and now we're living in the aftermath of it bursting.

Conclusion

IN THE INTRODUCTORY CHAPTER OF THIS BOOK, IT WAS suggested that the preceding interviews could be understood as an earnest attempt to instigate, suggest, and at times model a kind of cross-community dialogue between those who play games, those who make games, and those who research them. For that reason, the individuals who provided interviews were selected for their ability to speak in ways that might traverse different game-related communities and for their enthusiasm in fostering others to do the same. It was also suggested at the outset that, like the points of overlap found in those communities, there were substantial connections between the ideas explored in each section of the book (history, economy, and culture) that would emerge through a processes of accumulation and juxtaposition. To the extent that the previous chapters have succeeded in arguing for building those relationships and highlighting those connections, any kind of concluding chapter that attempts to summarize the interviews risks becoming extraneous and redundant. Instead, and as a way of concluding, this chapter offers some thoughts about what shared concerns these various communities face and suggests some additional provocations that push the arguments offered by the proceeding chapters toward a particular telos.

Though the primary goals of these three groups might be different (economic viability, identity and community, analysis and understanding, and so on), the content addressed in the preceding chapters suggests several overlapping areas of shared concern about the current status of video games and all that they touch.

SHARED PROBLEM 1: RESPECTABILITY

Video games are relatively unique among other contemporary media forms in that they had a prolonged period of time, early in their existence, where they were primarily marketed to male children and young male teens. As such, there was a solid decade or more of advertisements that emphasized fuzzy mascots, independence from parents and teachers, and all the trappings of male pubescence. Though games began to gain more traction with adults and the larger public toward the end of the twentieth and start of the twenty-first centuries, this image persisted then and to a large extent still persists today for a number of reasons, some of which can be controlled and some of which cannot.

Video games are often thought of as something that "wastes time" or "takes away" from an engagement with more pressing and more important social, political, or cultural issues. They are often blamed for the decline of "real men" in the popular press (Hingston, 2012). They are seen as youthful pursuits and as "nonserious" media (unlike film and literature). Kirkpatrick has suggested that "as computer gaming culture has grown in confidence and become more mainstream, it has still not managed to secure complete confidence in its own legitimacy as a 'pastime' with intrinsic value. . . . [T]here is still a question mark over the activity" (*Computer Games*, 186–187).

There are several ways to think about the issue of respectability. In the industry this problem often haunts people at the level of their career choice (Why did you go into video games if you are so smart and talented? Do you just want to play games all day?), at their level of professional and popular recognition (How many game writers, directors, voice actors, composers, and other artists are known to the public compared to those in film and television?), and at the level of salary compared to other tech and entertainment fields. All of this criticism comes despite the industry being very competitive financially and having a very large cultural impact globally.

In gamer culture respectability is wrapped up with all the trappings of the "nerd" and "geek "designation – there is still a strong sense that interest in video games (especially beyond the newest *Madden* or *Call of Duty* titles) signals unattractiveness, obsessiveness, poor hygiene, and social awkwardness. Even though people like Steve Jobs and Bill Gates are held up as "nerds par excellence," the number-one comedy in the United States (*The Big Bang Theory*) succeeds in getting its yuks by making fun of people who can explain the best strategies for reaching a level cap quickly in the newest Blizzard game. In academia the issue of respectability lingers in that many game studies scholars have to push against disciplinary norms and expectations for research, teaching, and publishing in order to study games in an interesting way.

SHARED PROBLEM 2: DIFFERENCE

The problem in the industry regarding a lack of diversity and difference is one that is easily summarized with some basic statistics, such as those offered in *Gamasutra*'s 2014 survey of more than 4,000 game developers. It reported that women make up only 5 percent of all programmers and engineers and 20 percent of management positions and earn, on average, about 15–20 percent less than men in these jobs. Previous studies have also shown that racial and ethnic minorities make up 10 percent or less of the total American game industry (see the 2005 IGDA report "Game Developer Demographics").

Like many other tech fields, the game industry has been and continues to be predominantly male and, in the United States and Europe, predominantly white. There is a bit of a vicious cycle here: (1) games were long marketed to primarily boys; (2) an interest in games as a career often directs people to mostly STEM fields, which are, again, historically and predominantly male; and then (3) in the industry the people who do the hiring and who define the culture are largely white and male. That said, there does seem to be an increased awareness of this among prominent figures in the industry, including some of those interviewed for this book. There is a new interest in bringing in fresh perspectives to game creation, changing the culture around games and the industry to be more inclusive, and reaching new audiences of consumers.

There is a recognition across many of the interviews in this book that games need to be more diverse, not only in terms of appealing to a wider demographic, but also in accounting for a wider variety of play styles and interests. For example, Casey Hudson's comments in chapter 10 about the inanity of the "casual versus hard-core" debate among gamers are indicative of how a lot of those in the game industry see the self-imposed divisions that players create. And while there is a long-festering culture of online competitive gaming mired in anonymous sexist and racist epitaphs delivered via headsets (Gray, 2012), and though harassment of women at gaming conventions and competitions persists (Amini, 2013), there is a growing number of groups created by gamers designed to address these problems. Websites such as GayGamer.net and BlacksinGaming.org address issues of cultural diversity, as do panels and meetings for underrepresented interest groups at conferences and conventions (for example, PAX and E3) that are tailored to the culture more broadly.

It is worth mentioning that the demographic makeup of those interviewed for, cited in, and discussed in this book is also closely aligned with gaming's problem with diversity both historically and today. Put simply, there was a very small percentage of women or minorities that are closely associated with gaming's historical development and economic ascendancy to consider for interviews, and many of those who are best known (such as Roberta Williams or Carol Shaw) rarely grant them or cannot be easily reached. This concern extends to the references following this chapter as well, where women and minority researchers, writers, and designers are underrepresented among those who have published video game–related materials.

This problem extends to academia, where although questions of race, gender, and other categories of difference have been generally well addressed in critical scholarship (especially that of the past few years), there is not a lot of racial and gender diversity in the actual field of game studies. Where schools have game-related majors, enrollment is predominantly male. When I first offered the seminar course I alluded to in the introduction, the enrollment was entirely male. When one sits on panels dedicated to games at academic conferences or reads the lists of keynote speaker at places such as Digital Games Research Association conferences, the speakers are, again, predominantly male and predominantly white. For game studies as a field to find increased relevance, these numbers and the logics that foster them need to shift.

SHARED PROBLEM 3: STAGNATION

While the video game industry is generally thought of as one that moves quickly to embrace new technological possibilities, there is a growing sense across communities that the industry is witnessing a creeping stagnation. It was a theme that came up regularly in the interviews in the preceding chapters and one that can be located in everything from recurring design choices in the industry to narrowing interests among players to redundant research in academia.

Stagnation has occurred before in the industry. It was at least one of the causes for the historic 1983 crash, which witnessed a lethargic transition between console generations (DeMaria and Wilson 105). Stagnation has been blamed for the reliance on a few select series as "tent poles" for studios and publishers; stagnation has also been blamed for the slow sales of many games that attempt something novel. While there might be an ongoing creative "boom" among independent game development, it is one that, according to some observers, seems ready to slow down or come to an end as an increasingly smaller percentage of small studios launch products that sustain future development (Fearon, 2014; Vogel, 2014).

PROVOCATIONS TOWARD SOLUTIONS

This book has suggested that these shared problems might be productively addressed through more conversation and collaboration across communities interested in games, bringing people with a variety of perspectives and expertise together. In closing, there are some specific strategies and provocations that are worth highlighting.

For those who research games, the provocation is one that Bogost, Lowood, and Castronova all touched on: an imperative to adapt to new audiences or risk obsolescence. That imperative is not meant to suggest that there is no value in doing academic research primarily for academic audiences or that processes of peer review, journal publishing, and attending scholarly conference meetings have no value for either understanding a subject or conveying that understanding to students who can parse the theories or methods that illuminates it. Rather, it is an imperative to do additional publishing, speaking, and research that can be productively considered by nonacademic audiences who are closely engaged with the same subject matter.

The "game" of finding success in academia is often one of "proper" name-dropping, careful sentence gymnastics, IRB-friendly research projects, grant-worthy proposals, and the corresponding acknowledgment of established academic prestige. For example, in "critical game studies," much of the game-based research is, by design, derivative of that found in other "critical" research fields, such as literary studies, rhetorical studies, cultural studies, media studies, and the like. There are politics at play in choosing these various models and writing for specific audiences. Key theorists from appropriate disciplines are regularly invoked; there are the requisite French postmodernists, the Frankfurt-school thinkers, the Canadian media ecologists, and so on. At the current rate, before long Marx, Foucault, Derrida, Habermas, Baudrillard, Adorno, Lacan, and McLuhan will have all had a romp with *Super Mario Bros., Ico, Portal,* and *World of Warcraft.*

To the extent that these theorists wrote about the function of popular culture, about the work of discourse, about the intervention of media into more areas of public and private life, or about the grand dilemmas of the late twentieth century makes them all obvious and sometimes useful figures. But they are also especially comfortable and politically prudent. In most cases, though, applying their ideas to the "critical analysis" of games likely does more to confuse their writing than it does to tell us something interesting about video games. More important, many of them are difficult for anyone without a graduate-level education in the humanities to begin to understand with any confidence or competence. This kind of writing and thinking about games cannot, *by itself,* be the future of game studies. If it is, game studies will miss a tremendous opportunity to provoke changes in how games are designed, marketed, played, taught, preserved, reviewed, or otherwise considered by audiences outside of a very select and only marginally influential audience. If scholars believe that an important reason to study a popular medium like video games is to understand their power to shape culture, they must find more ways to translate their research to those audiences who might be able to respond to it as they engage games. One way to do that is to address underexplored topics as well as underrepresented populations of gamers and game makers and to turn scholarly attention to subjects that are of interest to those outside of academic venues.

For those who make games, the provocation is slightly different: actively, bravely experiment with new models of game development. Across the interviews in this book with Fries, Santiago, Hudson, Jarvis, and others, one unifying theme was that innovation is born through systemic changes to studio development practices. They spoke of how new structures provided freedom to explore concepts and ideas that were novel to game design, how incorporating external voices into the development process functioned to shape more engaging titles, and how some of the lessons learned in contexts where those outside the industry think about games, such as game online communities and academia, proved to be productive in creating games that found critical and commercial success. While financial stability in media entertainment industries might be modeled on iteration or in technology industries on advancement, the largest cultural impact that video games can have comes through the introduction of creativity and novelty.

Such creativity and novelty are fostered not merely by refiguring existing models of game production, but specifically by incorporating new types of expertise into those processes. This expertise is represented primarily by individuals who think about games but do not (currently) make them. They are the most engaged and vocal members of online game communities, they are game journalists, they are individuals who do not match with the current demographic makeup of most development studios, they are scientists and artists whose own innovative work is adapted to game production, and they are researchers and theorists who contemplate the medium's historical significance and popular appeal. Directly incorporating these outside voices into the work of game production is a risky proposition; it can create uncomfortable discussions, hurt feelings, misunderstandings, territorialism, damaging public relations, and awkward transitions. It can be economically risky. But if the industry is to continue to move the medium of games toward the kind of cultural significance that comes from an ability to create social change and stimulate new ways of thinking, it will need to find ways to innovate that extend simply beyond offering new IPs.

The final provocation is for the largest community, those who play games. Put simply, it is this: invite criticism of your practices. Like any form of entertainment, games offer a certain escape from the tedium of life, and thus most people tend not to think much about the kinds of design considerations, cultural contexts, or artistic expressions found in the games they enjoy. If and when they do evaluate games, it is often from the perspective of a review. The provocation is to push those baseline forms of criticism further, to seek out critical perspectives that are not concerned with reading the same criteria, to consider more kinds of games from these perspectives, and to then turn that same advanced analytical thinking toward those places where others come together to discuss or enjoy games, where "game culture" emerges.

The interviews with Dillion, Grant, Melissinos, and Hudson (among others) all offer a kind of vision about what possibilities might exist for a more engaged, self-reflexive, and critical video game culture. Communities of gamers might become more involved in working with and within broader nongaming communities, they may become more aware of marginalizing discourses within their own communities, they may reimagine the relationships between game players and game makers, and they may work to become ambassadors for the social and cultural value of games themselves. When these processes occur, the kinds of cross-community discussions that this book brings together will happen organically, by necessity, with regularity, and the shared problems among those invested in the medium's future can be meaningfully addressed.

Notes

PREFACE

1. MobyGames, a database of games released from 1971 to the present, currently (as of late 2013) lists about 80,000 titles but excludes many foreign, arcade, and independent games released during that period. By comparison, an IMDb search of "released feature films" from that same period nets about 166,000 results.

INTRODUCTION

1. See, for example, the multipart "Game Theory" that ran in December 2012's *New York Times'* art blog and addressed issues such as gender, economics, violence, and more in the game industry.

2. From a modern perspective of selling products and enhancing the bottom line, there is some reckless abandon on display from tech-company representatives. On the other hand, there is also sincerity present here that should provoke greater skepticism about positions that are now taken for granted.

3. This argument persists, of course, in both formal modes (such as games criticism or award shows) and informal modes (such as debate among players). In both forms, we hear variations on statements like "*Call of Duty 4* is not art, but *Unfinished Swan* is," "*Super Mario Galaxy* is not art, but *Braid* is," "*Uncharted* is not art, but *Journey* is," and so on.

4. This is especially true for women in these spaces. See, for example, the essays "The Creepy Side of E3," by Kotaku contributor Tina Amini following her experiences at E3 2013, or "So What If I'm a Woman? Let Me Play the Damn Game," by Kotaku contributor Katie Williams following her experiences at E3 2012.

GAMES AND HISTORY

1. Kirkpatrick's *Computer Games and the Social Imaginary* (2013) has an excellent treatment of the contemporary significance of video games emerging in the postwar era.

2. It may, in fact, be helpful to think about games as the archetypical medium for illustrating a larger temporal shift in how, when, and why pop culture artifacts become designated "classic," "retro," "old-school," and so on. Part of this is due to the industry's own marketing of new technologies in terms that are meant to distinguish them from older systems.

3. The selection and emulation of the titles in these collections are often the subject of criticism in online retrogaming communities (Heineman, "Public Memory").

1. NOLAN BUSHNELL

1. For example, in an NPR interview from 2007, Bushnell remarks that after the golden age of the arcade, "the games evolved, the games morphed, games got very complex and lost a lot of the casual game play. I'm glad to see the casual game play coming back now on the Internet, games that aren't violent, that aren't complex that you can sit down and you can have some fun" (Hansen).

2. For an elaboration of this argument, see Neil Postman's *Amusing Ourselves to Death: Public Discourse in the Age of Show Business* (1985).

GAMES AND ECONOMY

1. This section of the book is composed of interviews with people with expertise in the North American game industry primarily, and the contours provided here are largely representative of that particular geographic segment of what is an increasingly global enterprise.

2. These categories are not always mutually exclusive, of course, as many publishers also have development studios that are closely aligned (for example, the same employees work to make the game and to sell it). As a general rule, the smaller a publisher is, the more closely affiliated with the developer(s) they are.

3. For some earlier book-length treatments of e-sports, Sirlin (2006) and Kane (2009) provide well-researched resources.

6. KELLEE SANTIAGO

1. The documentary *Indie Game: The Movie* does an excellent job of capturing the atmosphere in and around indie games

by following the development of three critically acclaimed independent titles: *Braid, Super Meat Boy,* and *Fez.*

2. For example, her 2010 TED talk prompted the Roger Ebert article mentioned in chapter 2.

3. One notable exception is Martin and Deuze's 2009 essay in *Games and Culture,* which is largely critical of the ways in which practices and conventions of major studio production have been taken up by independent developers.

GAMES AND CULTURE

1. There are multiple books and essays that address this topic already, of course. Notable examples would include the October 2006 volume of *Games and Culture,* devoted to *World or Warcraft* and its players; Adrienne Shaw's essay "What Is Video Game Culture? Cultural Studies and Game Studies" (2010), which takes a look at gamer culture through the lens of cultural theory; Steven Downing's case study on piracy in "Retro Gaming Subculture and the Social Construction of a Piracy Ethic" (2011); or the recent mass-market paperback by Anna Anthropy, *Rise of the Videogame Zinesters: How Freaks, Normals, Amateurs, Artists, Dreamers, Drop-outs, Queers, Housewives, and People Like You Are Taking Back an Art Form* (2012).

2. For example, Critical Distance, a website that works "to bring together and highlight the most interesting, provocative and robust writing, video and discussion on games from across the web," chose to highlight black authors covering a variety of topics in February 2014 to highlight their presence in games criticism.

Works Cited

Aarseth, Espen. "Game History: A Special Issue." *Game Studies* 13.2 (2013): n. pag. *GameStudies.org*, Dec 2013. Web.

Alexander, Leigh. "Grunge, Grrrls and Video Games: Turning the Dial for a More Meaningful Culture." *Gamasutra*. N.p., 13 Aug. 2013. Web.

———. "Taking on the Challenges of Being a Mom in Game Development." *Gamasutra*. N.p., 23 Jan. 2014. Web.

Allen, Samantha. "An Open Letter to Games Media." *ReAction*. N.p., 19 June 2013. Web. 16 Sept. 2013.

Amano, Yoshitaka. *The Sky: The Art of "Final Fantasy."* Milwaukee, OR: Dark Horse Books, 2013. Print.

Amini, Tina. "The Creepy Side of E3." *Kotaku*. N.p., 19 June 2013. Web. 16 Sept. 2013.

Anthropy, Anna. *Rise of the Videogame Zinesters: How Freaks, Normals, Amateurs, Artists, Dreamers, Drop-outs, Queers, Housewives, and People Like You Are Taking Back an Art Form*. New York: Seven Stories Press, 2012. Print.

"The Authoritative Video Game Database – Reviews and Information – MobyGames." *The Authoritative Video Game Database – Reviews and Information – MobyGames*. N.p., n.d. Web. 16 Sept. 2013.

Barwick, Joanna, James Dearnley, and Adrienne Muir. "Playing Games with Cultural Heritage: A Comparative Case Study Analysis of the Current Status of Digital Game Preservation." *Games and Culture* 6.4 (2011): 373–390. Print.

Baughman, Susan S., and Patricia D. Clagett, eds. *Video Games and Human Development: A Research Agenda for the 80's: Papers and Proceedings of a Symposium Held at the Harvard Graduate School of Education, Cambridge, Massachusetts, May 22–24, 1983*. Cambridge, MA: Monroe C. Gutman Library, Harvard Graduate School of Education, 1983. Print.

Bednarz, Anne. "Q&A: Chris Melissinos on Curating Smithsonian's *The Art of Video Games*." *Network World*. N.p., 15 Mar. 2012. Web. 16 Sept. 2013.

Benjamin, Walter, and Rolf Tiedemann. *The Arcades Project*. Cambridge, MA: Belknap, 1999. Print.

Bogost, Ian. *How to Do Things with Videogames*. Minneapolis: University of Minnesota, 2011. Print.

———. *Unit Operations: An Approach to Videogame Criticism*. Cambridge, MA: MIT Press, 2006. Print.

———. "You Played That? Game Studies Meets Game Criticism." *Ian Bo-*

gost – *Video Game Theory, Criticism, Design,* 5 Sept. 2009. Web. 16 Sept. 2013.

Burden, Michael, and Sean Gouglas. "The Algorithmic Experience: Portal as Art." *Game Studies* 12.2 (2012): n. pag. *GameStudies.org,* Dec. 2012. Web. 16 Sept. 2013.

Burnham, Van. *Supercade: A Visual History of the Videogame Age, 1971–1984.* Cambridge, MA: MIT Press, 2001. Print.

Campbell, Colin. "Magnavox Odyssey Inventor Baer Is Certain of His Own Legacy | Polygon." Polygon. N.p., 13 July 2013. Web. 16 Sept. 2013.

Capcom. *Mega Man: Official Complete Works.* Richmond Hill, ON: UDON Entertainment, 2009. Print.

Casablanca. Dir. Michael Curtiz. Warner Brothers, 1942. Film.

Castronova, Edward. *Exodus to the Virtual World: How Online Fun Is Changing Reality.* New York: Palgrave Macmillan, 2007. Print.

———. "On Virtual Economies." *Game Studies* 3.2 (2003): n. pag. *GameStudies. org.* Web.

———. *Synthetic Worlds: The Business and Culture of Online Games.* Chicago: University of Chicago, 2005. Print.

Child's Play Charity. *Child's Play Charity Press Kit.* N.p., n.d. Web. 16 Sept. 2013.

Chou, Kevin. "Why Tablets Are the Future of Gaming." *Fortune,* 27 Nov. 2012. Web. 16 Sept. 2013.

Citizen Kane. Dir. Orson Welles. RKO, 1941. Film.

City of Mesquite v. Aladdin's Castle, Inc. 455 U.S. 283 (1982). *Justia.* http://supreme .justia.com/cases/federal/us/455/283/.

Cohen, Scott. *Zap! The Rise and Fall of Atari.* New York: McGraw-Hill, 1984. Print.

Consalvo, Mia. *Cheating: Gaining Advantage in Videogames.* Cambridge, MA: MIT Press, 2007. Print.

Cousins, Ben. "When the Consoles Die, What Comes Next?" Presentation at the Game Developers Conference, San Francisco, 5–12 Mar. 2012. Web version at http://www.slideshare.net/bcousins /when-the-consoles-die-what-comes -next.

Deen, Philip D. "Interactivity, Inhabitation and Pragmatist Aesthetics." *Game Studies* 11.2 (2011): n. pag. *GameStudies. org,* May 2012. Web. 16 Sept. 2013.

DeMaria, Rusel, and Johnny L. Wilson. *High Score! The Illustrated History of Electronic Games.* Berkeley, CA: McGraw-Hill/Osborne, 2002. Print.

"DiGRA Conference 2013: DeFragging Game Studies." *DiGRA Conference, 2013.* N.p., 2013. Web. 16 Sept. 2013.

Downing, Steven. "Retro Gaming Subculture and the Social Construction of a Piracy Ethic." *International Journal of Cybercrime* 5.1 (2011): 750–772. Print.

Dyer-Witheford, Nick, and Greig de Peuter. *Games of Empire: Global Capitalism and Video Games.* Minneapolis: University of Minnesota Press, 2009. Print.

Ebert, Roger. "Video Games Can Never Be Art." *Roger Ebert's Journal.* N.p., 16 Apr. 2011. Web. 16 Sept. 2013.

Fearon, Robert. "Popping the Indie Bubble." *Gamasutra,* 26 May 2014. Web.

Gallagher, Rob. "No Sex Please, We Are Finite State Machines: On the Melancholy Sexlessness of the Video Game." *Games and Culture* 7.6 (2012): 399–418. Print.

"Game Developer Demographics: An Exploration of Workforce Diversity." Rep. N.p., International Game Developers Association (IGDA), 2005. Web.

"Game Theory – *ArtsBeat* Blog – NYTimes. com." *New York Times,* Dec. 2012. Web. 16 Sept. 2013.

Gaudiosi, John. "The 10 Most Powerful Women in Gaming." *Fortune,* 24 Oct. 2013. Web.

Gillespie, Greg, and Darren Crouse. "There and Back Again: Nostalgia, Art, and Ideology in Old-School Dungeons and Dragons." *Games and Culture* 7.6 (2012): 441–470. Print.

Goldberg, Marty "Retro Rogue." "Video Game Misconceptions: The Magnavox Odyssey Is Analog and Not Digital." *Classic Gaming.* N.p., 17 Aug. 2007. Web. 16 Sept. 2013.

Goombs, Michael, et al. *The Legend of Zelda: Hyrule Historia.* Milwaukee, OR: Dark Horse Books, 2013. Print.

Grant, Chris. "This Is a Goodbye Post." Joystiq. N.p., 27 Dec. 2011. Web. 16 Sept. 2013.

Gray, Kisjonna L. "Deviant Bodies, Stigmatized Identities, and Racist Acts: Examining the Experiences of African-American Gamers in Xbox Live." *New Review of Hypermedia and Multimedia* 18.4 (2012): 261–276. Print.

Hansen, Liane, and Nolan Bushnell. "*Pong:* The Ping Heard 'Round the World." Interview. *NPR.org.* N.p., 7 Dec. 2007. Web. 16 Sept. 2013. http://www.npr.org/templates/story/story.php?storyId=16816188.

Harris, Blake. *Console Wars: Sega, Nintendo, and the Battle That Defined a Generation.* New York: IT Books, 2014. Print.

Heineman, David S. "Public Memory and Gamer Identity: Retrogaming as Nostalgia." *Journal of Games Criticism* 1.1 (2014): n. pag. Web. 8 Aug. 2013.

———. "Review: *Journey* (PSN) | Yard Sale Gaming." *Yard Sale Gaming.* N.p., 9 Mar. 2012. Web. 16 Sept. 2013.

Helgeson, Matt. "The Changing Definition of 'Gamer.'" *Game Informer,* 20 Feb. 2014. Web.

Hingston, Sandy. "The Sorry Lives and Confusing Times of Today's Young Men." *Philadelphia Magazine,* 20 Feb. 2012. Web.

Holkins, Jerry. "Child's Play and *Retake Mass Effect.*" *Penny Arcade.* N.p., 22 Mar. 2012. Web. 16 Sept. 2013.

"How They Got Game." *How They Got Game.* Ed. Henry Lowood, Stanford University, 8 Aug. 2014. Web.

Icons. G4. 1 May 2001. Television.

Indie Game: The Movie. Dir. Lisanne Pajot and James Swirsky. Gowdy Manor Productions, 2012. Film.

James, E. L. *Fifty Shades of Grey.* New York: Vintage, 2012. Print.

Jan, Matej. "Congratulations, Your First Indie Game Is a Flop." *Gamasutra.* N.p., 27 June 2012. Web.

Jarvis, Eugene. "Intelligent Design or Artificial Stupidity: The Evolution of Video Game Design." DePaul University, Chicago, 6 Jan. 2008. Lecture.

Jin, Dal Yong. *Korea's Online Gaming Empire.* Cambridge: MIT Press, 2010. Print.

Kalata, Kurt, ed. *Hardcoregaming101.net Presents: The Guide to Classic Graphic Adventures.* Charleston, SC: Createspace Independent Publishing Platform, 2011. Print.

Kane, Michael. *Game Boys: Triumph, Heartbreak, and the Quest for Cash in the Battleground of Competitive Videogaming.* New York: Penguin Group, 2009. Web.

Kent, Steve. *The First Quarter: A 25-Year History of Video Games.* Bothell, WA: BWD Press, 2000. Print.

———. *The Ultimate History of Video Games, from "Pong" to "Pokémon" and Beyond: The Story behind the Craze That Touched Our Lives and Changed the World.* Roseville, CA: Prima, 2001. Print.

Keogh, Brendan. *Killing Is Harmless: A Critical Reading of "Spec Ops: The Line."* N.p.: Stolen Projects, n.d. Kindle ed.

Kerr, Peter. "Issue and Debate: Should Video Games Be Restricted by Law?" *New York Times*, 3 June 1982, C1. Print.

Kirkland, E. "Discursively Constructing the Art of *Silent Hill*." *Games and Culture* 5.3 (2010): 314–328. Print.

Kirkpatrick, G. *Computer Games and the Social Imaginary.* Cambridge: Polity Press, 2013. Print.

———. "Controller, Hand, Screen: Aesthetic Form in the Computer Game." *Games and Culture* 4.2 (2009): 127–143. Print.

Kushner, David. *Masters of Doom: How Two Guys Created an Empire and Transformed Pop Culture.* New York: Random House, 2003. Print.

Lessard, Jonathan. "*Adventure* before Adventure Games: A New Look at Crowther and Woods's Seminal Program." *Games and Culture* 8.3 (2013): 119–135. Print.

Lyons, Daniel. "Why Behavioral Economists Love Online Games." *Newsweek*, 18 Mar. 2010. Web.

Malone, Krista-Lee. "Dragon Kill Points: The Economics of Power Gamers." *Games and Culture* 4.3 (2009): 296–316. Print.

Martin, Chase Bowen, and Mark Deuze. "The Independent Production of Culture: A Digital Games Case Study." *Games and Culture* 4.3 (2009): 276–295. Print.

McDonough, Jerome P., et al. *Preserving Virtual Worlds Final Report.* Rep. N.p., 2010. Web. 16 Sept. 2013.

Mechner, Jordan. *The Making of "Karateka": Journals, 1982–1985.* ICG Testing, 2012. E-book.

———. *The Making of "Prince of Persia": Journals, 1985–1993.* ICG Testing, 2012. E-book.

Melissinos, Chris, and Patrick O'Rourke. *The Art of Video Games: From "Pac-Man" to "Mass Effect."* New York: Welcome, 2013. Print.

Milner, Ryan N. "Contested Convergence and the Politics of Play on GameTrailers.com." *Games and Culture* 8.1 (2003): 3–25. Print.

Montfort, Nick, and Ian Bogost. *Racing the Beam: The Atari Video Computer System.* Cambridge, MA: MIT Press, 2009. Print.

Moriarty, Tom. "Uncensored Videogames: Are Adults Ruining It for the Rest of Us?" *Videogaming and Computergaming Illustrated* (Oct. 1983): 18–20, 61. Print.

Murphy, David. "Hacking Public Memory: Understanding the Multiple Arcade Machine Emulator." *Games and Culture* 8.1 (2013): 43–53. Print.

Nintendo of America, Inc. v. Magnavox Co. http://www.leagle.com/decision/1987 1553659FSupp894_11391. United States District Court, S.D. New York, 21 May 1987. Print.

"The Oatmeal." *The Oatmeal: Comics, Quizzes, and Stories.* N.p., n.d. Web. 16 Sept. 2013.

O'Donnell, Casey. "The Nintendo Entertainment System and the 10NES Chip: Carving the Video Game Industry in Silicon." *Games and Culture* 6.1 (2011): 83–100. Print.

O'Malley, Harris. "Nerds and Male Privilege." *Kotaku.* 16 Dec 2011. Web.

Patents | Game Politics. N.p., n.d. Web. 16 Sept. 2013.

Pétronille, Marc, and William Audureau. *The History of "Sonic the Hedgehog."* Thornhill, ON: UDON Entertainment, 2013. Print.

Planes, Trains, and Automobiles. Dir. John Hughes. Paramount Pictures, 1987. Film.

Postman, Neil. *Amusing Ourselves to Death: Public Discourse in the Age of Show Business.* New York: Viking, 1985. Print.

Retro Gamer, 2004–present.

Sarkar, Samit. "Tackling Sexism in Gaming, 140 Characters at a Time." Polygon. 28 Nov. 2012. Web.

Sarkeesian, Anita. "The Mirror" (participant and presentation, TEDxWomen Conference, San Francisco, 1 Dec. 2012). Web version at http://tedxwomen.org /speakers/anita-sarkeesian-2/.

———. "Tropes vs. Women in Video Games by Anita Sarkeesian – Kickstarter." Kickstarter. N.p. 16 June 2012. Web.

Schulzke, Marcus. "Moral Decision Making in Fallout." *Game Studies* 9.2 (2009): n. pag. *GameStudies.org.* Web. 16 Sept. 2013.

Schut, Kevin. "Strategic Simulations and Our Past: The Bias of Computer Games in the Presentation of History." *Games and Culture* 2.3 (2007): 213–235. Print.

Shaw, Adrienne. "What Is Video Game Culture? Cultural Studies and Game Studies." *Games and Culture* 4.3 (2010): 228–253. Print.

Sirlin, David. *Playing to Win: Becoming the Champion.* Philadelphia: Xlibris, 2006. Print.

Smith, Jonas Helde. "The Games Economists Play: Implications of Economic Game Theory for the Study of Computer Games." *Game Studies* 6.1 (2006): n. pag. *GameStudies.org,* Dec. 2006. Web.

Steinkuehler, Constance. "The Mangle of Play." *Games and Culture* 1.3 (2006): 199–213. Print.

Stewart, Zolani. "This Week in Videogame Blogging: February 25th." *Critical Distance,* 25 Feb. 2014. Web.

Taylor, T. L. *Raising the Stakes: E-Sports and the Professionalization of Computer Gaming.* Cambridge: MIT Press, 2012. Print.

"TEDxUSC – Kellee Santiago – 3/23/09." Online video clip. *YouTube.* YouTube, 17 Aug. 2009. Web. 16 Sept. 2013.

"Top 100 Games Ever." *Electronic Gaming Monthly* (Nov. 1997): 100–160. Print.

Transitions: "Gamasutra" Salary Survey, 2014. Rep. *Gamasutra.* N.p., 2014. Web.

2013 Sales, Demographic and Usage Data Essential Facts about the Computer and Video Game Industry. Rep. N.p.: Entertainment Software Association, 2013. Print.

"UNF – Media Relations – Project Atrium Debuts Button-Pushing Videogame." *UNF – Media Relations – Project Atrium Debuts Button-Pushing Videogame.* Ed. Carl Holman. University of North Florida, 18 Oct. 2012. Web. 16 Sept. 2013.

Veerapen, Maeva. "Where Do Virtual Worlds Come From? A Genealogy of *Second Life.*" *Games and Culture* 8.2 (2013): 98–116. Print.

Vogel, Jeff. "The Indie Bubble Is Popping." *Bottom Feeder,* 21 May 2014. Web.

Williams, Katie. "So What If I'm a Woman? Let Me Play the Damn Game." Kotaku. N.p., 18 June 2012. Web. 16 Sept. 2013.

Zagal, J. P., C. Fernandez-Vara, and M. Mateas. "Rounds, Levels, and Waves: The Early Evolution of Gameplay Segmentation." *Games and Culture* 3.2 (2008): 175–198. Print.

VIDEO GAMES CITED

Asteroids. Coin-op, Atari VCS, many additional ports. Developed and published by Atari, Inc., 1981.

Baldur's Gate. Macintosh, Windows. Developed by Bioware. Interplay Productions, 1998.

Bejeweled. Browser, Macintosh, Windows, and many more. Developed and published by PopCap Games, Inc., 2000.

Big Buck Hunter series. Coin-op. Developed and published by Raw Thrills, 2000–.

Braid. Linux, Macintosh, PlayStation 3, Windows, Xbox 360. Developed by Number None, Inc. First distributed by Microsoft Game Studios, 2008.

Call of Duty. Macintosh, PlayStation 3, Windows, Xbox 360. Developed by Infinity Ward. Activision, 2003.

Call of Duty 4: Modern Warfare. Macintosh, PlayStation 3, Windows, Xbox 360. Developed by Infinity Ward. Activision, 2007.

Cloud. Windows. Developed and published by USC Interactive Media, 2005.

Computer Space. Developed by Nolan Bushnell and Ted Dabney. Nutting Associates, 1971.

Conker's Bad Fur Day. Nintendo 64. Developed by Rare, Ltd. Nintendo of America, 2001.

Crimzon Clover. Windows. Developed and published by Yotsubane, 2011.

Cruis'n series. Coin-op. Developed and published by Midway Games, 1994–2007.

Custer's Revenge. Atari VCS. Developed and published by Mystique, 1982.

Dear Esther. Macintosh, Windows. Developed and published by thechineseroom, 2012.

Defender. Coin-op. Developed and published by Williams Electronics, 1980.

Diablo III. Macintosh, Windows. Developed and published by Blizzard Entertainment, 2012.

Donkey Kong Country. Super Nintendo. Developed by Rare, Ltd. Nintendo, 1994.

Doom. Windows and many other platforms. Developed and published by id Software, 1993.

DOTA 2. Linux, Macintosh, Windows. Developed and published by Valve Corporation, 2013.

The Elder Scrolls V: Skyrim. PlayStation 3, Windows, Xbox 360. Developed by Bethesda Game Studios. Bethesda Softworks, LLC, 2011.

Eve Online. Windows, Macintosh, Linux. Developed and published by CCP Games, 2003.

Everquest. Windows. Developed by Verant Interactive. 989 Studios, 1999.

The Fast and the Furious series. Coin-op. Developed and published by Raw Thrills, 2004–.

Fez. Windows, Xbox 360. Developed by Polytron Corporation. Microsoft Studio and Trapdoor, Inc., 2012.

flOw. Browser, Macintosh, PlayStation 3, PSP, Windows. Developed by thatgamecompany, LLC. Sony Computer Entertainment, 2006.

Flower. PlayStation 3. Developed by thatgamecompany, LLC. Sony Computer Entertainment, 2009.

Gears of War. Windows, Xbox 360. Developed by Epic Games, Inc. Microsoft Game Studios, 2006.

God of War. PlayStation 2. Developed by SCE Studio Santa Monica. Sony Computer Entertainment America, 2005.

GoldenEye 007. Nintendo 64. Developed by Rare, Ltd. Nintendo of America, 1997.

Grand Theft Auto series. Various platforms. Developed and published by Rockstar Games, 1997–.

Halo: Combat Evolved. Windows, Xbox. Developed by Bungie Studios. Microsoft Game Studios, 2001.

Halo 2600. Atari VCS. Developed by Ed Fries. Published by AtariAge, 2010.

Ico. PlayStation 2. Developed by Team Ico. Sony Computer Entertainment America, 2001.

Journey. PlayStation 3. Developed by that-gamecompany, LLC. Sony Computer Entertainment America, 2012.

Killer Instinct. Coin-op Game Boy, Super Nintendo. Developed by Rare, Ltd. Nintendo of America, 1995.

Killzone. PlayStation 2. Developed by Guerilla B.V. Sony Computer Entertainment America, 2004.

King's Quest, series. Windows. Developed and published by Sierra Entertainment, 1984–1998.

League of Legends. Windows and Macintosh. Developed and published by Riot Games, 2009.

Leisure Suit Larry series. Various platforms. Developed by Sierra Entertainment, High Voltage Software, Team 17, and Replay Games. Various publishers, 1987–.

Link: The Faces of Evil. CD Interactive. Developed by Animation Magic. Philips Media, 1993.

Little Big Planet. PlayStation 3. Developed by Media Molecule, Ltd. Sony Computer Entertainment America, 2008.

Madden NFL 2012. Android, iOS, PlayStation (various), Xbox 360, Wii. Developed by EA Tiburon and HB Studios. Electronic Arts, 2011.

Manhunt. PlayStation 2 and Xbox. Developed by Rockstar North. Rockstar Games, 2003.

Marathon. Macintosh. Developed and published by Bungie Software Products Corporation, 1994.

Mass Effect. Windows, Xbox 360. Developed by Bioware. Electronic Arts, 2007.

Mass Effect 2. PlayStation 3, Windows, Xbox 360. Developed by Bioware. Electronic Arts, 2011.

Mass Effect 3. PlayStation 3, Wii U, Windows, Xbox 360. Developed by Bioware. Electronic Arts, 2012.

Mega Man. Nintendo Entertainment System. Developed and published by Capcom, 1987.

Metal Gear series. Various platforms. Developed and published by Konami, 1987–.

Metropolis Street Racer (a.k.a. *MSR*). Dreamcast. Developed by Bizarre Creations, Ltd. Sega of America, 2001.

Microsoft Flight Simulator 2002. Windows. Developed and published by Microsoft Corporation, 2001.

Minecraft. Browser, Linux, Macintosh, Windows. Developed and published by Mojang AB, 2010.

N.A.R.C. Coin-op. Developed and published by Williams, 1988.

Neverwinter Nights. Linux, Macintosh, Windows. Developed by Bioware. Infogrames, Inc., 2002.

Oddworld, Munch's Oddysee. Xbox. Developed by Oddworld Inhabitants, Inc. Microsoft Corporation, 2001.

OutRun Online Arcade. Xbox 360, PlayStation 3. Developed by Sumo Digital. Sega, 2009.

Pac-Man. Coin-op. Developed and published by Namco, 1980.

Papo and Yo. PlayStation 3, Windows. Developed and published by Minority, 2012.

Pong. Coin-op. Developed and published by Atari, 1982.

Portal. Macintosh, Windows. Developed and published by Valve Corporation, 2007.

Project Gotham Racing. Xbox. Developed by Bizarre Creations, Ltd. Microsoft Corporation, 2001.

Putt-Putt series. Macintosh, Windows. Developed and published by Humongous Entertainment, 1992–.

Quake. DOS, Macintosh, PlayStation, Windows, and many more platforms. Developed and published by id Software, Inc., 1996.

Robotron: 2084. Coin-op. Developed by Vid Kidz. Williams Electronics, 1982.

Satan's Hollow. Coin-op. Developed by Bally Midway, 1982.

Sea Wolf. Coin-op. Developed by Dave Nutting Associates. Midway, 1976.

Second Life. Macintosh, Windows. Developed and published by Linden Lab, 2003–.

Shadow of the Colossus. PlayStation 2. Developed by Team Ico. Sony Computer Entertainment, 2005.

Sid Meir's Civilization. Amiga, Atari ST, DOS, Macintosh, PC-98, PlayStation, Super Nintendo, Windows. Developed by MPS Labs. Microprose Software, 1991.

Smash TV. Coin-op. Developed and published by Williams, 1990.

Space Invaders. Coin-op. Developed by Taito. Midway, 1978.

Spacewar! PDP-1. Developed by Steve Russel, 1962.

Spec Ops: The Line. PlayStation 3, Windows, Xbox 360. Developed by Darkside Game Studios, Inc., and YAGER Development GmBH. 2K Games, Inc., 2012.

Starcraft. Macintosh, Windows. Developed and published by Blizzard Entertainment, 1998.

Star Wars: Knights of the Old Republic. Macintosh, Windows, Xbox. Developed by Bioware. LucasArts, 2003.

Super Mario Bros. Nintendo Entertainment System. Developed by Nintendo. Nintendo Co., Ltd., 1985.

Super Mario Galaxy. Wii. Developed by Nintendo EAD. Nintendo of America, 2007.

Super Meat Boy. Windows, Xbox 360. Developed and published by Team Meat, 2010.

Target Terror. Coin-op. Developed and published by Raw Thrills, 2004.

Tennis for Two. Developed by William Higginbotham, 1958.

Terminator Salvation. Coin-op. Developed and published by Raw Thrills, 2010.

Tetris. Various platforms. Developed by Alexey Pajitnov. Spectrum Holobyte, 1987.

To the Moon. Windows. Developed and published by Freebird Games, 2011.

Two Brothers. Windows. Developed and published by Ackk Studios, 2013.

Uncharted: Drake's Fortune. PlayStation 3. Developed by Naughty Dog. Sony Computer Entertainment America, 2007.

The Unfinished Swan. PlayStation 3. Developed by Giant Sparrow. Sony Computer Entertainment America, 2012.

Wizardry, series. Windows. Developed and published by Sir-Tech, 1981–2001.

Wonderbook: Book of Spells. PlayStation 3. Developed by SCE Studio London. Sony Computer Entertainment Europe, 2012.

World of Goo. Linux, Macintosh, Wii, Windows. Developed and published by 2D Boy, LLC, 2008.

World of Tanks. Windows. Developed and published by Wargaming.net, Inc., 2011–.

World of Warcraft. Macintosh, Windows. Developed and published by Blizzard Entertainment, 2004–.

Zelda: The Wand of Gamelon. CD Interactive. Developed by Animation Magic. Philips Media, 1993.

Zelda's Adventure. CD Interactive. Developed by Viridis. Philips Media, 1994.

Index

DAVID S. HEINEMAN is an Associate Professor of Communication Studies at Bloomsburg University of Pennsylvania. His primary research interests are located at the intersection of rhetorical theory and criticism and new media technologies. He has written about the role of social media, hacktivism, and other emergent technologies in American politics; about the video game industry and gamer culture; and about digital rhetoric more broadly. He enjoys podcasting and kayaking.

6/15/16

CPSIA information can
Printed in the USA
BVOW05s1048260416

445642BV000

017154